THE MUSICIAN'S Ai HANDBOOK

Enhance And Promote Your Music With Artificial Intelligence

BOBBY OWSINSKI

FIRST EDITION

The Musician's Ai Handbook
by Bobby Owsinski

Published by:
Bobby Owsinski Media Group
4109 West Burbank, Blvd.
Burbank, CA 91505

© Bobby Owsinski 2023
ISBN: 978-1-946837-31-8

ALL RIGHTS RESERVED. No part of this work covered by the copyright herein may be reproduced, transmitted, stored, or used in any form and by any means graphic, electronic or mechanical, including but not limited to photocopying, scanning, digitizing, taping, Web distribution, information networks or information storage and retrieval systems, except as permitted in Sections 107 or 108 of the 1976 Copyright Act, without the prior written permission of the publisher.

For permission to use text or information from this product, submit requests to office@bobbyowsinski.com.

Please note that much of this publication is based on personal experience and anecdotal evidence. Although the author and publisher have made every reasonable attempt to achieve complete accuracy of the content in this Guide, they assume no responsibility for errors or omissions. Also, you should use this information as you see fit, and at your own risk. Your particular situation may not be exactly suited to the examples illustrated herein; in fact, it's likely that they won't be the same, and you should adjust your use of the information and recommendations accordingly.

Any trademarks, service marks, product names or named features are assumed to be the property of their respective owners, and are used only for reference. There is no implied endorsement if we use one of these terms.

Finally, nothing in this book is intended to replace common sense, legal, medical or other professional advice, and is meant to inform and entertain the reader.

To buy books in quantity for corporate use or incentives, email office@bobbyowsinski.com.

Thanks so much for purchasing this book!

Here Are 2 Free Bonuses
The Ai Music Cheat Sheet PDF Download,
and free regular Ai updates.

(use the QR Code or go to bobbyowsinskicourses.com/cheatreg)

TABLE OF CONTENTS

Introduction 1

   What This Book Is About 2

   Did I Use Ai To Write This Book? 3

PART I

The Foundations Of Ai 7

   A Little Ai History 7

   How Ai Works 11

   Ai Tools 16

   How Ai Generates Music 18

   Summing It Up 20

Ai Copyright 23

   Copyright Basics 23

   The Confusing World Of Ai Copyright 27

   Summing It Up 32

PART II

Ai Composition 37

   Ai Text-To-Music Platforms 37

   Ai Music Composition Idea Platforms 43

   Using A Chatbot As A Composition Tool 45

   Ai Lyric Generation 47

   Summing It Up 49

Ai Music Production Tools ... 51
- *Ai Sound Generation* ... 51
- *Ai Tonal Morphing* ... 55
- *Ai Accompaniment* ... 58
- *Voice Cloning* ... 60
- *Ai Song Analyzers* ... 61
- *Summing It Up* ... 64

Ai Audio Tools ... 65
- *Ai DAWs* ... 65
- *Ai Track Separation Tools* ... 67
- *Ai Audio Plugins* ... 70
- *Ai Noise Reduction Tools* ... 80
- *Ai Signal Paths* ... 82
- *Summing It Up* ... 87

Ai Mixing And Mastering ... 89
- *Ai Mixing And Balance* ... 89
- *Ai Mastering* ... 96
- *Summing It Up* ... 104

PART III

Ai Graphics Platforms ... 109
- *Ai Text-To-Image Platforms* ... 109
- *Ai Stock Images* ... 122
- *Ai Photo Tools* ... 123
- *Ai Art Platforms* ... 124

  Ai Branding Platforms 127

  Summing It Up 129

Ai Video Platforms 131

  Ai Music Video Creation 132

  Ai Lyric Video Creation 140

  Limitations Of Ai Video Generators 143

  Summing It Up 144

Ai Marketing Platforms 145

  The Big 3 Chatbots 146

  Prompt Engineering 153

  Summing It Up 158

The Future Of Ai Music 159

  Building Your Ai Toolset 159

  Your Ai Music Future 162

  Finally. 164

Glossary 165

Ai Music Tools And Services 169

About Bobby Owsinski 177

INTRODUCTION

Are you worried that artificial intelligence (Ai) is going to be so advanced that it will make your musical skills obsolete?

Do you fear that it will will come up with ideas so good that there will be no need for your creativity anymore?

Maybe you're concerned that Ai is evolving so rapidly that you'll always be playing catch up, or that knowledge you gain now about it will be outdated in no time?

I can certainly understand your feelings because they're commonly shared, thanks to the many sensationalistic click-bait headlines that we read online. And I have to admit that I felt somewhat the same before I began the research for this book.

You'll be relieved to learn that I discovered that these fears where truly myths. In fact, Ai can serve as a fantastic time-saving tool that can enhance our music in unprecedented ways.

I came to that revelation when I began to examine what Ai really is, and I found that I really liked it. Not just for the outcomes that it promised but also the technology itself.

I began to study computer science and Deep Learning (more on what that really means later) through online courses offered by MIT, IBM and Metacademy to try to get my arms around the subject.

Just what is the difference between machine learning, neural networks and deep learning? You see these terms (many say they're buzzwords) used interchangeably all the time, but as you'll soon learn, they each mean something different even though they're related. When I started my Ai journey, I wanted to find out not only what they meant but also how the underlying technology works.

Of course, the overwhelming reason that I got into the subject in the first place is I wanted to know how Ai fits into music.

Despite some of the impressive fake Drake, Weeknd, Ariana Grande, and John Lennon tracks available, I soon found out that it was a lot harder than it seems to create really good Ai music.

I took a journey where I sampled over 100 Ai's (most of them music) just to get a feel for what was available, what was actually helpful to musicians, and what was hype.

I dedicated months to testing not only music Ai's, but lyric, video, graphics, branding and marketing Ai's as well. I discovered that music and audio Ai's actually lagged behind some of the consumer Ai giants like OpenAi, Anthropic, and Microsoft in terms of technology.

The reason why I share this journey with you, and the reason for this book, is that I made all the mistakes with the technology so you won't have to.

There are a lot of Ai platforms that are supremely simple, but don't provide a professional result as they're aimed at consumers or music neophytes. On the other hand, there are Ai platforms, apps and plugins that require a steep learning curve to where it feels like you're almost learning a new language. I don't want that, and I'm pretty sure neither do you. What we both want is for the technology to:

A) accelerate our music creation process

B) give us new ideas and fresh inspiration when we're creatively stuck, and

C) ideally, provide results better than we could have come up with on our own.

Achieving even one of those objectives will make the time invested learning about Ai worthwhile, but a combination will take you to places you never thought possible.

WHAT THIS BOOK IS ABOUT

This book aims to:

- Provide you with a foundational understanding of Ai so that you're never baffled by the basics
- Bust the many myths about Ai, both good and bad
- Enlighten you about copyright restrictions on a global scale and highlight potential hidden clauses in platform or app fine prints
- Teach you how to craft effective prompts for optimal results, and
- Show you how Ai can help you do these things faster than you could on your own

As musicians, artists, songwriters, engineers and producers, we may want Ai to help us with multiple creative or business tasks or just one. That's why I've divided this book into three parts:

- **Part 1** covers **Ai basics**, where you'll understand why Ai behaves like it does, it's restrictions and limitations, bust its many myths, and make you aware of copyright restrictions both on a global and an application/plugin level.

- **Part 2** covers **Ai Composition And Production** - Yes, Ai can produce entire songs for you, but they won't be that good unless you personally get involved on a deeper level. We'll look at ways to get fresh ideas for melodies, lyrics, chord progression, and then use Ai production techniques to help discover new sounds or transform existing ones into something brand new.

    Also included in Part 2 is a chapter on **Ai Audio Apps** that dives into Ai plugins tailored for EQ, compression, limiting, gating, reverb, mix separation, and noise reduction.

And we finish Part 2 with **Ai Mixing and Mastering** where we'll look at the various ways that Ai can help your mixing, as well as online and plugin mastering services.

- **Part 3** cover's **Ai Marketing**, where we delve into creating music and lyric videos, graphics and branding, and using Ai chatbots to help with marketing chores like release launches, merch plans, and email sequences.

By the the time you get to the end of this book you're going to know more about Ai than 99% of all musicians on the planet! And you'll know how to harness it to make your music creation and promotion easier as well.

Let me finish by saying that the genie's out of the bottle, the cow's out of the barn, the cat's out of the bag (plug in your cliche of choice) - they're not going back and neither is Ai. Whether you're skeptical about Ai or not, it's not going away. It's time to make it work for you.

DID I USE AI TO WRITE THIS BOOK?

I bet you're asking yourself that question right about now.

No, Ai didn't write this book, but it helped. As you will soon read, Ai is a great collaboration tool. I believe that it works best when you use it for getting ideas, and that's exactly what happened in this case.

I started by asking ChatGPT to generate multiple lists of topics for me, then I asked Bing Ai and Google's Bard as well. From there I cherry-picked the resultant topics, but not as many as you might think as I already had a well-rounded list. It was more of a "what did I forget" situation than anything else.

If there was a topic that I felt I wasn't explaining clearly, I fed it into ChatGPT and asked if it could do better. Sometimes it could and sometimes it couldn't, but it usually came up with a little something (maybe just a word) that I felt improved the overall clarity.

Finally, I would feed a section of a chapter of the book into ChatGPT and ask it to find grammar and spelling mistakes, and then suggest word substitutions to help express an idea better.

Although it was usually great at finding grammar errors, I didn't always use it's other suggestions if I felt it altered my voice at all, since people buy my books because it feels like I'm talking directly with them (or so I'm told) so I didn't want to lose that.

And this is the essence of Ai. As you'll see in various spots in this book, if you use it to 100% generate a result, be it music or social posts or even a book like this, it might do a nice job, but there will be something missing from it. That something is YOU - the nuances, subtleties, and refinements that make your creation distinctly you.

You are the crucial ingredient and driver of the creation. Your essence is distinctly different from a machine, and that's what makes your creation better.

PLEASE NOTE: *Just to be clear, I abbreviate artificial intelligence as "Ai" rather than "AI" because AI is too easy to confuse with a person named "Al." Ai just reads so much better.*

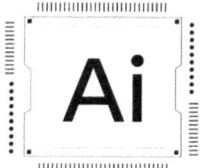

PART: 1

Ai BASICS

In this section of the book we'll discuss some of the more important, but overlooked, aspects of Ai, like it's fundamentals and copyright. Knowing the basic Ai terms means that you can easily transverse through artificial intelligence technology without any confusion. This will get you to your ultimate result with a particular platform faster. It will also let you sort through the massive amounts of misinformation and clickbait found on the subject.

Understanding copyright basics, then how Ai fits into them, is also essential so that you can always be sure of the ownership of the Ai-generative results that you create.

I've tried my best to lay both subjects out in an understandable, easy to digest way with a limited amount of technical and legal jargon so you can get on with the all the fun that Ai has to offer as soon as you can.

THE FOUNDATIONS OF Ai

Sometimes it's tempting to bypass a "Basics" chapter because you might assume it's dull, but I promise that you'll find enough of those "Ohhhh, so that what that means!" moments to make reading this one worthwhile.

Here's the thing - the more you know about how Ai works, the better you can make it work for you. Plus you'll lose your fears about it and come to realize that it's just a tool, and a pretty remarkable one at that.

What's even more exciting is that once you've absorbed the content of this chapter, you'll likely know more about Ai than 99% of musicians out there, and it can help you in other facets of your life beyond music as well.

So let's dive in. First of all, what exactly is Ai? Here's the textbook definition:

> *Ai refers to the science and engineering behind crafting intelligent machines, particularly intelligent computer programs. Ai achieves this by assimilating vast amounts of data, processing it, and subsequently learning from past experiences to enhance outcomes in the future.*

Yep, it's just a computer and some software that's doing what a human usually does, only a lot more efficiently. As you'll soon see, it's been a dream of humans almost from the beginning scientific thinking.

A LITTLE Ai HISTORY

The concept of "artificial intelligence" actually goes back thousands of years to the ancient philosophers as they pondered the biggest questions of life. Back then, inventors created what was called "automatons," which were rudimentary machines that moved without human intervention.

One of the earliest records of an automaton comes from 400 BCE and refers to a mechanical pigeon created by a friend of the philosopher Plato. Fast forward to 1495 and inventor Leonardo da Vinci created one of the most renowned automaton's called "Leonardo's Robot" (see Figure 1.1)

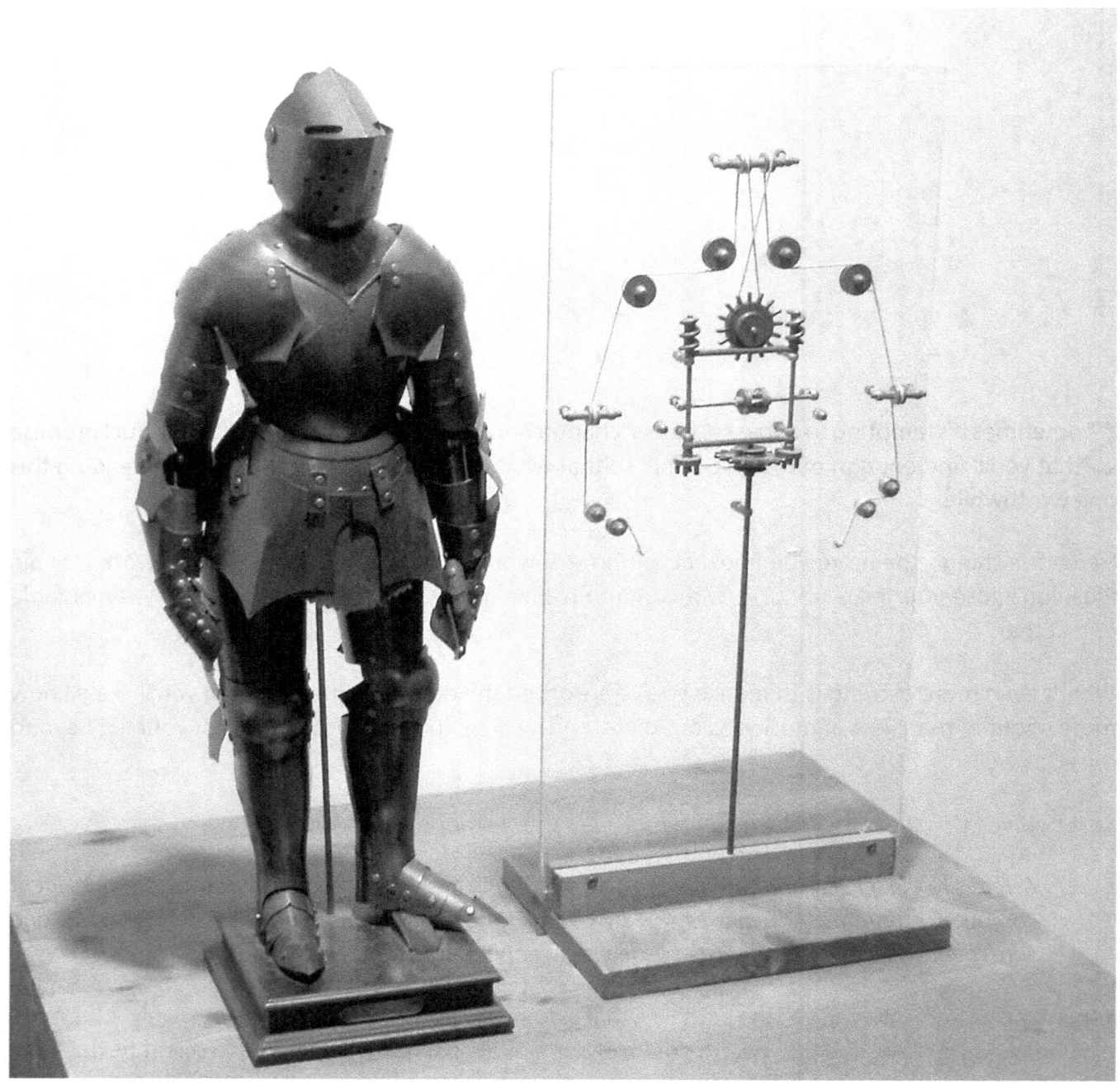

Figure 1.1: Model of a robot based on drawings of Leonardo Di Vinci
[Photo by Erik Möller. Leonardo da Vinci. Mensch - Erfinder - Genie exhibit, Berlin 2005]

The idea here was to have a machine that could act on it's own free will, but the concept was envisioned centuries before the technology could make that dream even remotely possible.

The Birth Of Ai

The true birth of what we've come to know as Ai occurred between the years of 1950 to 1956 when a series of scientific papers were published that coined the phrase "artificial intelligence" and set the stage for where we are today.

First came Alan Turing's famous work from 1950 called "Computer Machinery and Intelligence." This set the stage for what's known as The Turing Test, a benchmark that experts still use to gauge computer intelligence even today (although many argue that it needs to be replaced with one that's more up-to-date).

In 1952 a computer scientist named Arthur Samuel developed a program that mastered checkers, which is the first example of a computer that could learn to play a game independently.

Then in 1955 scientist John McCarthy hosted a famous workshop at Dartmouth University centered around "artificial intelligence" (marking the first time the term was ever used).

The reason why these three scientists are mentioned is because not only did they outline the basics concepts and structure of Ai, but they continued to be influential in the field even after their initial contributions.

Ai Matures

The late 1950s through the 1960s was a time of both rapid growth and simultaneous struggles for funding for Ai research. New programming languages like LISP were created (and they're still in use to this day), the concepts of Machine Learning and Expert Systems (an Ai focused on one particular field) were introduced, and General Motors integrated the first industrial robot into their assembly line. During this period Ai became a mainstream idea quickly.

In 1961 four engineers at Bell Labs taught an IBM 7094 computer to sing "Daisy Bell" (a song that most of us know as "A Bicycle Built For Two"), which became the first example of a computer being used to produce music.

In 1968, ELIZA, the first "chatterbot" (later shortened to chatbot, the term we use today) that was able to converse with humans, was created. This was the first example of a new approach to data handling called natural language processing (NLP) that eventually we've come to know as "generative Ai."

In the 1970s the first robot with human traits was built in Japan, while an engineering graduate student constructed the inaugural autonomous vehicle—the "Stanford Cart."

While all this sounds exciting, the industry faced challenges as both the U.S. and U.K. governments weren't all that interested in the technology at the time, and decreased its research funding.

This changed in the 1980s as new breakthroughs led to governments finally understanding Ai's commercial potential as it began to find it's way into industry, leading to additional research funding. One of the successes was an early expert system known as XCON, which was designed to assist in the ordering components for computer systems by automatically picking items based on the customer's needs.

The 1980s also witnessed the introduction of the first driverless car capable of reaching speeds up to 55 mph on obstacle-free, human driver-free roads. Deep Learning techniques and the use of Expert System gained prominence, both of which allowed computers to learn from their mistakes and make independent decisions.

Ai Finds Consumer Uses

By 1997, Ai technology was finally introduced into consumer products, exemplified by the Dragon Systems computer speech recognition system. The trend continued in 2002 with the introduction of the first Roomba automated floor vacuum cleaner.

In 2006 online companies like Twitter, Facebook, and Netflix began utilizing Ai into their advertising and user experience algorithms. Then in 2011, Apple released Siri, the first popular voice-activated virtual assistant.

Ai really came of age in 2020 with the beta-testing GPT-3 by OpenAI, a model that uses Deep Learning capable of creating computer programming code, poetry, marketing plans, and other language and writing tasks. While not the first Ai of its kind, it's the first that could rival human-produced content.

In 2021 OpenAI then developed DALL-E, which can process and understand images enough to produce accurate captions, and use simple text to create images, moving Ai one step closer to understanding the visual world.

Which brings us to today, with hundreds of Ai's that range from chatbots like ChatGPT to dedicated music creation and production platforms, to plugins and stand-alone audio apps.

How You're Using It Right Now

As you've seen from the previous section, you might not realize it but you've been using Ai for a lot longer than you think. Today it's so ingrained in our everyday digital lives that we almost completely take it for granted. Just consider some of the times that you might have used it just today:

- Social media algorithms (Recommended for you, or your newsfeed)
- A Google search
- Digital assistants (Siri, Alexa)
- Online shopping (People also bought)
- Unlocking your phone (facial recognition)
- Location apps (Waze, Google Maps, etc)
- Editing graphics and videos (object selection, photo cutout)
- Writing a post or text (autocomplete)

- Video games (you play against the machine)
- Listening to music (personalized recommendations)

If Ai is such a big part of our everyday lives, then why shouldn't we use it for helping us create music too? As you'll soon see, it's both a valuable tool and innovative collaborator.

HOW Ai WORKS

Before we begin, understand that we're not going to get into the weeds with math and advanced concepts that a computer scientist would use. I intend to make this as easily understandable, yet as accurate, as possible.

First, it's important to note that artificial intelligence is just one area of computer science, which is the study of computers and computational systems. Unlike other engineering disciplines, computer scientists deal mostly with software and software systems, which includes computer systems and networks, security, database systems, human computer interaction, vision and graphics, numerical analysis, programming languages, software engineering, bioinformatics and theory of computing - and, of course, artificial intelligence.

Artificial intelligence is actually composed of a number of sub-categories, each one going further into a specific domains. For instance:

- **Machine Learning** (ML) is a subset of Ai that centers on the notion that systems can learn from data, identify patterns, and make decisions without explicit programming.

  Machine learning can be used to analyze audio signals and extract features, such as pitch, tempo, timbre, genre, mood, etc. It can also be used to generate new musical content based on existing data, such as samples, loops, and MIDI files. For example, Melody Sauce 2 is a plugin that uses Machine Learning to generate original melodies based on user input and preferences.

- **Neural Networks** are computing systems inspired by the biological neural networks in the human brain. The network is trained by feeding it a large amount of data, and the nodes gradually learn to perform the desired task.

  Neural Networks can be used to model complex relationships between inputs and outputs, such as audio synthesis, sound design, or audio effects. For example, Solaris Virtual Vocalist is a plugin that uses a neural network to synthesize realistic vocal sounds based on user input and parameters.

- **Deep Learning** is a subset of ML that uses neural networks with many layers (hence "deep"). It's capable of learning from larger quantities of data and can make more complex predictions.

Deep Learning can be used to achieve state-of-the-art results in various areas of music production, such as source separation, noise reduction, transcription, recognition, and enhancement. For example, iZotope RX 10 is a plugin that uses deep learning to remove unwanted noise and repair audio issues with high accuracy and quality. Figure 1.2 shows exactly how these fit together.

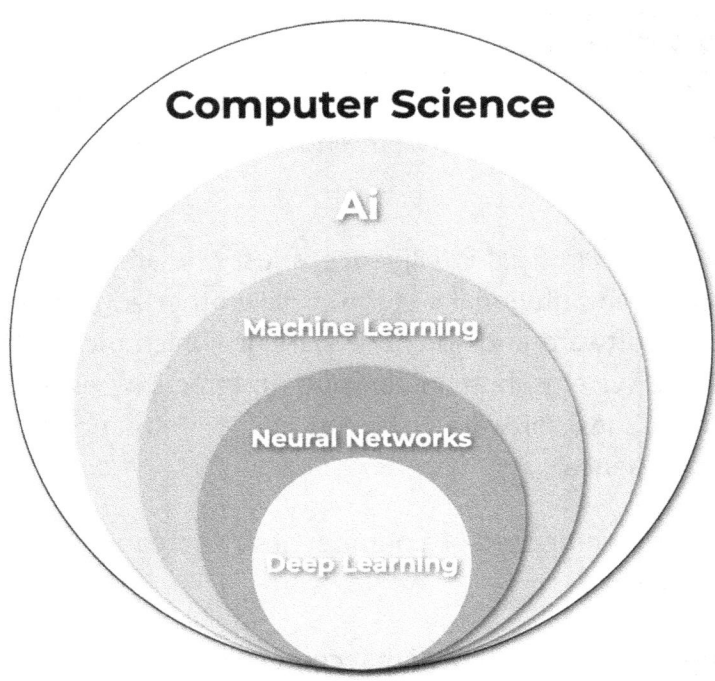

Figure 1.2: Ai sub-categories of computer science
© 2023 Bobby Owsinski

As you can see, Machine Learning, Neural Networks and Deep Learning all relate to one another in that they're all artificial intelligence, but they're not the same thing and the terms can't be used interchangeably.

Ai Training

Any flavor of Ai requires data to train it. This could be heavily curated data like in the case of Machine Learning for facial or voice recognition, or vast amounts of data that's been either intentionally fed into the Ai or scraped from the Internet. Scraping is the process of using automated bots to extract content or data from a website. The data collected can be in the form of text, graphics, or music.

As you're probably aware, scraping the Internet for training data has caused a huge controversy, as many believe there could be a possible copyright violation on every website that's been scraped (see Chapter 2 on Ai Copyright). While that's yet to be determined by the courts, most Ai platforms (especially for music) have acknowledged that there's a potential problem that leaves them open to lawsuits (some have already started) and have since installed data "guardrails" to make copyright violations less likely.

It's too late in the case of Ai's like ChaptGPT since the training has already been completed, but it's now possible to protect your website or online material from Ai webcrawlers, which wasn't in place prior until late 2023.

There are actually plenty of other legal ways to train an Ai. For instance, large datasets can be purchased from numerous vendors. There are also dozens, if not hundreds of free public datasets readily available online.

Ai Buzzwords

I'm sure that you've seen many of the following terms and have a general idea of what they mean, but aren't really sure. As I said before, these are not deep computer science explanations, but they are accurate.

ChatBot: A chatbot is a computer program that mimics human conversation, either in written or spoken form, allowing humans to interact with software or digital devices as if they were communicating with an actual person. Notable examples include ChatGPT, Bing Ai, Google's Bard, Anthrophic Claude, and Jasper Ai.

ChatGPT: ChatGPT stands for Generative Pre-trained Transformer, which basically means its an Ai that has been trained before you use it, and is able to transform data from one form to another, like changing languages or converting text into computer code.

Generative Ai: This is a type of Ai that creates new content, such as music, images, or text, based on the data it's been trained on. It's responses are often based on patterns it learns from existing data.

Large Language Models (LLMs): These are Ai models trained on a vast amount of text datasets, hence the "language" in the name. They use statistical models to analyze the training data, learning the patterns and connections between words and phrases. This allows them to generate new content, such as blog posts or articles, that can be similar in style to a specific author or genre. An example is GPT-3 and 4, which were developed by a company called OpenAI.

Machine Learning (ML): Machine Learning is a subset of Ai. It's a method of data analysis that automates data model building. It's based on the concept that systems can learn from data, identify patterns, and make decisions with minimal human intervention.

Most of the time the training data has to be labeled by a human so the algorithm understands the differences. For instance, if we were teaching it to recognize animals, a human would label a dog as a "dog" and a cat as a "cat," or when it comes to traffic signs, a STOP sign versus a SLOW sign (see Figure 1.3).

Machine Learning
Needs A Human To Label It

Label: Slow   Label: Yield   Label: Stop

Figure 1.3: Data labels for machine learning
© 2023 Bobby Owsinski

You can think of Machine Learning like cooking a nice spaghetti sauce. You have some ingredients (data), a recipe (algorithm) and a pot (model). You follow the recipe to combine the ingredients in the pot and cook them until the sauce is done (train the model). Then you taste the sauce (evaluate the model) and see if you like it or not. If not, you can adjust the recipe or the ingredients and try again without too much trouble.

Neural Networks: Neural Networks are computing systems inspired by the biological neural networks in the human brain. They are a key part of Machine Learning, and are designed to recognize patterns. Neural Networks go a step deeper though. They can train themselves to look for patterns, and they can also learn from their mistakes.

Neural Networks consist of an input layer that takes data inputs, one or more hidden layers that process the inputs, and an output layer that produces the final result (see Figure 1.4). Neural Networks can learn complex, non-linear patterns from data and are widely used for tasks such as image recognition, natural language processing, speech recognition, etc.

Neural Network
Figures It Out By Itself

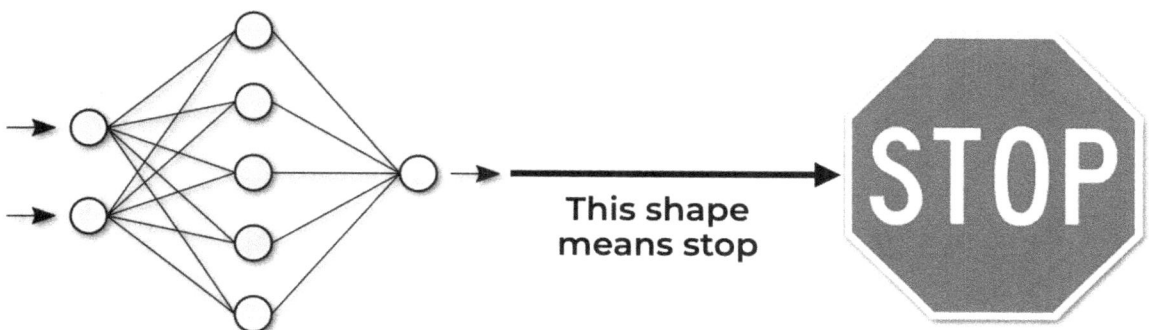

Figure 1.4: A neural network
© 2023 Bobby Owsinski

Following up on our cooking analogy, Neural Networks are like baking a cake. You still have some ingredients (data), a recipe (algorithm) and a pot (model), but this time the pot is a special one: it has many layers (neurons) and each layer can perform some transformations on the ingredients. You still follow the recipe to combine the ingredients in the pot and cook them until they're done (train the model), but this time you can't really see what's happening inside the pot. You just hope that the cake will come out nice and fluffy (accurate and generalizable).

Deep Learning: Deep Learning is basically a Neural Network on steroids. Just like our brain can not only see an object, but smell it, feel it, and hear it at the same time without us even thinking about it, deep learning can do multiple tasks at the same time as well. In music, for example, a Deep Learning Ai might be analyzing the style, tempo, rhythm, timbre and chordal complexity all at the same time in order to generate a new composition.

Deep Learning is a subset of Maching Learning that uses Neural Networks with many layers (hence the term "deep"). It's capable of learning from larger quantities of data and can make more complex predictions as a result (see Figure 1.5). Anything more than 3 neural layers is consider Deep Learning.

Deep Learning
A Neural Network With More Layers

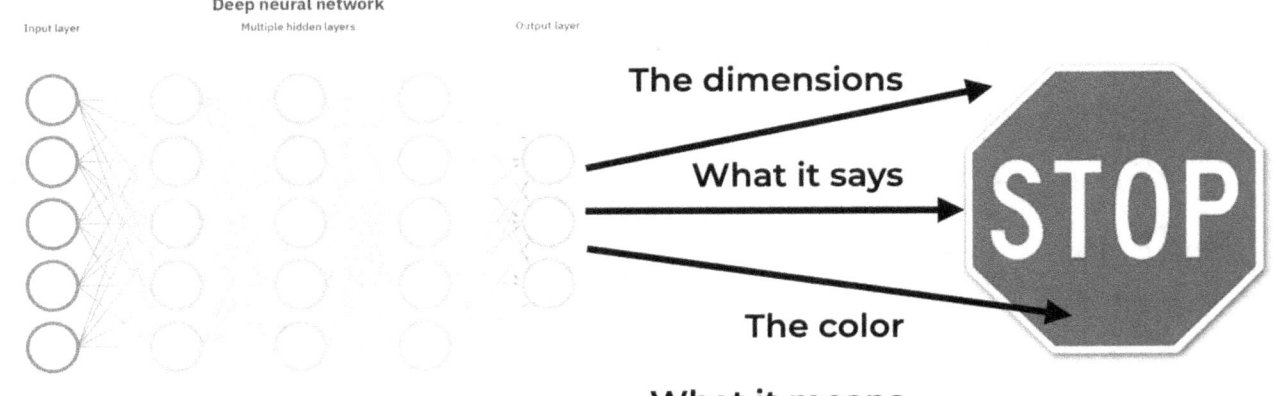

Figure 1.5: Deep Learning
© 2023 Bobby Owsinski

Once again we can use cooking as an analogy, but this time Deep Learning is like making an elaborate wedding cake. You still have ingredients (data), a recipe (algorithm) and a pot (model), but this time the pot is a very complex one: it has many layers (neurons), each layer can perform different transformations on the ingredients, and some layers can even communicate with each other. You still follow the recipe to combine the ingredients in the pot and cook them until they're done (train the model), but this time you need a lot of time, patience and resources to make it work. You also need to decorate the cake with some icing and flowers (hyper-parameters) to make it look beautiful and tasty.

Ai TOOLS

Indeed, Ai is a tool—a vast array of tools, in fact. Let's explore what these tools can offer your music. There are well over 100 different music-related Ai tools for you to choose from covering a variety of areas, and there are new ones coming online every day.

Some of these will wow consumers and be of no use to a music pro. Some are intended for professionals but are so deep that you need to dedicate a lot of time to explore the possibilities. Regardless, lets look at some of the categories and possibilities they provide.

- Composition tools allow us to create full songs, backing tracks, chord ideas and melodies.
- Lyric generators help us with lyric ideas.
- Production tools help with crafting new sounds and arrangements.
- Audio processors use Ai for to determine compression, EQ and reverb plugin settings that automatically adapt to the sound source.

- Audio separation tools allow you to isolate the different mix elements in a fully mixed track.
- Noise reduction tools eliminate intrusive background noises in a track.
- Mastering tools are capable of delivering pro-level quality masters of our mixes.
- Music and lyric video creation tools that work by just feeding the Ai platform our music.
- Ai graphics tools help us to create graphics for videos or social media.
- Ai branding tools can help us create logos and graphics for merch.
- And finally Ai marketing tools can help us to write copy for everything from bios to websites to social media posts.

Not only is Ai being used for new music operations that we haven't thought of yet, but more and more tools for each category are being released every week.

Some Things To Remember

When it comes to using Ai tools for music creation, there are a number of things to remember.

- First of all, music Ai tools in general are not nearly as sophisticated as apps like ChatGPT or any of the chatbots. That's because the needs of a creative musician are fairly focused when compared with most industrial and consumer Ai's. It also takes a lot of time and money to train and maintain models as large as what the big consumer Ai's use.
- In general the Ai music creation tools can generate full songs, just the chords, or only the melodies if you want. While the results can be good to very good, your input and creativity are still needed to make the results great.
- Some Ai tools are very good at generating new sounds. For instance you can ask that your voice be changed into a saxophone or violin. In most cases this seems like magic to non-musicians but the results may not be up to a professional level that can be used in recordings, unless you're looking for something that sort of sounds like a sax, but not really.
- Ai is really good at generating lyrics, although again, don't expect the songs they generate to be on the level of Bob Dylan or Bernie Taupin. Nevertheless, you can usually find some really good nuggets that will inspire you.
- When it comes to Ai audio plugins and apps, in many cases these are even less sophisticated than an Ai music generator, mostly because they don't really have to be as sophisticated because their job focus is really narrow. In many cases, all they have is a *Learn* button that will will either figure out the plugin's settings based on the audio you play in, or by learning from a reference track that you upload.
- In fact, there are some apps that claim to be Ai-driven that aren't interactive at all. Instead of using a technique like convolution to model a piece of analog hardware, they use a neural network to determine the sound at different parameter settings. This may be more or less

accurate than other ways of modeling gear, but maybe not enough to make a difference to the average user. Many times you can't access the Ai directly.

- Ai can help us write copy for bios and ads, or create music videos, branding and graphics. Just about any music promotion benefit by augmenting what you already have with Ai.

In essence, there are Ai tools for just about any need an artist, songwriter or band might need during the course of making and promoting their music. The trick is to find one that not only meets your need but is easy to use as well.

HOW Ai GENERATES MUSIC

A common question is "How does an Ai music generator make music?" Let's delve into this because the topic is not only fascinating, but highlights some of Ai music's limitations as well.

Like other Ai's, a music generator's Neural Network has to be trained. This is done by using a dataset of songs, like you would expect. These could come from either scraping existing music, which could be a vast collection of songs in a particular genre or style. It could also come from licensed music from a popular artist or producer, as is more recently the case with newer music Ai's.

The algorithm examines the patterns and structures in the music using an audio spectrogram (see Figure 1.6), and then examines the patterns and structures in the music such as the chords, melodies, beats, rhythms, and instrumentation. It then uses this information to create new music that is similar in style and structure to the training material.

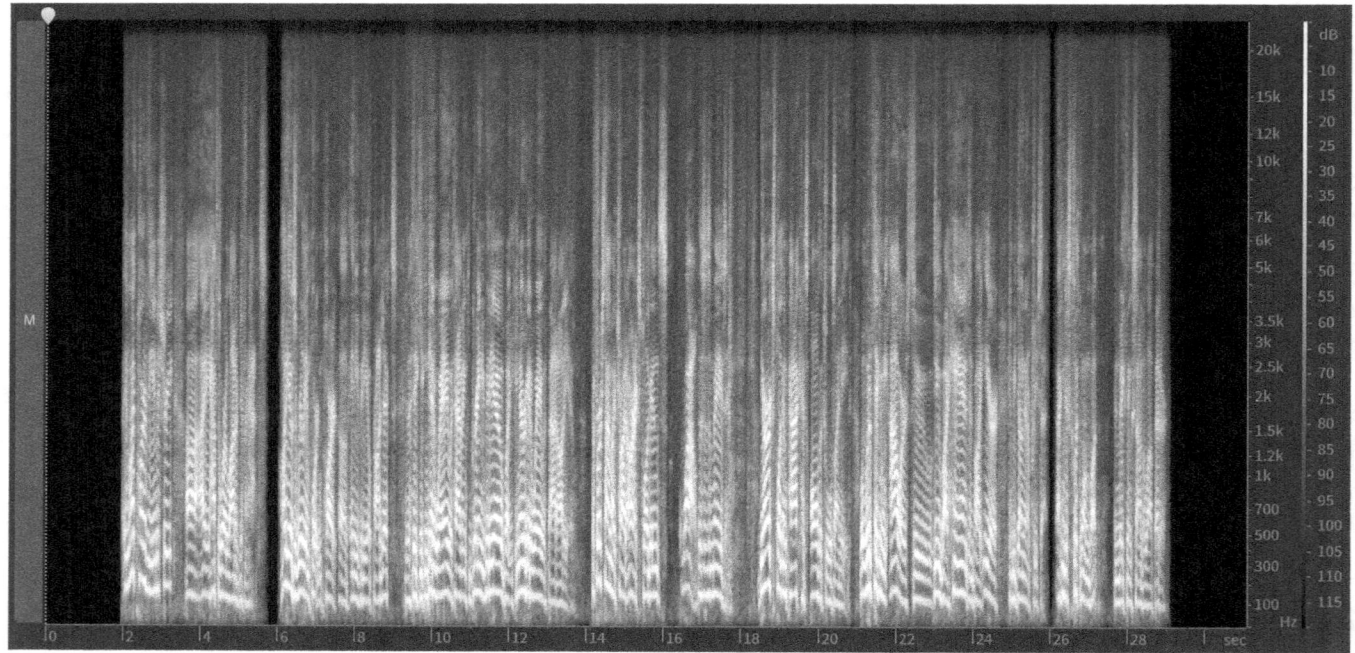

Figure 1.6: An audio spectrogram
Courtesy of iZotope

The thing to remember is that all this requires a large amount of computer horsepower either based in the cloud or from your computer. The limitations begin to emerge when it comes to generating music.

When you ask graphics Ai to generate an image, it only has to do it once. Sure it knows what colors to use, how to bend the curves and adjust lighting and shadows, but it adjusts all these parameters just one time to create your image.

For a video, the Ai now needs to generate an image 30 times a second, and for gaming the frequency typically reaches 60 times a second. This puts more strain on an Ai's system, but it usually has no trouble handling it except for the wait time to generate the result.

The complexity amplifies considerably when it comes to music though, as a music Ai typically generates music anywhere from 8,000 to 44,100 times a second (see Figure 1.7)! Since operating at this pace is so taxing, it usually begins to throw away frequency data in the same manner as MP3 encoding which is referred to as frequency masking.

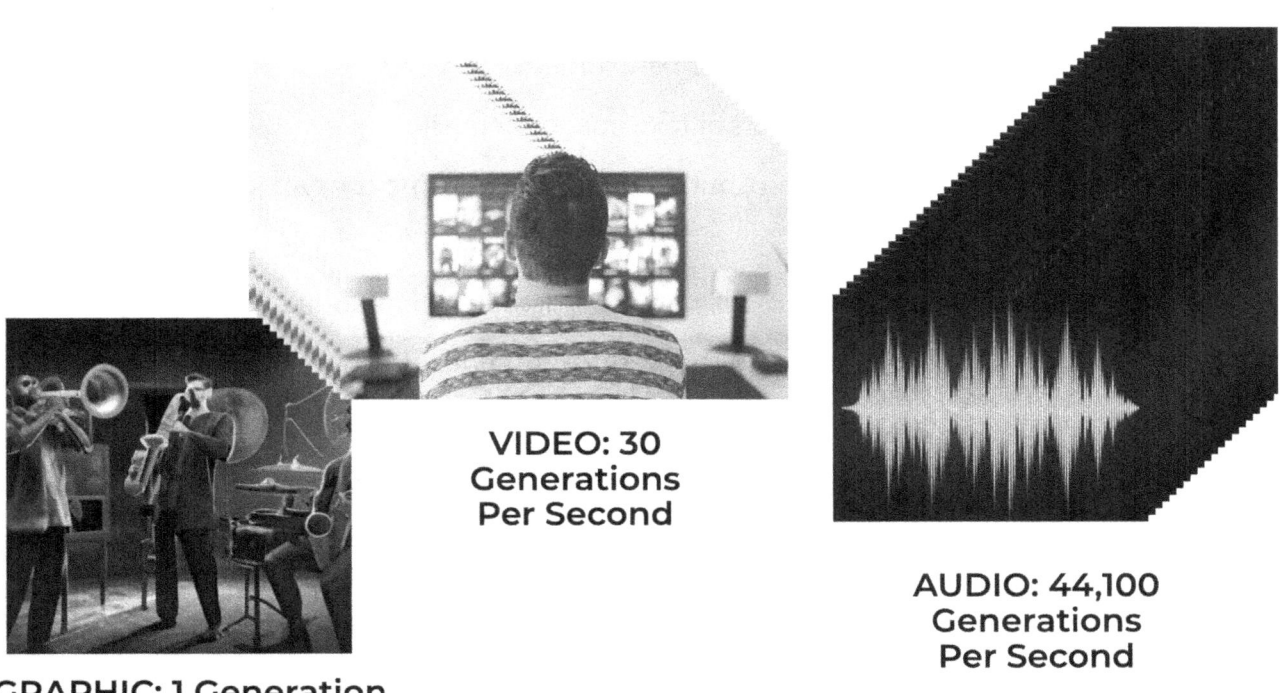

Figure 1.7: Generations required for graphic, video and audio
© 2023 Bobby Owsinski

This means that the audio resolution of most Ai generated songs is just not that good - certainly not up to professional standards. It's possible that a full 44.1kHz/16 bit CD-quality file can be generated, but you usually have to pay a subscription premium for that to happen.

If you require an audio resolution higher than 44.1/16 (most record labels now require 96kHz/24 bit mix files in their delivery specs), then your best approach is to download the MIDI file (which is usually a free option on most music Ai's), import it into your DAW, then use virtual instruments to generate the sounds you want at a higher resolution (we'll go over this more in depth in Chapter 3).

To finish up the question of "How does an Ai music generator make music?", the music generator doesn't use a voice chip or oscillators like in a synthesizer to make its sounds. It's just a stream of 1's and 0's that it sends to your computer's audio interface digital-to-analog convertor, the same as playing back any audio from your computer.

SUMMING IT UP

To summarize this chapter, these are the primary takeaways:

- Ai performs tasks that usually would take human intelligence to perform
- You're using Ai already
- Machine Learning, Neural Networks, and Deep Learning are all part of Ai, but they're not the same
- Generative Ai takes input and creates new content
- Ai training relies on huge datasets of text, images or music
- Building an Ai is straight forward, but training it is hard, time consuming, and expensive
- Ai is just another tool
- Whatever you learn in this book will not be outdated anytime soon
- Ai for music spans composition, lyrics, production, audio plugins, mixing, and mastering
- Ai for marketing includes writing bio or ad copy, creating videos, branding and graphics
- Music Ai apps are generally not as sophisticated as chatbots like ChatGPT
- Some Ai audio plugins are rather limited in functionality
- A few Ai audio plugins have no user interaction at all
- Ai marketing is only as good as the prompt you provide it
- The larger the Neural Network, the more parameters it can analyze
- The more layers the Neural Network has, the more realistic the generated music can be
- Ai Music NEEDS A HUMAN

To illustrate just how much Ai needs a human touch, take a look at Figure 1.8 below.

 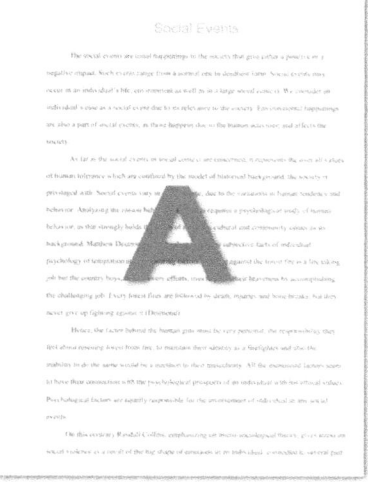 

Figure 1.8: Ai with a human's input
© 2023 Bobby Owsinski

Imagine that you were in school and asked to submit a term paper on "Social Events." You can't think of anything to write, so you turn in a blank page. Of course you can expect the paper to get an F as a result.

Now imagine you consult a chatbot like ChatGPT, Bard, or Bing Ai and ask it to write the term paper for you. It will provide decent work, but the most you could hope for (unless your teacher figured out you used a chatbot) would get a C+ or maybe a B- grade.

Now imagine that you take the output that the chatbot gave you, and you used some of its best stuff, tweaked some others, and added your own outlook on the subject. Get ready for that A that you wanted.

It's the same with music. If you ask an Ai music generator to write a song for you, you'll probably be disappointed if you depend solely on its outcome. Add your own production ideas and it can turn into something great.

We'll look at this more in depth in Chapters 3 and 4.

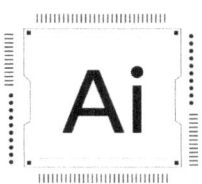

Ai COPYRIGHT

Please note that this chapter is not a substitute for professional legal advice. Seek the advice of a licensed copyright attorney in the appropriate jurisdiction before taking any action that may affect your rights.

One of the biggest issues with not only Ai music, but Ai-generated content, is ownership. To say that there's still a lot of gray areas is an understatement.

If you generate a song, a graphic, a video or a text response from ChatGPT, who owns it? Is it the owner of the platform you used? Is it the person who wrote the code, or the one who trained the Ai? Is it the owner or owners of the material used to train the Ai? Is it the person who typed in the prompt requesting the content (you)? Is it all of the above, or none of the above?

I'm sorry to say that the answer is a little bit of all of these, although the law is evolving (rather slowly I might add) as you read this. Before we get into that, it's time to take a quick look at the basics of copyright first so you can better understand all the confusion around it when it comes to Ai.

COPYRIGHT BASICS

First let's look at the classic definition of copyright.

> *Copyright is a legal protection given to creators of original works, including music. It allows the creator to control how their work is used and prevents others from using it without permission.*

The purpose of a copyright is to make sure that creators benefit from their work to encourage them to keep creating.

What Can Be Copyrighted

What can be copyrighted when it comes to music? There are actually two copyrights attached to every song:

- The **Composition,** which includes the song's melodies, rhythms, and lyrics. It's the publishing aspect of the song (musical work or underlying work).
- The **Sound Recording**: This is the actual recording of a performance. For example, if a band records a song in a studio or a producer creates a song in his or her home studio, that specific recording is protected.

It should be noted that ideas, styles, or techniques can't be copyrighted. Only the tangible expression of those ideas can be. That means that an idea that you might have for what you think is a unique chord progression or a recording technique can't be copyrighted.

When it comes to Ai-generated music, most of the time only the sound recording is mentioned and the composition (a big part of the revenue stream of the song) is overlooked. This is actually a big deal and something that we'll get into more in depth in a bit.

Obtaining A Copyright

Many artists, songwriters and composers aren't aware that you get automatic protection as soon as you create and record your music in a tangible form (like writing it down or recording it). Even better, as soon as the song is published online on either social media or a streaming service, it's timestamped, which might be helpful to prove that you wrote it first if there's ever a dispute.

The traditional way of obtaining a copyright was to register your work with the U.S. Copyright Office (copyright.gov/registration). In the pre-internet days this was always recommended but it's no longer required thanks to the ability to publish online. It's more of a hassle as well because the process involves filling out a form, paying a fee (from $45 to $125), and submitting a copy of the work. It does provide some additional legal benefits, like the ability to sue for statutory damages, and is a powerful tool to have when it comes to an infringement lawsuit.

Obtaining a copyright provides benefits for a long time. The copyright lasts for the life of the creator plus 70 years. If there are multiple creators, it lasts for the life of the last surviving creator plus 70 years. If it's a work for hire (like a buy-out for a film), the protection lasts 95 years from publication or 120 years from creation, whichever is shorter. After this period, the work enters the "public domain" and can be used by anyone without permission.

Rights of Copyright Holders

Holding a copyright is useful because it gives you a number of rights, such as:

- **Reproduction**: Only the copyright holder can make copies of the song or allow others to do so.
- **Distribution**: The holder controls the right to sell, lease, or rent copies of the music.
- **Performance**: This includes playing the song in public, on the radio, or online.

- **Adaptation**: Only the copyright holder can change the song or create derivative works based on it, like remixes or samples.
- **Digital Transmission**: This pertains to the right to stream or digitally transmit recordings.

Exceptions And Misconceptions

There's a portion of copyright law widely misunderstood and misused called Fair Use. Fair use allows limited use of copyrighted material without permission for purposes like criticism, commentary, parody, news reporting, education, and research.

Where the problems arise is that just because something is labeled as "educational" or "commentary" doesn't automatically make it fair use. Each case is unique.

Factors that are looked at closely include:

- **Purpose and character of the use** (e.g., commercial vs. educational). Non-profit educational uses are more likely to be fair use than commercial uses. However, commercial use doesn't automatically rule out fair use.
- **Nature of the copyrighted work.** It makes a difference whether the work is fact or fiction. Factual works (like news articles) are more likely to be subject to fair use than highly creative works (like novels or songs). Also, whether a work is published or unpublished makes a difference. Using unpublished works without permission is less likely to be considered fair use.
- **Amount used in relation to the whole work.** Using a small portion of a copyrighted work may favor fair use, but there's no specific percentage that's automatically safe. Even if a small portion is used, if it's the most significant or recognizable part work (like the major hook of a song), it might weigh against fair use.
- **Effect on the market value of the copyrighted work.** If the new work acts as a substitute for the original, harming its market, it's less likely to be considered fair use.

As you can see, there's a lot of misunderstanding about what actually constitutes fair use, and that especially applies to Ai-generated content. What might be fair use in one case might not be in another.

Here are a few common areas of confusion of fair use and copyright:

- **"Non-profit means it's fair use."** While non-commercial use is a factor, it's not an automatic pass.
- **"Giving credit avoids infringement."** Crediting the original creator is a good practice, but it doesn't automatically make it use fair.
- **"There's a specific percentage that's safe."** There's no "magic number" or percentage that guarantees fair use. Even a short clip can be a violation if it captures the essence of the song.

- **"If I don't profit from it, it's not a violation."** Even if you don't make money from using someone else's music, it can still be a copyright infringement.

- **"I bought the song, so I can use it however I want."** Buying a song or album either digitally or physically (like a CD or vinyl album) gives you the right to listen to it personally, but not to use it for other purposes, like in videos or public performances.

Copyright Licenses

If you want to use someone else's music, you often need to get a license or permission which will most likely involve paying a fee for the privilege. There are three types of licenses that can be obtained:

- **Mechanical License**: Needed in order to reproduce and distribute a sound recording made of a musical work
- **Performance License**: Needed for playing a song in public
- **Synchronization License**: Needed for using a song in visual media, like movies or TV shows. Remember that a song consists of both the musical work and the sound recording and a license if required for both.

So what happens if you don't get a license? There can be a legal action where the copyright holder can sue the infringer for damages, which can be substantial. For instance, if the work was registered with the Copyright Office, the holder can sue for set amounts, which can range from $750 to $150,000 per each work that is infringed. In severe cases, copyright infringement can even lead to criminal charges, fines, and even imprisonment.

The reality of the situation is that legal fees are substantial for any copyright lawsuit, so unless a song is a huge hit and bringing in considerable revenue, suing is just not affordable. That said, that doesn't mean that you're off the hook. It might take years for a legal action to be brought, but as soon as a song reaches a certain revenue threshold, here comes the lawsuit. That's why it's best to get your legal ducks in a row as soon as possible and obtain a license if needed.

One of the ways that fear of legal action has changed songwriting is the fact that you now see so many co-writers on a song (as many as 20 or more!). Some producers now feel that instead of worrying about who made what kind of contribution during the creation of a song, if you were in the room while it was being written, then you get credit. That's obviously not an ideal situation but it does solve a potential problem before it even starts (Nashville handles this differently by having an unwritten rule that if two people write a song, it's split 50-50; if three people write a song it's a third each, etc. This works particularly well if the same people cowrite lots of songs).

THE CONFUSING WORLD OF Ai COPYRIGHT

When it comes to the world of Ai copyright, it all boils down to who owns what, and this is directly a result of the fact the U.S. copyright law is out of date. The last time it was updated was with the Digital Millennium Copyright Act of 1998, which, despite having the word digital in its title, was written before the internet became a widely used source of music and creative content distribution.

While updating the law seems like such an easy solution to the problems and confusion, that requires a lot of study because of the issues that we're about to cover are complex and have far-reaching effects. Even if a wise and fair law was crafted, it might have trouble passing both Houses of Congress in these politically divided times.

That leaves us with many unanswered questions, most of which are slowly getting worked out based on the fact that, just like our multi-songwriter credits, it's very expensive to enter litigation. The deeper your pockets though, the more likely that will happen.

Ai Copyright Ownership

As stated in the very first paragraph of this chapter, the issue of ownership is at the heart of all the confusion. Again, who owns it? Is it the owner of the platform you used? Is it the person who wrote the code, or the one who trained the Ai? Is it the owner or owners of the material used to train the Ai? Is it the person who typed in the prompt requesting the content? Is it all of the above, or none of the above?

The U.S. Copyright Office provided guidance on this in March of 2023 that takes a significant step in clearing up the confusion when it stated that a 100% Ai-generated work could not be copyrighted.

Then in August of 2023 a federal judge ruled that Ai-generated artwork cannot be copyrighted because it lacks human authorship. In essence, it agreed with the previous ruling that music or any creative content that's 100% generated by Ai cannot be copyrighted, but this time clarified why.

The judge ruled that copyright law only extends to human beings, and works created by animals, forces of nature (even those claimed to have been authored by divine spirits like religious texts), and Ai can't be copyrighted.

This ruling was not a total surprise since it heralds back to this picture (see Figure 2.1).

2.1: Naruto selfie

It's a selfie of an Indonesian crested macaque monkey named Naruto who was left with a camera, took some pictures of itself, and those excellent pictures consequently became famous and helped sell a lot of books and magazines. The fact that the photo was commercialized led to a court case that contended that since the monkey took the picture, it owned the copyright.

The court saw differently and stated that since the monkey wasn't human, it couldn't receive a copyright, which leads to the most recent ruling against Ai being a copyright owner.

But How Much?

So if a human must be involved in the creation, how much of an involvement is required? There's the rub - there's been no determination yet, and maybe there won't be. It could be just like fair use, where each case is unique and has to be ruled on separately. All we know for sure is that for a copyright to be issued with Ai content, a human must participate in the creation in some way.

These dual rulings did leave an impression on the music business though. The Recording Academy immediately stated that a Grammy would not be awarded to a 100% Ai-generated song. Many online distributors like Tunecore stated they would not distribute 100% Ai-generated songs going forward, and Spotify removed a full 7% of its catalog because it found it was Ai generated.

One problem solved, but perhaps a bigger one remains - how much does a human need to be involved, and does the human have to name the Ai as a co-writer?

Ai Content Licensing

While the official word on ownership is still somewhat up in the air, the fact is that different Ai platforms make different claims about how much of the content generated they own and how much they'll let you license or own yourself. This is something that any user has to be aware of before you actually decide to use to use an Ai platform of any kind.

Typical Licenses

The typical license categories generally are divided along three payment tiers that a platform might offer.

The first tier is usually free or low cost. In this case you may be instructed that the platform owns any content that's generated, and while you're permitted to use it for personal use, you may be restricted to certain platforms like YouTube or Facebook, or maybe restricted from using it at all, and you're not permitted to monetize it. In other words, you can play with the content you helped generate but you can't do anything with it.

Also, the resolution of the content might be restricted as well, so if it's audio the quality might be limited to a low-bandwidth MP3, and if it's a video, it might be a smaller standard resolution 720x480 size.

The second tier usually asks a modest monthly fee. For that you still don't own the copyright (the platform keeps that) but you're licensed to freely use the content where you like and even monetize it. Plus, you might have access to higher resolution content as well.

What's not always clear is the term of the license. Does the license end if you stop paying the monthly subscription for the service? It's time to read the fine print on its Terms and Conditions page.

The third tier is usually a premium tier where you pay the highest amount per month. That means if it's a consumer-leaning platform it will cost $19 to $29 per month. If it's aimed at professionals, it may cost as much as $99 per month.

For that you will granted the copyright with no restrictions where you can use the content, and also have access to the highest resolution the platform can create.

It's Still Not Determined

While an Ai platform might tell you that it's keeping or granting the copyright to you, that doesn't mean it has the right to do so, as this still hasn't been determined by the Copyright Office. It's possible that you're being asked to pay for a copyright that doesn't exist.

What's worse, because of the vagueness of copyright ownership as it exists now, you might unknowingly be liable and sued for infringement of intellectual property in the future if the music you use is too similar to an existing song!

Before you get frightened off from ever using Ai to help you create music again, remember that the only time you're likely to be sued is if your song is generating a massive amount of revenue (again, this is not legal advice!). By then you, your publisher and record label, will most likely have a team of intellectual property attorneys that can attempt to sort this out for you.

However, you're still left open to take-down notices on Youtube and other social networks, which may make your content inaccessible. Or another ruling by the Copyright Office or even a new law can take this in a direction that we can't foresee today.

The Composition Copyright Dilemma

One of the more interesting aspects of Ai music copyright is that the composition (publishing) copyright is seldom mentioned on the terms and conditions page of any Ai music platform. It's as if it doesn't exist.

In almost all cases the copyright that's referred to is for the recording. Who owns this second copyright? Some might assume that because you're the one that entered the prompt, that means that you're the creator and therefore own the composition copyright, but that's rarely spelled out in an Ai music platform's terms and conditions. As of now, this is yet to be determined.

The Training Question

One battle that's already happening is whether the material that was used to train the Ai was copyrighted or not, and how does that play into the ultimate copyright of the content that you, the user, asked to be generated.

If high-powered Ai's like ChatGPT, Google's Bard, and Bing Ai have used datasets scraped from across the web, undoubtedly some copyrighted material was scraped in the process. This leaves them open for copyright infringement lawsuits and in fact there are dozens currently in play over this.

Their argument is that the scraped data was fair use, but the lawsuits claim that the companies violated privacy and property rights, and copyright laws. The thought is that it's impossible to train on a sound recording without making a copy of it and, without getting permission to do so, making a copy of it is probably a copyright infringement.

These training datasets may actually turn out to be a new source of income for songwriters and copyright holders in the future. For instance, if a music Ai wanted to ingest Elton John's entire catalog to get the ultimate Elton sound, his management and publisher could say, "No problem. Give us $50 million and a percentage of the revenue and we're good."

To some degree, this is already happening with artists like Holly Herndon and Grimes offering Ai virtual versions of their voices in exchange for a percentage of the revenue that the song that it's used in makes.

Name, Image, And Likeness

Using a virtual Grimes or Holly Herndon brings up the point of Name, Image and Likeness or NIL. If you're a college football fan, you've probably heard of NIL, where star college players can finally get paid for the use of their name, or image, or likeness, as in their names on football jerseys or ability to endorse products.

The same applies to virtual voices. Just because you pay to use a vocal clone of a person, that doesn't mean that you also get the name, image and likeness rights to use as well. In fact, NIL rights are explicitly spelled out in all agreements involving virtual vocalists, virtual images or virtual voices.

That means that you can't use Grimes vocals on a track and then use her name to get views, publicity or streams without getting permission first.

This also brings up possible NIL issues in other mediums like Ai graphics and videos as well. If you were to ask an Ai graphics generator to create an album cover that includes Taylor Swift, and then use it for your album, you can bet that you'll be hearing from her attorneys unless you've received permission first.

In truth, Ai generators of all types have recognized this problem and have included what they call "guardrails" (meaning restrictions) around their image or music generation. That means that if you ask an Ai music generator to create music like Ed Sheeran, or a likeness of Ariana Grande, you'll most likely get a polite message back that says, "I'm sorry but I can't do that!"

Regardless, be careful when generating media other than music that involves someone famous, since NIL infringement is just as serious as with music.

Where Ai Copyright Sits Today

As you've read, there's a lot of confusion about Ai copyright because the current laws are outdated and don't directly apply to the situation today. The fact of the matter is that copyright law around the world was written for the last century and not for today's digital world.

While the U.S. looks like it will be slow at adopting new law, new guidance from the Copyright Office and lawsuit judgements could shape how we view copyright much more quickly and provide a roadmap of what could work going forward.

That said, other areas of the world are moving much faster to figure this out as the European Union, Japan and even China race to address the uncertainty head on. As you might expect, their approaches are different, with the EU proposing a much more stringent copyright law wanting to control and restrict how Ai is used, Japan taking a relatively loose "anything goes" attitude, and China using a combination of the two - loose for research and the military but somewhat stringent for commercial use.

A potential loophole may exist where if the Ai, and therefore the training, was done in another part of the world, then it would be subject to the laws of that jurisdiction. That means that if the training was done in Japan and that country has looser copyright laws than that United States, then things that would be considered infringement here might not be there. Hence, no infringement.

These new copyright laws are not passed yet and are just early proposals, so many things could change during the process.

Now here's the good news!

This book shows you how to use Ai as a tool to help you enhance your music creations and promotions. It's all about your creativity with a bit of its help, which means that in most cases, you should own the copyright, just like when you write a song.

If you use an Ai to help you with some chord progression ideas or ChatGPT helps you write marketing copy, as it sits now, you're the owner (again, not legal advice). The problems with copyright begins to apply if you use a 100% Ai creation or you have minimal interaction (but we don't know how much yet).

This is what happens when we use technology on the cutting edge. Sometimes there are more questions than answers.

SUMMING IT UP

The following applies to Ai copyright as of the writing of this book.

- Ai copyright is confusing right now because the copyright laws around the world are outdated.
- The U.S. Copyright Office has ruled that you can't copyright a 100% Ai-generated piece of content (song, artwork, graphics, video). A human must be involved, but it hasn't been worked out exactly how much yet.
- Many music distributors will not distribute a 100% Ai-generated song, streaming services are deleting them, and it won't be eligible to win a Grammy either.
- Many online Ai content generators contend that they own the copyright to the generated content. You can either license it from them or own it depending upon the subscription tier to register for.
- Some online Ai content generators restrict you from distributing the content online or monetizing it unless you register for a higher tier.

- You may not get the highest resolution content unless you register for the highest subscription tier.
- When it comes to music, all of the above applies to the recording copyright. The composition (publishing) copyright is rarely mentioned. Who owns it? Read the terms and conditions.
- In most cases you can avoid any of these problems if you download the MIDI file, load it into your DAW, and use your own virtual instruments to build the track.
- Ai training datasets may become a new source of revenue for artists and songwriters in the future.
- Complicating matters, proposed copyright laws in other territories of the world may be more or less strict than what we adhere to in the United States.

PART 2

Ai MUSIC PRODUCTION

Ai music production encompasses both music composition and music production, and they both need a bit of a clarification.

The Ai Music Composition chapter consists of sections on Ai text-to-music platforms, which actually generate music and MIDI files; Ai music idea platforms, which are more for melody and chord change suggestions, how to use ChatGPT as a compositional tool; and Ai lyric generation, again to give you ideas for words and phrases when you're stuck.

The chapter on Ai Production Tools covers platforms that create new sounds, transform current sounds into different ones, some Ai's that are smart enough to play along with you, Ai song analysis, and Ai voice cloning, a hot topic for many.

Chapter 5 covers all sorts of Ai audio plugins and standalone apps, from Ai DAWS, track separation tools, noise reduction tools, plugins like Ai-driven compressors, limiters, EQs, gates and reverbs, to where to place them in the signal path of your DAW.

Ai COMPOSITION

While many think that using Ai for writing a song is simply typing in a prompt that says, "Create a song that sounds like Drake," there's much more to it than that. A music Ai like Loudly or Boomy might output something that might be in the ballpark, but the surprise is that you'll probably only get about 30 seconds and not a full-length song. If you're a musician or songwriter, that's not what you're looking for.

Ai composition is really more than that. It's asking one of the many Ai tools to help you generate a melody, a lyric or a chord progression that you might find useful in your daily songwriting. It's learning how to form the exact prompt that will give you an idea for a new beat or melody twist that you never would have thought of otherwise.

As you might imagine, there are now dozens of tools that can help us do that, with more coming online all the time. Some are platforms that you access in a browser, some are standalone apps, and some are DAW plugins. They range from being remarkably simple to deeply intricate, some requiring a steep learning curve to navigate.

This is not a book about mastering a specific platform or plugin so we won't go down the rabbit hole of learning a particular Ai, although I will point out the features and nuances of some of the ones that I find more interesting.

Instead, we'll look at how we can have these help us in our songwriting, so that no matter which one you use or if a new one comes along, your approach can remain consistent in order to get the best results.

Ai TEXT-TO-MUSIC PLATFORMS

There are a number of platforms that are user-friendly and don't require much music skill, and these fall into the "consumer" platforms category. They tend to respond to simple prompts (in fact, they won't allow you to get too complicated) and produce results that impress consumers or music beginners, but aren't likely to be useful in a professional setting. They can be very helpful in certain situations though, as long as you don't expect a result that's beyond the capabilities of the platform. Unfortunately, the music that gets generated is disappointing much of the time, and it's all because of one song.

The Viral Track That Changed Everything

The song that significantly heightened Ai awareness within the music industry was a track created by the anonymous *ghostwriter977* called "Heart On My Sleeve," released in March of 2023. This would be just another track by an unknown composer except that it featured superstars Drake and The Weeknd, or so it seemed.

It turned out that neither of these artists actually performed on the track. Their voices were Ai-generated. That didn't stop the song from becoming a viral hit though, as "Heart On My Sleeve" quickly accumulated 600,000 streams on Spotify, 275,000 views on YouTube, 6.9 million views on Twitter, and 15 million views on TikTok before a take-down was forced by Universal Music Group, the parent company of these artists record labels.

The quick success of the track sent ripples through the music industry, as a slew of new superstar imitation songs soon flooded social media and online distributors. It also misled casual music fans into thinking that all they had to do was sign into a music Ai and input a prompt that simply said, "Make a song like Drake," and out would pop a flawless imitation.

What most people didn't understand was that "Heart On My Sleeve" and all the other similar tracks that followed were actually meticulously crafted mostly *without* the use of Ai.

While *ghostwriter977* never revealed the Ai that he used, he did state that he was a ghostwriter for a record label with a great deal of music production experience. He crafted the song manually, and only used Ai to clone the voices of Drake and The Weeknd, which then replaced his vocal performance.

The fact of the matter is that the various Drake, John Lennon, Michael Jackson, Kanye West, and Ariana Grande (and others) Ai songs that you can find online require far more than just a prompt to create, as all of them involve good old-fashioned music production to create the backing track first.

The effect of these "fake" songs was that millions flocked to Ai music generators like Boomy and Loudly only to be disappointed that their creations weren't even in the same universe as the originals. On the positive side, these same creators were exposed to producing music via Ai, but the downside was that online music streamers were suddenly flooded with millions of these tracks.

The music industry's reaction was fast and furious, as record labels issued take-down notices on Ai-generated fake tracks, and music distributors like Spotify and Tunecore deleted and rejected not only obvious fake tracks, but 100% Ai-generated tracks as well.

Regardless of its limitations, consumer-level Ai generated music is here to stay.

Ai Consumer Composition Platforms

Ai consumer platforms can generate a song for you with just a text prompt. In some cases you're additionally asked to provide the genre and profile of the song, the energy level, the instruments that you'd like to hear, and the duration. It will then generate up to five examples that you can choose from (see Figure 3.1).

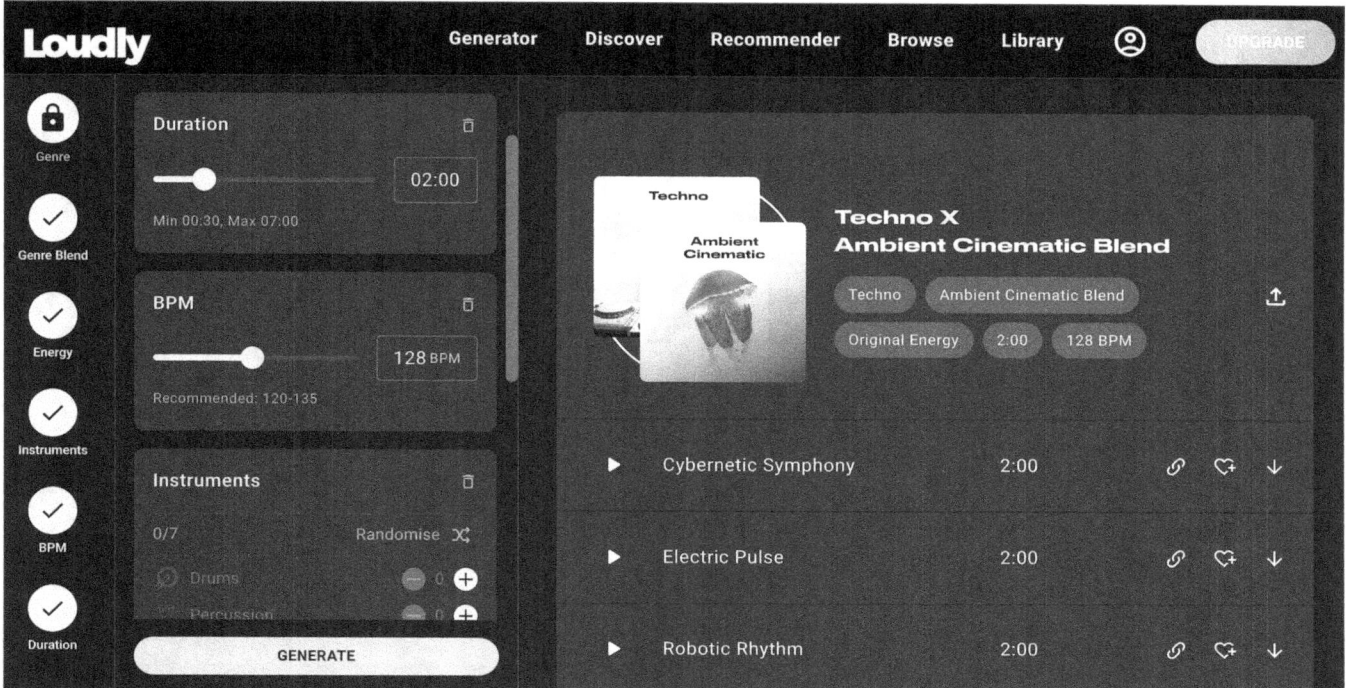

Figure 3.1: Loudly song creation with 3 examples
© 2023 Bobby Owsinski

Limitations

On the surface all this might seem like magic to a non-musician, but these types of platforms do have some limitations.

- In some cases the profiles are limited (usually veering towards sub-genres of electronic music), and the music that's generated tends to have only a verse and chorus.

- Another limitation is the fact that if you choose to download the audio file of the song, the best you can hope for is a 44.1kHz/16 bit file as its highest resolution. Although this is CD quality, it's not quite at the level of what most pros would use the studio.

- The audio quality is highly variable. Some Ai's will generate a much higher quality audio file than others. It's worth it to do a comparison.

- Don't expect your first, second or even fifth try to yield a result you like. According to Dadabots, less than 10% of all Ai-generated music is acceptable. Don't get discouraged though - keep trying with a new prompt or just regenerating the one you have.

- Instead of settling for a mediocre download, you're better off to grab the MIDI file, load it into your DAW, and use the virtual instruments of your choice instead of the ones provided by the Ai (see Figure 3.2). This will give you a wider palette of sounds to choose from as well as the freedom to edit the song as needed.

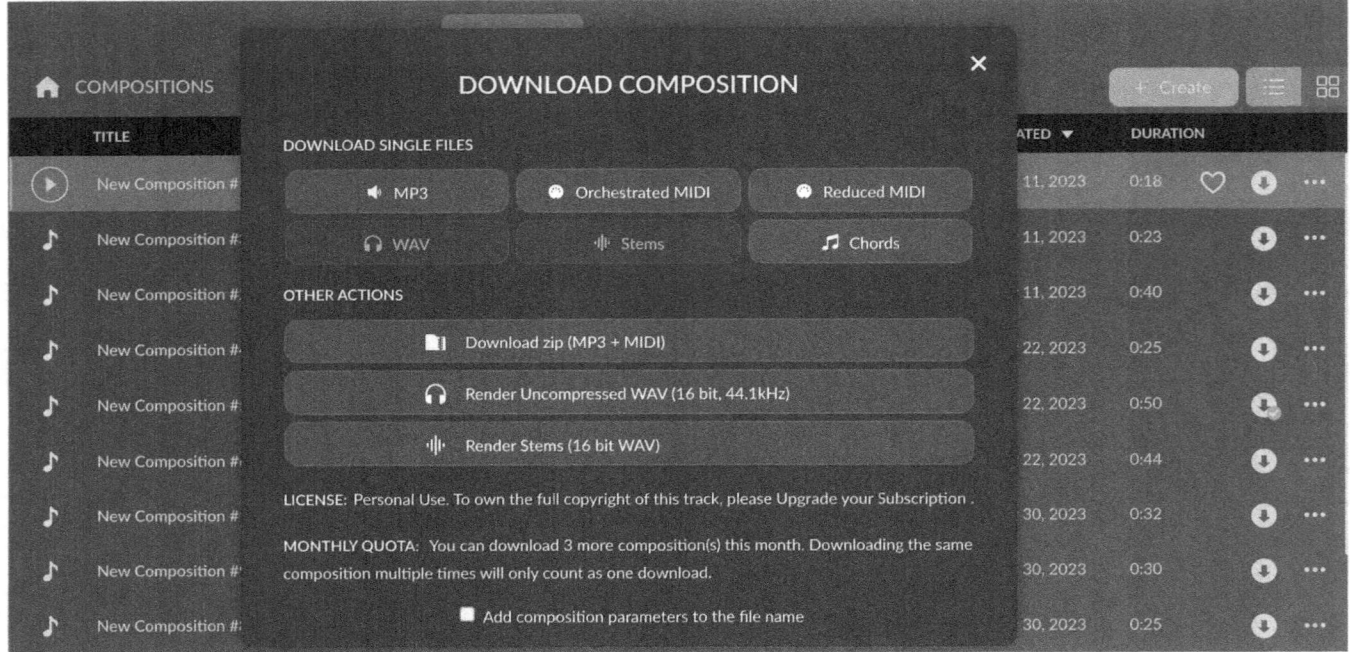

Figure 3.2: The various download options from Aiva
© 2023 Bobby Owsinski

- Be aware of the copyright and license. Most Ai music generators are subscription-based with three tiers. The free tier will allow you to generate music, but only for your own use as you'll be restricted from posting it anywhere. The middle tier will provide a license to use the song, post it and even monetize it, but you may be restricted to only certain platforms where that's allowed. The most expensive premium tier may assign the copyright of the song to you (read Chapter 2 for the potential pitfalls in this) and lift the restrictions on how and where it can be used. In all cases, be sure to read the fine print.

- Some Ai music generators are aimed at a very specific audience, such as video creators who are looking for music to play behind their visuals. Since the music isn't supposed to overshadow the picture, Ai can actually excel at the task since the output can be on the bland side.

The bottom line is that it will take more time to generate an acceptable track than you might expect, and then you may be restricted on what you can do with it based upon the payment tier you subscribe to.

Ai Text-To-Music Composition Platforms

As the name implies, a text-to-music platform takes a text prompt and generates music from it. The text prompt may be restricted to a simple phrase, or it may be long and complex, depending upon the platform. There may also be additional parameters that affect the music output, such as genre, energy, emotion and duration. These are just some of the platforms available at the time of writing this book. There are new ones coming online all the time, and some on this list might have folded or been acquired by the time you read this.

Here are some Ai text-to-music composition platforms to check out:

- Aiva - AIVA.ai
- Ai Test Kitchen - aitestkitchen.withgoogle.com/
- Beathoven - Beatoven.ai
- Boomy - Boomy.com
- Chordify - Chordify.net
- Ecrett Music - Ecrettmusic.com
- Loudly - Loudly.com
- Magenta - magenta.tensorflow.org
- Melodrive - Melodrive.itch.io
- Melobytes - Melobytes.com/en
- Musenet - openai.com/research/musenet
- Musico - Musi-co.com
- MusicGen - huggingface.co/spaces/facebook/MusicGen
- Splash Music - Splashmusic.com
- Soundful - Soundful.com
- Soundraw - Soundraw.io

Ai Music Generation Prompts

Regardless of the platform you use, crafting a prompt is your first step to generating music. Like with everything that's Ai-centric, the better the prompt, the better the outcome. Let's look at some prompt creation practices that will help you get the result you're looking for faster. These are the elements to consider in a prompt:

1. **The genre of music.** While generic terms like jazz, classical, or rock are a starting point, getting more specific like "upbeat, 80's-style synth-pop with a joyful melody" zeros in on a better result.
2. **The mood you're aiming for.** Using words like "melancholy," "upbeat," "dramatic," "dreamy," "intense," "mellow," or "rhythmic" can help guide the Ai in a specific direction.

3. **The instruments you'd like to be prominent.** If you have certain instruments in mind, spell it out. For example, "A soft ballad featuring a piano, cello, and female vocals." Also, what instruments you'd like to exclude (example: "A jazz combo without a saxophone.")

4. **The tempo and rhythm.** If you have a specific tempo in mind, indicate it via beats per minute (BPM). Likewise you're looking for a rhythmic pattern, include that. For instance, "A lively salsa at 180 BPM" or "A slow, melancholic waltz."

5. **Reference existing music.** If you have a specific sound or artist in mind, referencing them can be helpful.

6. **Structure or progression.** If you want a song with a specific structure (intro, verse, chorus, bridge, etc.), specify that in the prompt. For example, "A track with an ethereal intro leading into a powerful chorus, followed by a soft bridge and ending with an echoing outro."

7. **The duration of the song.** If you need a specific length for the music, state it. "A 2-minute cinematic intro for a sci-fi film."

8. **Refine the result.** Ai-generated music might not always match your vision on the first try. You might have to tweak your prompt or provide feedback on the generated output to refine the results. Provide feedback on what you liked and what you'd like to change for the next iteration.

9. **Test Different Prompts.** If the Ai allows it, run multiple prompts to see which one provides the desired result.

Remember that the punch your prompt packs can also be swayed by the capabilities and design of the specific Ai music generator you're working with. Some Ai's might vibe better with certain types of prompts than others. A dash of experimentation and iteration will go a long way in sharpening your prompts and bagging the best results.

How To Use

1. If available, use an appropriate prompt (see the section above)
2. Select the *Create* button
3. Select a music genre profile if offered
4. Select a key signature if offered
5. Select the tempo if offered
6. Select the number of compositions examples to be generated if offered
7. Either download as an audio or MIDI file if satisfied
8. If not satisfied, open the editor and make changes or add new parts
9. Either download as an audio or MIDI file if satisfied with the results

Ai MUSIC COMPOSITION IDEA PLATFORMS

The second type of composition platform is more oriented to a professional musician, composer, or songwriter. In this case you're looking more for chord pattern or melody ideas than a finished track, hence the name "Idea Platform." That means that the prompt approach is different since we're not looking for a entire arrangement, only bits of the skeleton.

Ai Composition General Prompt Guidelines

When using one of these tools, if you were to create a simple prompt like "create a memorable melody," you'd most likely get a repeating sequence of quarter notes from the C major scale that you most likely won't find very inspiring. To get something usable, try adding the following to the prompt:

- Ask for "a combination of quarter, eighth, and sixteenth notes" when prompting for a melody.
- Tell it what scale or key signature you want it to use.
- Try asking it for specific chord progressions using roman numerals.
- Ask for chord progressions that fit a genre's style, like a jazzy chord progression or a punk rock progression.

Ai Composition Idea Platforms

Ai composition idea platforms come in different flavors: some are browser-based, others are stand-alone apps, and some come as plugins. The following platforms vary in their focus—some are for fresh melody ideas, others are for discovering new chord patterns, while some are jacks of both trades. A select few can almost morph into a DAW.

Because some of the following platforms can get complex, I suggest finding one thing that it does well, and stick to that if you're not up for learning another new platform. A good example of this would be Scaler 2 (see Figure 3.3), which is an excellent platform for finding new chord substitutions and changes. As above, there are new ones coming online all the time, and some on this list might have folded or been acquired by the time you read this.

Figure 3.3: Scaler 2

Here are some Ai music composition sites to check out:

- Aiva - Aiva.ai
- Audiocipher - Audiocipher.com
- Audiomodern - Audiomodern.com
- Bandlab Songstarter - Bandlab.com/songstarter
- Captain Chords - Mixedinkey.com/captain-plugins/captain-chords/
- Flow Machines - flow-machines.com
- Lemonaide - Lemonaide.ai
- Melody Sauce - Melody Sauce
- Melody Studio - Melodystudio.net
- Neutone - Neutone.space
- Orb Producer - orbplugins.com/orb-producer-suite/

- Pilot Plugins - mixedinkey.com/pilot/
- Playbeat - audiomodern.com/shop/plugins/playbeat-3/
- Scaler 2 - Scalerplugin.com

Again, some of these platforms can present a steep learning curve, so don't go down the rabbit hole if all you want is a new way to generate a few melody suggestions. The idea is to make your music better in the most efficient way possible.

USING A CHATBOT AS A COMPOSITION TOOL

It's easy to think that a chatbot like ChatGPT is for text-only output, but we can also use it as quick composition tool as well. While it won't create music directly, it can help you with melodies and chord progressions. Let's take a look.

Use A Chatbot To Generate Chord Progressions

Try the following prompts in ChatGPT or other chatbot to generate interesting chord progressions. These go from simple to complex.

- Write a chord progression in [key signature].
- Write a complex chord progression in [key signature].
- Write a chord progression in the style of [example: Elton John].
- Write a chord progression for a jazz-rock song with a pulsating keyboard arpeggio.
- Write an 8 chord progression in [key signature].
- Write an 8 chord progression in [key signature] using closed-inversions.

Use A Chatbot To Generate Guitar Tabs

Once again, these go from simple to complex.

- Write a chord progression in guitar tablature
- Create guitar tabs for a ii7 V I chord progression in F Major.
- Write a rock guitar solo in the key of C in tablature.

Use A Chatbot To Generate Melodies

Since melodies are not easy to express through text prompts, ChatGPT itself suggests using this list of options for melody prompts:

- **Standard Notation:** Naming notes (e.g., "C-E-G") along with their durations (e.g., "quarter note C, half note E, quarter note G").

- **Scale Degrees:** Naming a melody in relation to the key it's in using scale degrees (e.g., "In the key of C Major: 1-3-5").

- **Guitar Tablature:** You'll get melodies as they appear on a guitar neck, but the rhythm will be missing (see Figure 3.4).

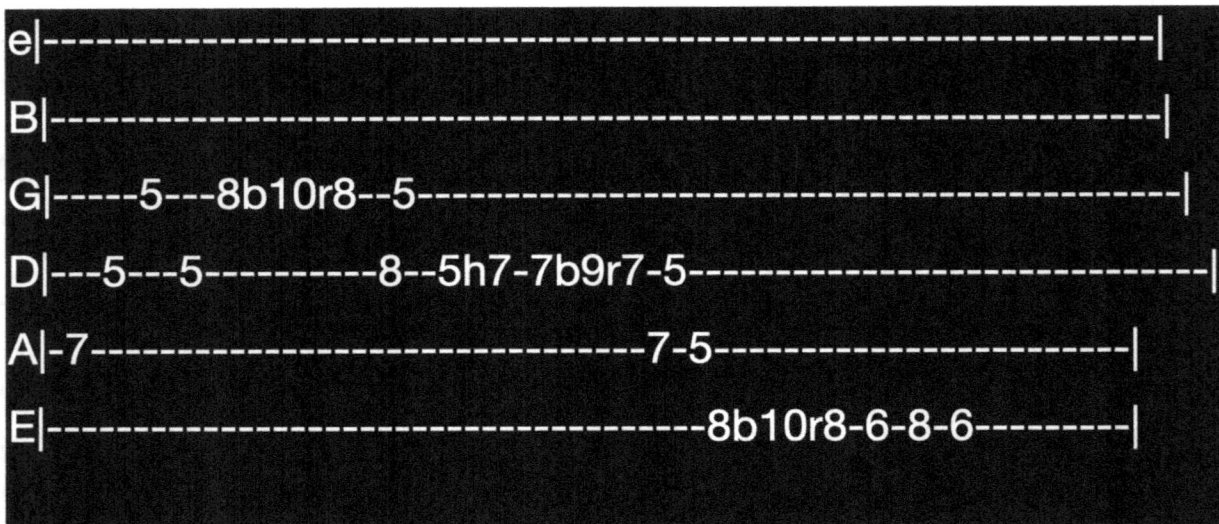

Figure 3.4: A guitar solo in tablature from ChatGPT
© 2023 Bobby Owsinski

- **Piano Roll Notation:** Describe the melody using MIDI note numbers, representing the values on your DAW's piano roll. For example, a C Major arpeggio would be represented as 60, 64, 67.

- **Solfège:** Describe simple melodies using the do-re-mi system. This lacks rhythmic input and will keep you fixed to a simple diatonic scale.

- **Alphanumeric Pitch Notation:** This system uses the letters A-G in combination with numbers 0-9 to represent pitches, with C4 often being set as "middle C". For example, a melody might go "C4-E4-G4-C5".

- **Pitch frequencies**: Name each musical note as a frequency (Hz) rather than using standard notation concepts like note names.

ChatGPT Melody Prompts

- Write a melody in <key signature> using alphanumeric pitch notation. Include indicators of rhythm.

- Use this same chord progression and give each chord four beats.

- Write a catchy melody in the same key signature using quarter and eighth notes. Be sure to indicate the duration of each note in the melody. If the melody contains notes outside of the chord, then it should only be used as passing tones to a note that is in the chord. Here is the progression: Dm7 - G7 - CM9 - Em7

How To Use

1. Select the chatbot that you want to use. You may want to try more than one since they all provide different results.

2. Design your prompt using the suggestions above. Remember, the more detail you provide the better the results you'll get.

3. Regenerate the results at least once.

4. Transfer the results to you favorite instrument and finish your composition.

Ai LYRIC GENERATION

If you have trouble coming up with lyrics for songs, you'll be pleased to know that writing lyrics is one area that Ai excels at. While you can't expect it to come up with lyrics on the level of Bob Dylan or Bernie Taupin, you will get something rather serviceable that just might contain a word or phrase that will spark your own lyric writing breakthrough.

Just like in every other Ai case, the better the prompt the better the results. Here are some prompt tips to follow for best results:

- The more you set the stage for the song, the better your results will be ("A boy away in the Navy longing for his girlfriend in New York City")

- Ask the Ai to imagine it's the songwriter ("Imagine you're a songwriter. . .")

- Add the mood, the concept, the intended audience, any related emotions, the hero and the goal ("Imagine you're a country music songwriter. Write a sad song aimed at teen-age girls about a boy that looks like Kid Laroi who's away in the Navy")

- Ask the Ai to become a person in the song ("Imagine you're a cowboy on a cool night on the open range.")

- Remember to tell it the form of the song you want (example: "The song should have 3 verses, 2 chorus, a bridge")

Ai Lyric Prompts

While you can ask the Ai to generate an entire song, sometime you only need help in a particular section. Here are some examples:

- "Write a chorus about a school romance that ends at graduation."

- "Craft a verse that describes the feeling of wandering through a city that you don't know late at night."

- "Write a bridge about the bittersweet feeling of a relationship breaking up that you knew had to end."

- "Compose a song in the style of a 1980s power ballad that captures the essence of a day at the beach where the sand pebbles are like memories."

- "Write a ballad about two stars in the sky that are destined to never meet."

You often get better results if you ask the Ai to act as a songwriter or coach. Here are some examples.

- "I want you to act as a songwriter. Write a song about a sad young boy trapped in New York City, longing to return to his country home. The song is aimed at teenagers. It should contain an intro, 3 verses, 2 different choruses, a bridge and an outro."

- "I want you to act as a songwriting coach and help me determine the specific aspect of my song that is causing writer's block."

- "I want you to act as my songwriting mentor, offering suggestions related to a particular song section. I will provide the lyrics of the song I'm working on and identify the part or parts I'm struggling with. Offer specific recommendations for revisions, alternative approaches, or exercises that can help me address the issue in that section. Share your insights on why you believe these suggestions will improve the overall song."

Ai Lyric Platforms

There are many Ai lyric writing platforms. Some are just a feature of an expanded Ai, while others are dedicated just to lyric writing. Then there's ChatGPT, which is very fast and can provide impressive results.

Here are some lyric generator platforms to check out:

- Chat GPT - openai.com/blog/chatgpt
- Bored Humans - boredhumans.com/?tool=46
- Deepbeat - Deepbeat.org
- Freshbots - Freshbots.org
- Keyword To Lyrics - lyrics.mathigatti.com
- LogicBalls - logicballs.com/tools/song-lyrics-generator
- Masterpiece Generator - song-lyrics-generator.org.uk/
- My Lyrics Maker - apps.apple.com/us/app/my-lyrics-maker/id1609300054
- Rytr - rytr.me/use-cases/song-lyrics

- Song Lyrics Generator - song-lyrics-generator.org.uk/
- These Lyrics Do Not Exist - theselyricsdonotexist.com

How To Use

1. Select the chatbot that you want to use. You may want to try more than one since they will all provide different results.
2. Design your prompt using the suggestions above. Remember, the more you set the stage regarding the song's story the better the results you'll get.
3. Be sure to indicate if you only want a verse, chorus, bridge, or multiple song sections.
4. Regenerate the results at least once.
5. Use a different platform and repeat as above.

SUMMING IT UP

- Don't be fooled into thinking a single prompt produces good music the first time
- Usually only about 10% of the music generated is acceptable
- Don't expect a full song to be generated without needing some tweaks
- It takes a lot of tweaking to get close to the examples that you hear online (many are mostly created manually using standard production tools)
- This can take hours
- And the audio quality is marginal at best (some platforms provide better audio quality than others)
- Remember - you can't copyright a 100% Ai-generated song
- A 100% Ai-generated song will be banned by distributors and streaming platforms
- You may be restricted where you can post Ai-generated music
- Monetization may also be restricted
- You usually need a paid Pro account to own the copyright (but read Chapter 2 for more details)
- You usually need a paid Pro account to download Wav files
- The highest resolution audio files are 44.1kHz/16 bit
- You're better off to download the MIDI file
- Some platforms are really complex and require a long learning curve, but you don't need to learn everything to make them useful

- Use them for inspiration
- Don't expect brilliance
- Expect to get some good ideas
- The more you paint the picture, the better the Ai response

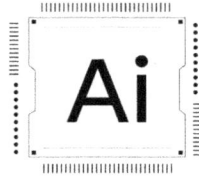

4
Ai MUSIC PRODUCTION TOOLS

Now that you've written the song it's time to produce it. That means putting together the arrangement and the instrumentation that's appropriate for the style of music that you're working in. While there's no Ai that will arrange a song for you yet, there are a lot of Ai's that will help you not only come up with new and unusual sounds, but suggest new musical parts that fit your song harmonically and rhythmically as well.

We're going to break these down into five categories: Ai Sounds, Ai Tonal Morphing, Ai Accompaniment, Ai Voice Cloning and Ai Song Analyzers. Each one has a particular focus on music production. You might only need one of the five, but don't be surprised if you find a need for all of them at one time or another.

AI SOUND GENERATION

Producers are often faced with a decision - "Do I use vintage sounds that everyone knows or do I look for sounds that no one has heard before?" Often a new and exciting sound can be a big part of why a song is a hit, so more and more producers are looking beyond sample libraries to something that's completely cutting edge and new. As you might imagine, there's an Ai for that.

Ai Samples

Many genres of music are based on samples, in which case an Ai like Output Arcade (see Figure 4.1) can be very useful. Although it features a diverse library of samples, it's also able to convert your tracks into samples as well. The platform then lays out a wide variety of tweaks like filters, slicing, pitch alterations, playback speed adjustments, re-sequencing options, FX, modulation (both LFO and step sequence), macros, and the list goes on.

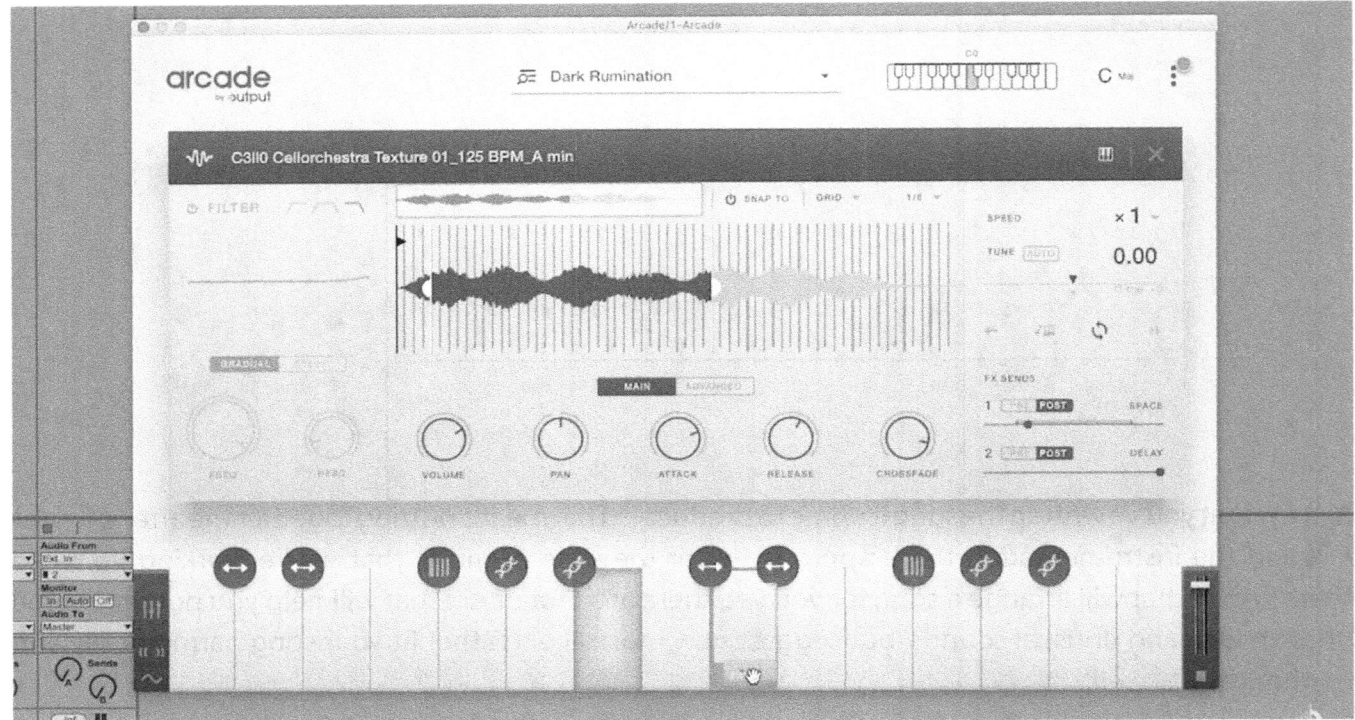

Figure 4.1: Output Arcade sample conversion

Samplab is another sample-oriented platform that has a wide assortment of features, including the ability to generate samples from a text prompt, turn audio samples into a MIDI file, stem separation, real time audio warping (time stretching), and more.

On the other hand, sometimes you're just looking for the right loop that fits with or augments your song. Even if you don't have a large library of samples to choose from, auditioning potential candidates can often seem like it's taking forever. Jamahook is a recommendation platform for loops and beats designed to be a massive time saver by quickly finding loops that work. As with many audio plugins (like you'll see in Chapter 5), after you play a short piece of your tune, it then finds rhythmically and harmonically suitable loops for each musical segment in real time.

Finally, many producers collect libraries like they collect t-shirts, and that can cause big problems when it comes to actually finding the right sound. Atlas 2 is an Ai-powered organizer focused on being used with large sample libraries that uses Ai to help you find what you need much faster than you ever could manually.

Ai Drum Sounds

Drums are the heartbeat of any song, and while many producers are satisfied with using their favorites over and over, others are more adventurous and want something new for every song.

Emergent Drums (see Figure 4.2) uses cutting-edge generative models trained to design novel drum samples bit by bit from scratch. No source recordings are used to generate the samples, so each one is truly original. It uses two different sound models, Crunchy and Creamy, to provide extensive variations in the samples you create. Not only that, you're able to drag in your own sample and have it create variations on that as well.

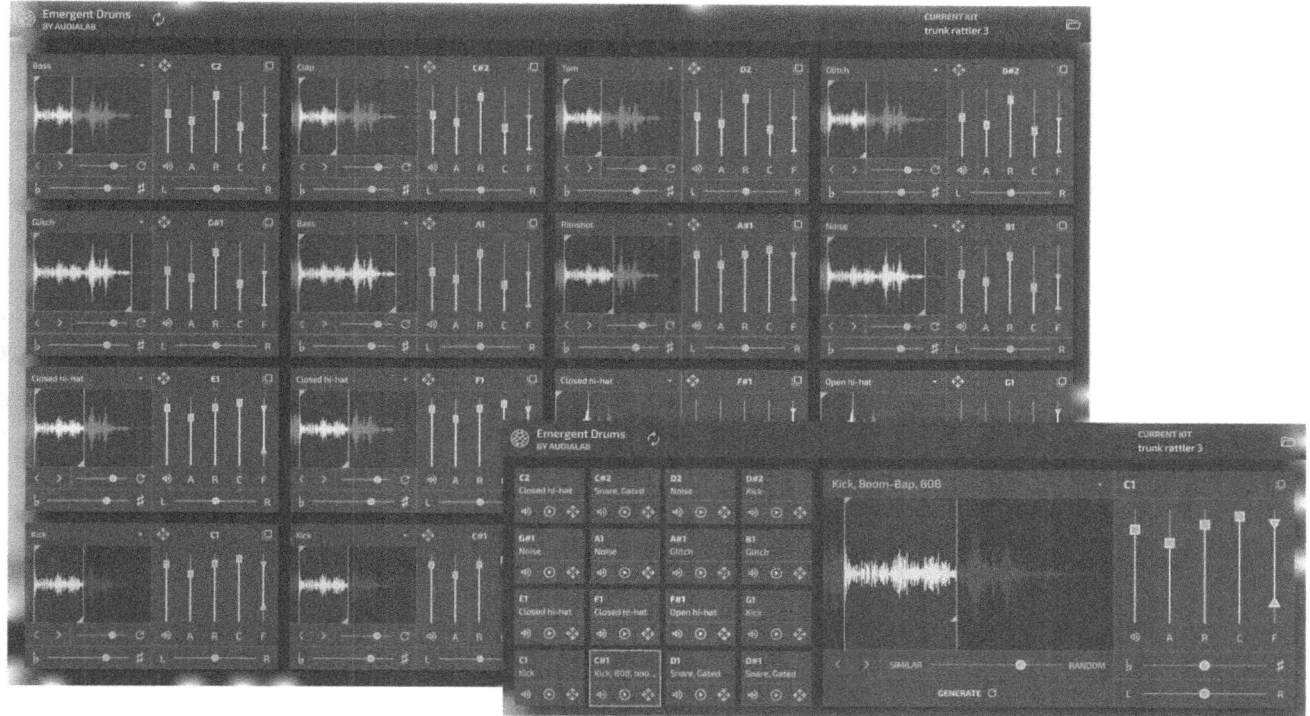

Figure 4.2: Emergent Drums

Steinberg Backbone uses a new Sony-built Ai called DrumGAN to create new kick drum, snare drum and cymbal samples in a very fast, intuitive way. It can also analyze samples that you feed into it and create numerous variations. All samples can be further adjusted using a number of Backbone's modules.

Both of these platforms have a pretty steep learning curve that might take longer than you'd like to get up and running. Plus they lean heavily towards electronic music, which may or may not be your focus. That said, if new drum sounds are what you're looking for, these two platforms are a good place to start.

Ai Synthesis

For synth sounds, Quantakor (see Figure 4.3) is a rompler that uses artificial intelligence along with a complex resynthesis algorithm to provide lush new soundscapes. If you're not familiar with the term "rompler," it's a musical instrument that plays pre-set sounds based on samples. Of course you can modify the sounds with various parameter controls, but you can't go beyond the original samples that the Ai has generated. Considering that what it does it does really well, that's probably enough for most producers.

Figure 4.3: Quantakor Ai Synthesizer

Sistema is an interesting synth plugin as it can use a text input to describe the sound in order to generate it, or it can create a new sound based on the parameters you set in the plugin's user interface. It has an equally interesting pricing model in that you can purchase it outright or rent to own, in which case the plugin will be yours in 5 months.

The idea behind all of these platforms and plugins is to help you find a new sound that better fits your vision or to discover entirely new sounds that no one has heard before

As said before, some of these platforms, like other music Ai's, tend to be oriented towards electronic music. This is because many of the programmers tend to prefer listening and making electronic music, but also because the generated sounds tend to fit that genre better than some that are more organic in nature. Also, most are available in AU and VST plugin formats only, so if you use Pro Tools, you'll need a VST wrapper like Blue Cat's Patchwork to use them.

Here's a list of some of the various platforms to check out:

- Algonaut Atlas 2 - Algonaut.audio
- Emergent Drums - audialab.com
- Jamahook - Jamahook.com
- Output Arcade - output.com/landing-pages/arcade/
- Eplex 7 Quantakor - eplex7.com/quantakor

- Samplab - Samplab.com/text-to-sample
- Sistema - guk.ai
- Steinberg Backbone - steinberg.net/vst-instruments/backbone

> **DAW Plugin Formats**
> There are three basic plugin formats that DAWs use.
> - VST stands for Virtual Studio Technology and is a plugin format developed by Steinberg. Popular DAWs like Cubase, Reaper, Ableton Live and FL Studio use this format.
> - AU (Audio Unit) is Apple's equivalent format for macOS users and is used by Logic Pro X, although it can read the VST plugin format as well.
> - AAX (Avid Audio eXtension) is a proprietary plugin format created by Avid specifically for use with Pro Tools. It's possible for Pro Tools to also use VST plugins, but it requires a small translation plugin called a wrapper to do so.
>
> Although plugins created by large developers are usually available in all plugin formats, some smaller developers sometimes choose not to make an AAX version because of development costs, as is the case with many Ai audio developers.

Ai TONAL MORPHING

Tonal morphing Ai's turn an existing sound into something else, like a voice into a violin, a flute into a trumpet, a male voice into a female voice, or even your voice into someone else's.

At the forefront of this category is singer, composer and artist Holly Herndon, who actually has a Doctorate from Stanford's Center for Computer Research in Music and Acoustics, where her research focus was on the interplay between machine learning and the voice. Holly launched her Holly+ platform back in 2021 so that a clone of her voice could be legally licensed. Anyone can upload a polyphonic audio file and receive a download of that music sung back in her distinctive processed voice.

If Holly's voice isn't quite what you're looking for, there are many more to choose from on Kits Ai (see Figure 4.4), Dreamtonics, or Uberduck (including one by pop artist Grimes). Speaking of Grimes, you can legally use her voice on one of your songs as long as you pay a 50% royalty fee at elf.tech.

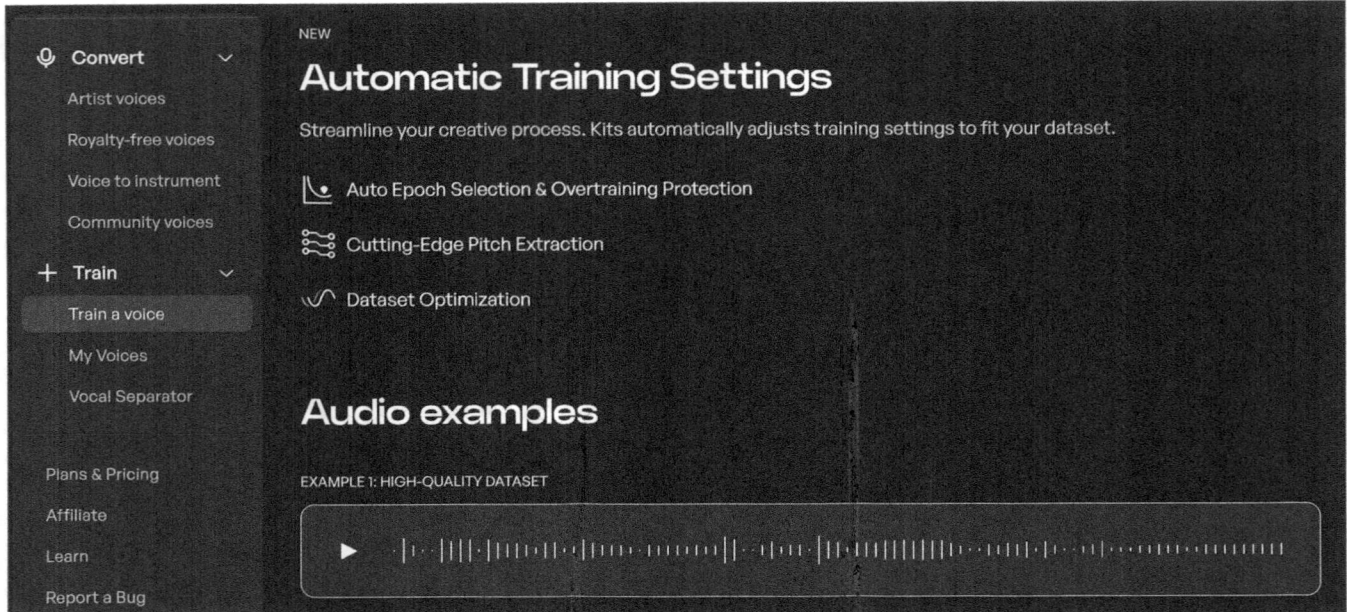

Figure 4.4: Kits Ai

Dreamtonics Synthesizer V (pronounced "V" as in vocal and not the Roman numeral) is a "vocal synthesizer" where the user inputs melodies or a MIDI file, then fills in the lyrics, and a selected virtual vocalist then sings them. It consists of an editor and a database of virtual vocalists, which are purchased separately. Synthesizer V can be used as a stand-alone app (PC, Mac or Linux) or as a VST3 plugin.

One of the vocal synthesis methods it uses allows a vocalist to sing real songs as samples, and the neural network learns all of its vocal characteristics, which then enables it to simulate the real vocal. Beyond that, the user is able to adjust the vocal with a wide range of parameter control that includes pitch deviation, vibrato envelope, loudness, tension, air, gender, vocal mode, and more. Plus it can even translate the vocals into other languages, although only English, Chinese and Japanese are currently available.

On the other hand, if you want to change your voice or any other track into a different instrument, there's Mawf (see Figure 4.5) and Tone Transfer (among others) to choose from.

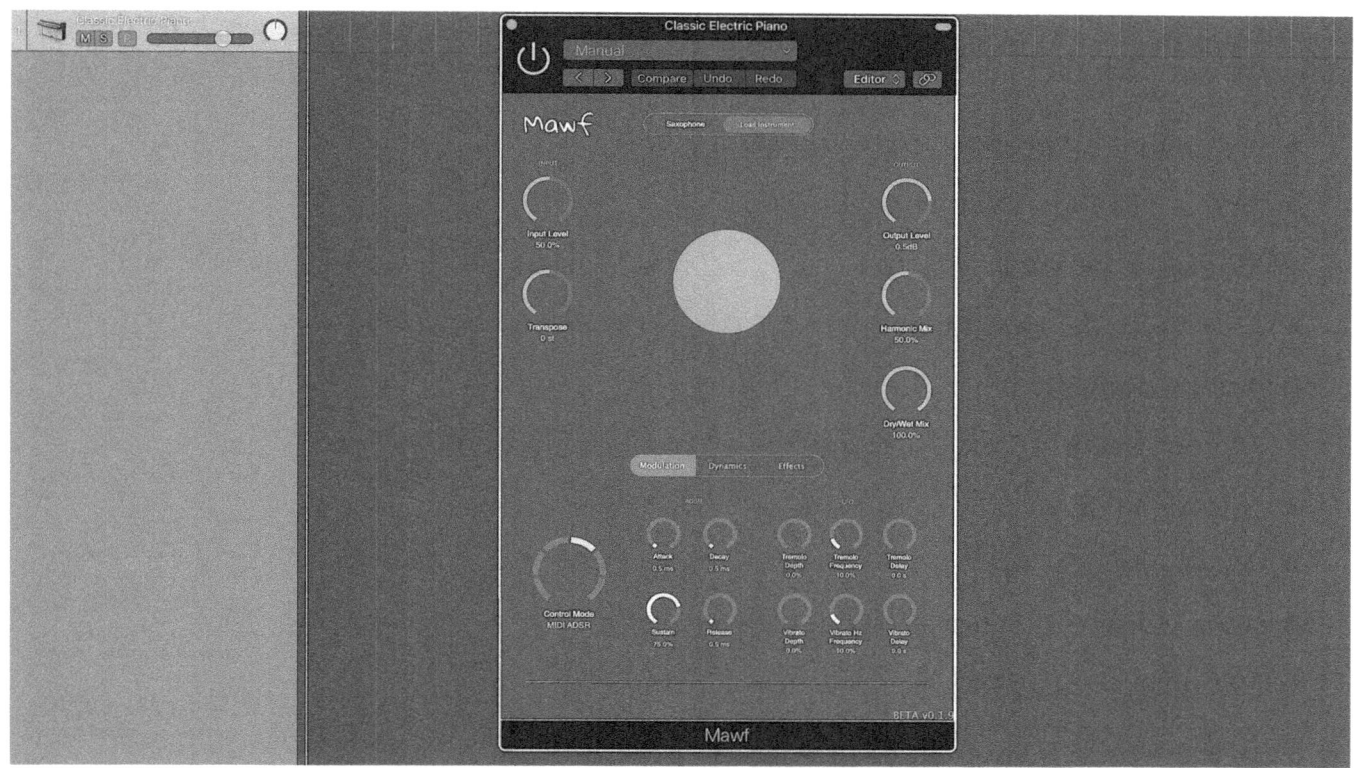

Figure 4.5: Mawf virtual synthesizer

Finally, iZotope's Nectar 4 has a module called *Backer* (see Figure 4.6) that allows you to choose from a variety of voices to instantly add backgrounds to your lead vocals.

Figure 4.6: iZotope Nectar 4 Backer feature

57 | Ai Music Production Tools

Of course, there are plenty more to choose from than the examples mentioned above, but these are a good place to start.

- Dreamtonics - dreamtonics.com/synthesizerv/
- Eclipsed Sounds- Eclipsedsounds.com
- Grimes virtual vocal - elf.tech
- Heard Sounds - Heardsounds.com
- Holly+ - Holly.plus
- iZotope Nectar 4 Backer - izotope.com/en/products/nectar.html
- Kits Ai - Kits.ai
- Mawf - Mawf.io
- Tone Transfer - sites.research.google/tonetransfer
- UberduckAI - Uberduck.ai

Ai ACCOMPANIMENT

We've now entered into the realm of Ai becoming your band member and playing along with you in real time. One of the most interesting Ai's in this category is EZDrummer 3 (see Figure 4.7), where its *Bandmate* feature will find the right drum part for your song without you having to program it. This is a very exciting development for those that aren't good at programming drums or simply don't want to take the time. Likewise, Playbeat 3 generates drum patterns and variations based on how you train it during your everyday songwriting life.

Figure 4.7: EZ Drummer 3 Bandmate

Two more Ai plugins that take a similar approach are Drum Monkey and Bass Dragon from Unison. Drum Monkey pulls from over 3,000 drum samples to provide beats in more than 30 different music genres. Bass Dragon searches from over 19,500+ custom-designed, genre-specific MIDI bass line fragments to come up with perfect bass lines and 808 patterns for your song.

Likewise, Orb Bass analyzes the entire harmony of a track and proposes the best bass lines for your song. Orb Arpeggio is an instant easy-to-use module for providing both simple and complex arpeggios, which many times can be the backbone element of a song. These are both part of the Orb Producer Suite, which also includes Orb Chords for finding chord progressions and Orb Melody for providing new melody options.

Musico is an Ai that uses gestures, movement or sound to generate music, so you could actually use it when playing live. On the other hand, Melodrive Instant Album (see Figure 4.8) is intended for gaming as it generates music in real time according to the gameplay.

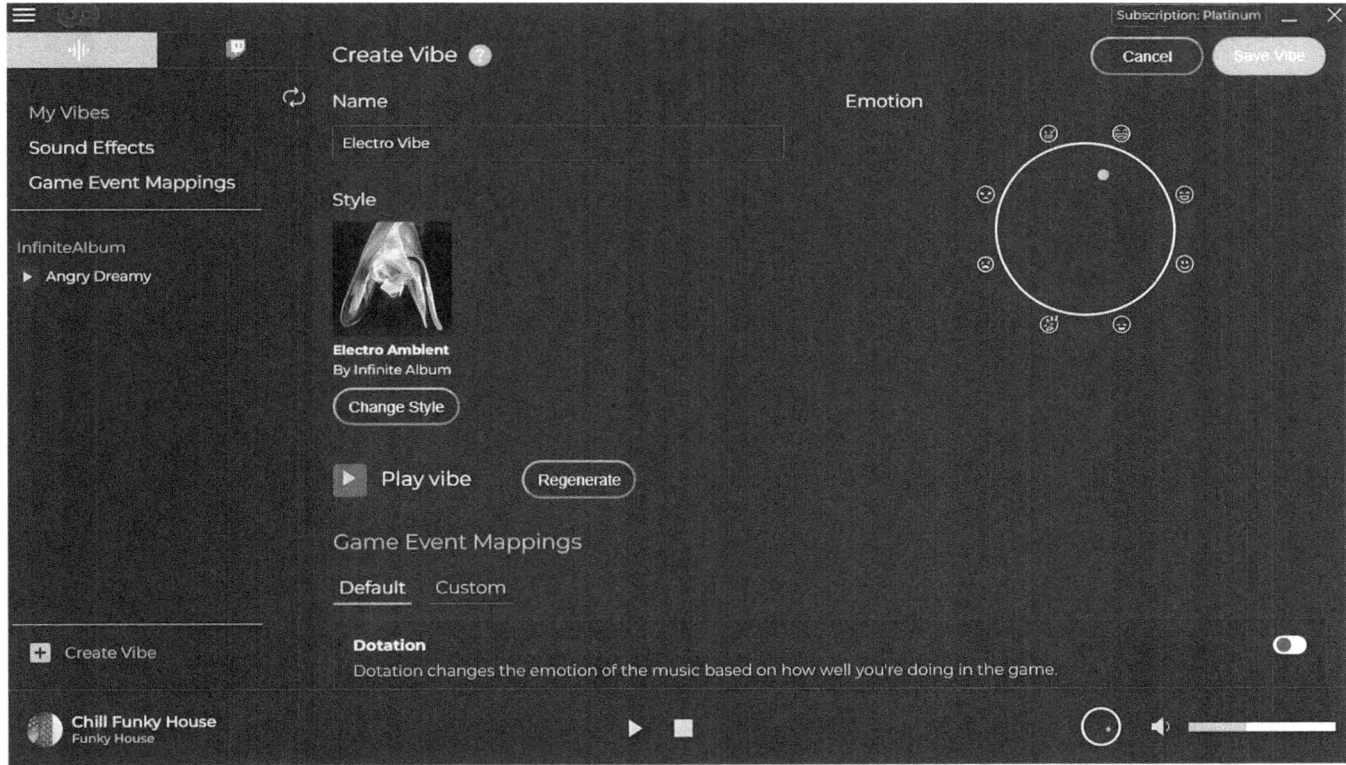

Figure 4.8: Musico

We're just scratching the surface when it comes to Ai accompaniment, so expect platforms in this area of music to get better and more useful as the training and neural networks grow. In the meantime, here are some Ai accompaniment platforms to check out:

- EZDrummer 3 - toontrack.com/product/ezdrummer-3/
- Melodrive Instant Album - infinitealbum.io/
- Musico - Musi-co.com

- Playbeat 3 - audiomodern.com/shop/plugins/playbeat-3/
- Orb Producer Suite - orbplugins.com/orb-producer-suite/
- Unison Bass Dragon - Unison.audio/bass-dragon
- Unison Drum Monkey - Unison.audio/drum-monkey

VOICE CLONING

Voice cloners allow you to either clone your own voice, or use other virtual voices to read your text. These are mostly intended for commercial applications that need a voice to read a written script, like for audiobooks, voiceovers, marketing videos or customer service.

Unlike many of the other Ai's that we've looked at, most of the music production Ai's don't require extensive prompting to get something that's usable, although regenerating the result a few times is still a good idea.

The exception is the voice cloners, which do require training if you use a voice that it hasn't been trained on before. For instance, if you were going to train one of them on your voice, it would require an upload of a clean audio file (meaning no background noise on it) with a duration of anywhere from 30 seconds to 30 minutes.

I've found that while the short audio files result in a pretty good audio representation of your voice, it requires a longer audio file to really train it on your vocal inflections so it sounds like you enough to fool the average listener. In some cases the Ai platform will recommend you read from a specialized script so that the neural network can compare it to other training material in order to understand the nuances of your voice better.

Regardless of the production category of Ai that you use, you'll find that they'll keep getting better at what they do as they're trained more, or new ones utilizing larger neural networks come on the market.

Plus, many singers will find that licensing their voice to one of these platforms will be yet another revenue source. While there's no standard on what kind of revenue is possible yet, the concept is new enough that everyone is still learning about what's possible, especially on the business side.

On the other hand, voice cloning has the potential for abuse, as it could easily be used to commit fraud, spread misinformation and generate fake audio evidence. As we've seen in the case of ghostwriter977 and "Heart On My Sleeve," the fact that a superstar's voice has been illegally cloned doesn't matter much to the general public when it comes to consuming a song. Look for legislation concerning illegal voice cloning soon, as multiple bills are pending in both the California legislature and United States Congress.

Here are some Ai voice cloners to check out:

- Delphi - withdelphi.com
- Eleven Labs - beta.elevenlabs.com
- Lovo Ai - Lovo.ai

- Murf Ai - <u>Murf.ai</u>
- Resemble Ai - <u>Resemble.ai/cloned</u>
- Respeecher - <u>Respeecher.com</u>

How To Use

1. Select the platform that you want to use. You may want to try more than one since they all provide different results.
2. Select the voice, the voice settings and model. Try different combinations as some will work better for you than others.
3. Enter the text that you want to convert to speech.
4. Generate the spoken audio. Regenerate again with different settings if not satisfied.
5. To clone your own voice, upload a recording of your voice. Anywhere from 30 seconds to 30 minutes is required, but the longer the duration of the file, the better it will capture your personal inflections. Be sure that the uploaded file of your voice is as noise-free as possible.
6. Repeat steps 2 through 4.
7. Download the generated file if satisfied.

Commercial Use Policies

This sounds like a broken record, but be sure to always check the terms and conditions of the platform to find out its commercial use policies.

In some instances you're free to use anything you generate, but there may be commercial use restrictions with some virtual vocalists databases.

In other words, you can use it for experimentation but you may have to pay extra to release the song that's using virtual vocalist commercially.

In some instances you must provide attribution to the virtual vocalist in order to use the song.

You're never allowed to use the virtual vocalist's name and likeness without prior agreement, which is negotiated separately.

Be sure to read the fine print to understand what's required to use the app, platform or database.

Ai SONG ANALYZERS

Song analyzers are somewhat focused in that they usually do only one thing, like finding the name, key, or BPM of a song, or maybe even determining its musical genre. For instance, if you've ever used Shazam to find out the name of a song that you just heard, you've just used a song analyzer. It's really good at only that one function, but that's exactly all we need it for.

While finding the name of a tune is a perfectly understandable and useful function for just about everyone, many professional musicians are quite capable of determining the key of a song or its tempo (beats per minute or BPM) just by using their ears and experience. That said, many music producers today are excellent at building songs via samples and loops, but might be a little light on the music theory, and this is where a song analyzer might be particularly useful. And when it comes to finding the genre and sub-genre of a song, most of us would gladly leave that to a friendly Ai.

Let's look at the different categories of song analyzers.

Key And Tempo Analyzers

One of the best key and tempo analyzers available is Mixed In Key, a simple utility that sits on your desktop, listens to the song or loop that's played, then tells you the key, scale and BPM (See Figure 4.9). Its graphic note visualizer also shows you the exact notes being played at any given time. You can also just drop an audio file onto its interface and it will extract the same information.

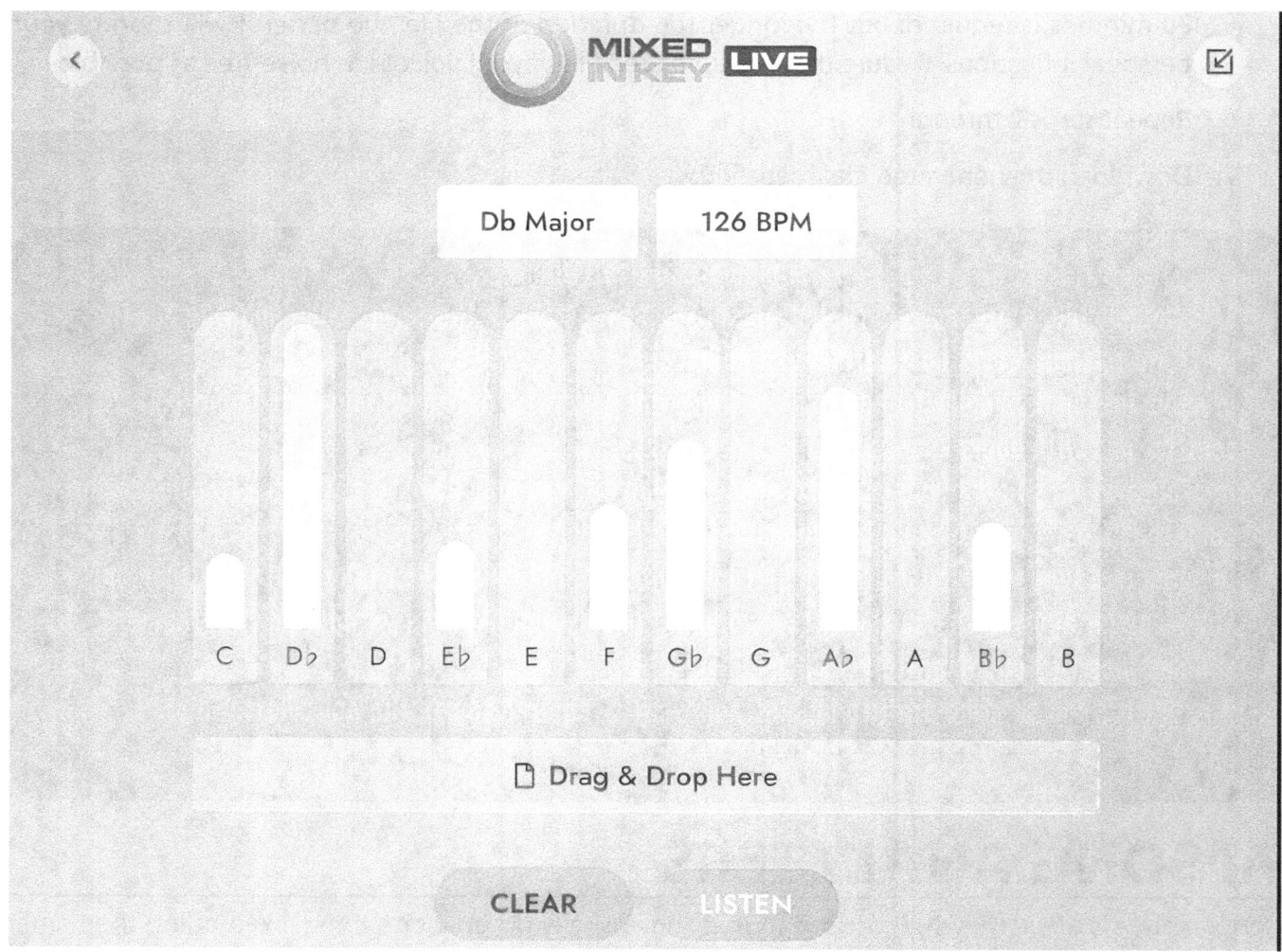

Figure 4.9: Mixed In Key

Vocal Remover has a Song Key and BPM Finder function that works from the desktop, as does Moises. The downside of these two is that the key and BPM functions are just features of a more sophisticated app, so you may end up paying for functions that you won't use.

Hook Theory has a unique function in that it will detect the chord progression in a song, and Mazmazika Chord Analyzer will outline the chords from any song from YouTube, Soundcloud or that you upload.

Song Genre Analyzers

If you were to try to generate a song by using any of the text-to-music Ai's, you'd find out soon enough that using a broad term like rock, rap, or electronic probably won't get you where you want to go. There are so many sub-genres attached to each musical genre that's it's hard to keep track of them all. But, as you've probably imagined, there's an Ai for that.

Music Genre Finder will instantly determine the genre of a reference song, provide the genres for Spotify and Wikipedia, and also provide a thorough track analysis that includes everything from Length, tempo, loudness level, key, popularity, happiness level, and more (see Figure 4.10). Make note of the genre and sub-genre and use that in your music-generation prompt.

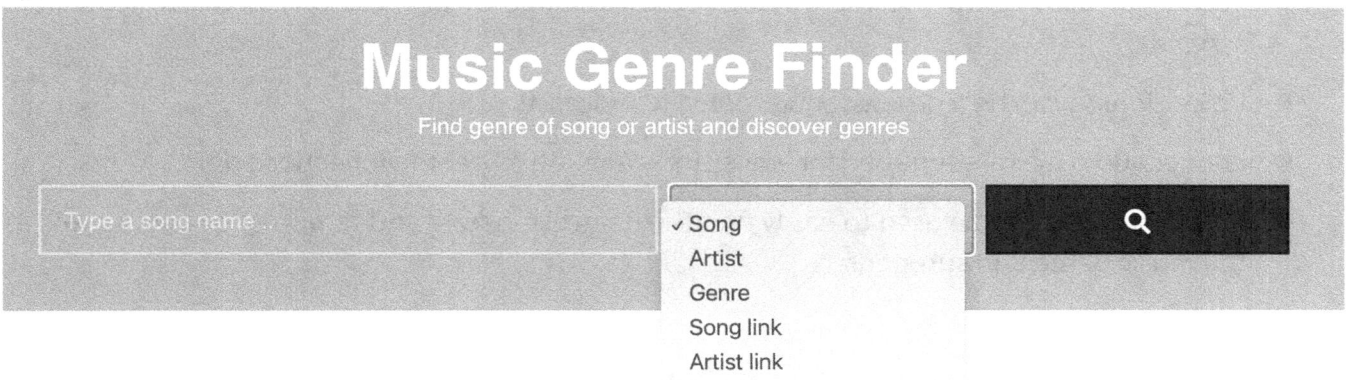

Figure 4.10: Music Genre Finder

Here are a number of Ai song analyzers to check out:

- Hook Theory - hooktheory.com/trends
- Mazmazika Chord Analyzer - mazmazika.com/chordanalyzer
- Miked In Key - mixedinkey.com/live/
- Moises - moises.ai
- Music Genre Finder - chosic.com/music-genre-finder
- Song Key And BPM Finder - vocalremover.org/key-bpm-finder

SUMMING IT UP

- Production Ai's are meant to generate new sounds or fill out productions
- They usually don't require complex prompting
- Many tend to be oriented towards electronic music
- As of the writing of this book, they're usually only available in VST and AU plugin formats
- The install is complicated for many of them
- Most have a bit of a learning curve
- There are many Ai's designed to find the right sample or loop for a song
- Some are designed to make searching a large sound library easier
- Using a virtual singer on a project is now a viable option
- You might have to pay extra and provide attribution when you use a virtual singer in a commercially released song
- You're not allowed to use the virtual vocalist's image or likeness unless that's negotiated separately
- Voice cloning can be a new revenue source for vocalists
- Longer audio files are required for voice clone training to get the inflections right
- Song analyzers can be used to easily find the name, key, scale and tempo or a song, as well as the music genre and sub-genre

5

Ai AUDIO TOOLS

While this book touches on all sorts of Ai's, some readers may be more focused on the many Ai audio tools than the other areas. In fact, Ai audio plugins shine in that they cut to the chase and make the setup of compressors, EQs and reverbs much easier by automatically adjusting their parameters for the song.

These audio tools will definitely get you into the ball park, but it should be noted that they require some tweaking in order to contribute to a professional mix. On the other hand, Ai track separation tools do what was once almost unthinkable by taking a full mixed stereo track and separating it into individual elements, while Ai noise reduction tools can take what a few years ago would have been an unusable recording and make it noise-free.

Before we get into those tools, let's take a look at what many consider the most important audio tool to a modern musician - the digital audio workstation.

Ai DAWS

Combining artificial intelligence with a digital audio workstation results in a new kind of DAW called a *Generative Audio Workstation*, or GAW. In this case, you get an Ai composition tool capable of generating audio from text, along with the elements of a DAW such as an editing timeline, audio processing and effects, and a digital mixer.

What's interesting here is the wide variety of approaches that different developers take. For instance, Aiva is touted for its music generation, but once the music is generated it can be manipulated via a browser-based DAW. Since the number of tracks that it can work with is limited, for anything more advanced you have to export the MIDI file, import it into your favorite DAW, and manipulate it via virtual instruments and plugin processors from there.

Magix Music Maker uses a different strategy in that it's a dedicated stand-alone DAW. You select the genre and a few instruments and its "Song Maker Ai" will generate all the other parts for you (see Figure 5.1). You can then edit and process the session as if you have recorded all the parts yourself.

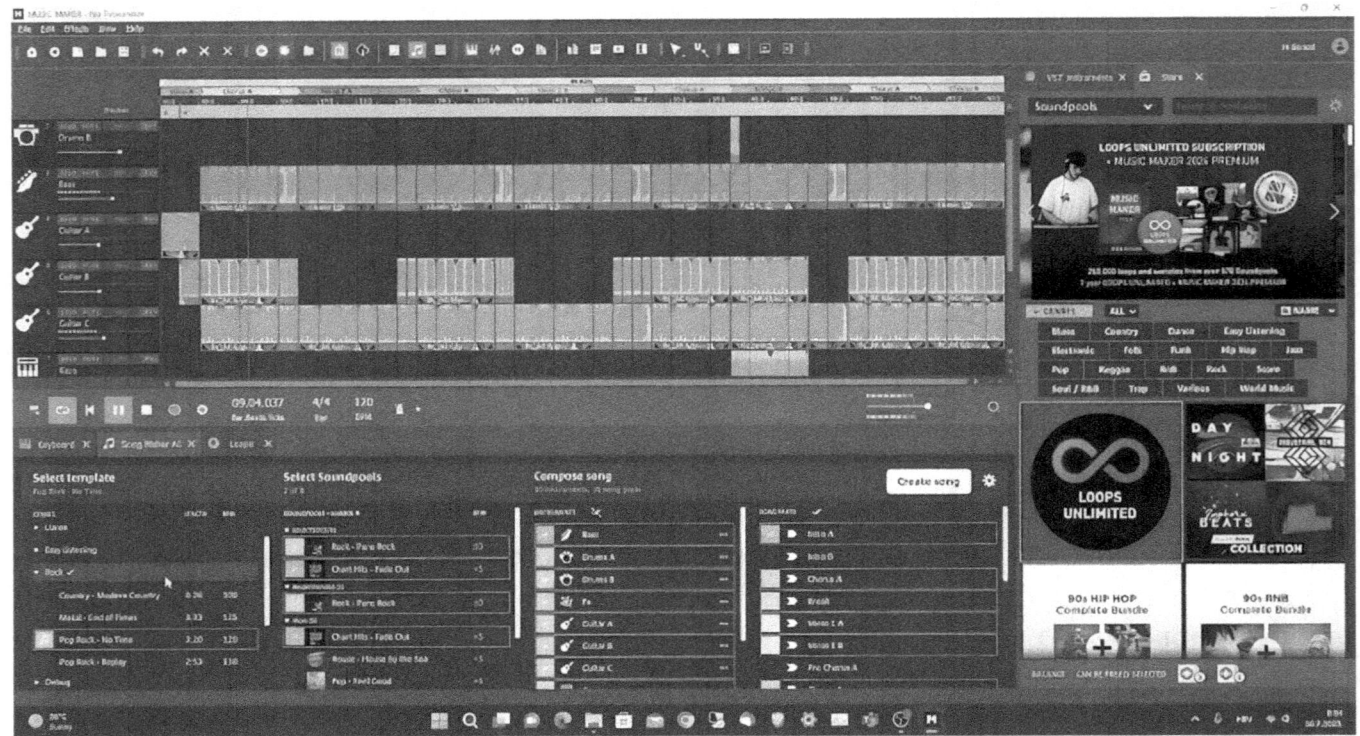

Figure 5.1: Magix Music Maker Song Maker Ai
Courtesy: Magix

Wavtool does something similar only it's fully in your browser. Not only will it suggest parts and sounds, but after you're settled on what you want you can ask it via text to make processor changes. For instance, if you type in, "Add distortion to the vocal" it will do that automatically for you. You can also ask it questions like, "What is mix buss compression?" and it will explain it to you, then ask if you want it added to your track.

Polymorph is another stand-alone software tool, but it's a completely new approach to a DAW in that the layout is very different as it's totally gesture-based. That means that instead of relying on MIDI or a traditional keyboard, the app uses mouse input to create sweeping musical gestures in real-time. According to Jay Tobin, Polymorph's creator, the "gesture-based paradigm significantly lowers the barrier of access for those looking to try experimental approaches to music production, and makes for a program equally at home on a stage mid-performance as it is in a studio setting."

As you can see from Figure 5.2, Polymorph looks way different than any other DAW, yet it makes perfect sense after you've played with it a bit. As you might imagine, anything that varies that much from what we're used to requires some retraining, but the manual and tutorials are well done and easy to follow.

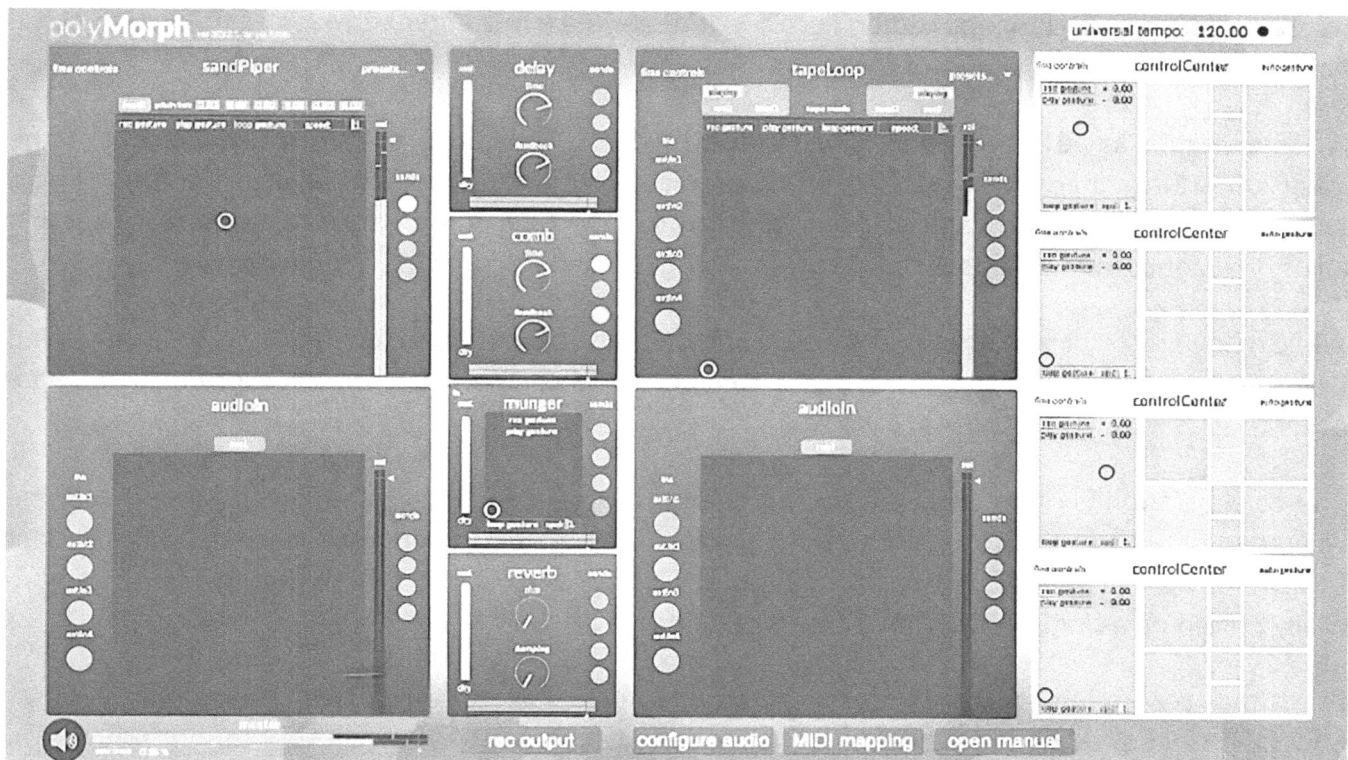

Figure 5.2: Jay Tobin Polymorph
Courtesy Jay Tobin

There will no doubt be other GAW approaches as we go along since there's no reason to stick within the current constructs if we're making music in a different way anyway. Plus, anything that can keep you from switching platforms during the music creation process keeps it simpler with fewer possibilities for technical glitches and mistakes.

Here are some GAWs to check out:

- Aiva - Aiva.ai
- Magix Music Maker - magix.com/us/music-editing/music-maker/
- Nodal - Nodalmusic.com
- Polymorph - jaytobin.com/polymorph/
- Wavtool - Wavtool.com

Ai TRACK SEPARATION TOOLS

Almost since the beginning of modern recorded music there's been a desire to separate out the individual mix elements from the full mix. This came to the commercial forefront in the 1980s, when karaoke gained popularity in the United States, there was a strong demand for backing tracks without vocals. Engineers would routinely flip the phase of one of the stereo channels to see if the vocal might disappear, which happened on occasion if the original mix engineer wasn't careful with phase correlation during the final mix of the song.

Track separation as we know it today didn't truly evolve until Ai was incorporated into the process in the early 2000s. Since then it's jumped to a whole new level, with many inexpensive platforms performing simple vocal, bass, drums and music bed extraction, to film maker Peter Jackson's process for extracting all of The Beatles instruments and vocals from a single mono track for the *Get Back* movie.

While many artists, producers and engineers immediately think of track separation (sometimes called de-mixing or stem separation) for its ability to rebalance a song or replace a vocal or track, there are other uses as well.

Source separation is often used in film and television shows to replace the music when it can't be cleared for a reissue, or recover dialog from a noisy location track. DJs use track separation to extract just the vocals of a track for a remix, and it's now being used in hearing aids so that the user can more easily zero in on a single voice from a crowd of people.

Most track separation tools are browser-based like Audioshake (see Figure 5.3), Cyro-mix, Demixer and Sounds.Studio. Other tools like Lalal and Moises are stand-alone desktop applications, while RipX DeepReMix and Audionamix have more sophisticated packages meant for serious pros.

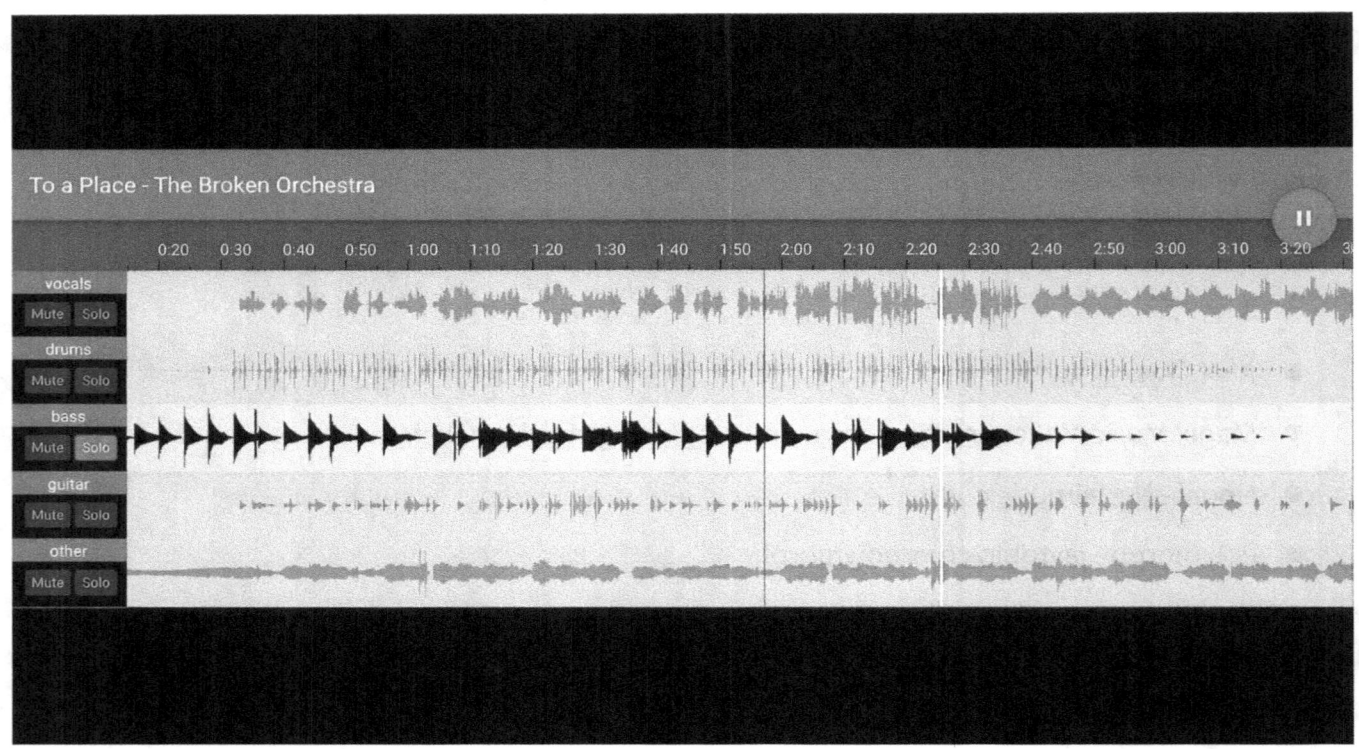

Figure 5.3: Audioshake
Courtesy Audioshake

Spleeter, developed by Deezer Technologies, is a free Ai source separation library that can recreate multitracks from an already mixed audio file. It's used as part of the streaming service's recommendation engine where it's used to separate vocal and instrumental tracks in oder to analyze and then enrich its metadata, although it can also be used by the general public for audio separation.

Acon Digital's Remix plugin (see Figure 5.4) is interesting in that it separates 5 stems (vocals, piano, bass, drums and other) in real time. You can control the sensitivity of the detection to control the leakage, solo or mute, and control the balance of each track with its own level control.

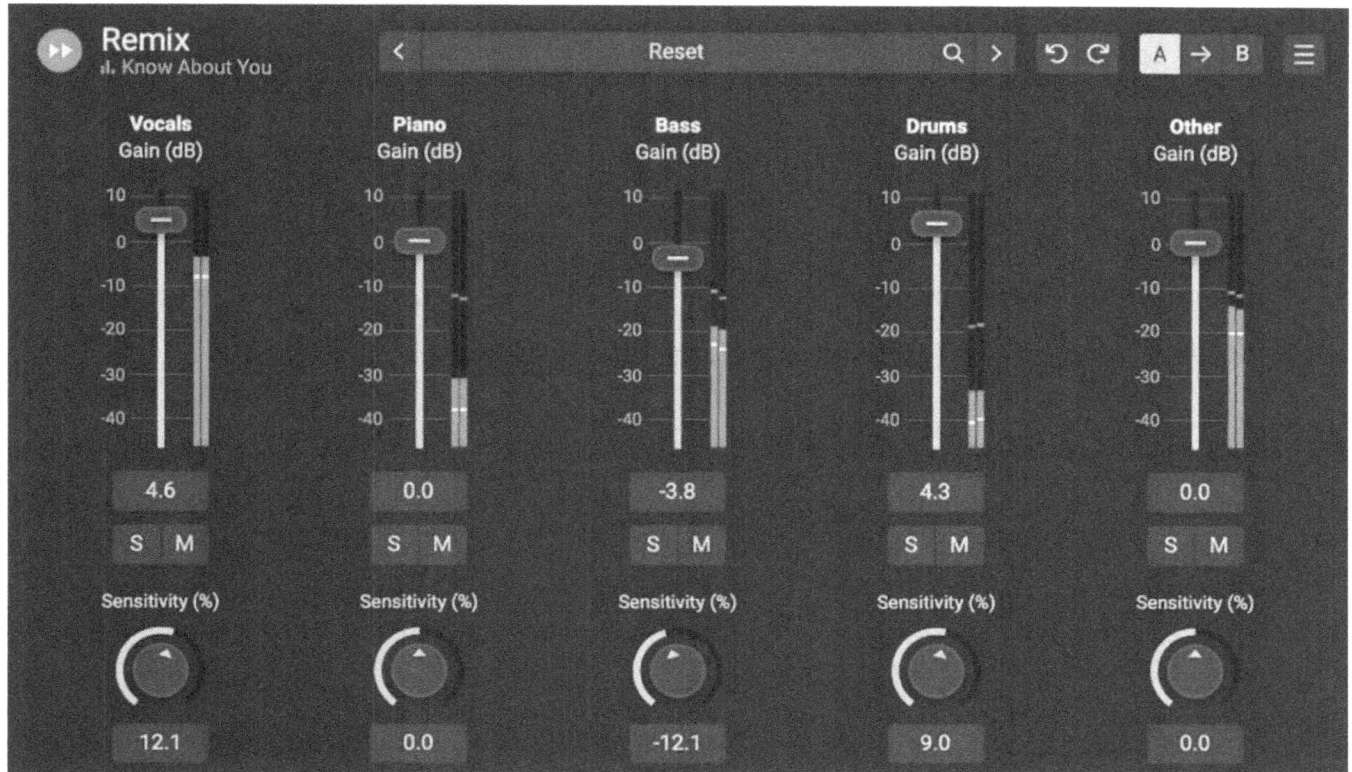

Figure 5.4: Acon Digital Remix plugin
Courtesy Acon Digital

How To Use

Use the highest resolution audio track possible. The better the audio track quality, the better the separation.

1. Upload the stereo track to the platform or application.
2. If offered, select a stem separation option.
3. Refine the stems with a de-bleed or sensitivity adjustment if offered.
4. Export the stems to your DAW.

Here are a few track separation platforms to check out:

- Audionamix - Audionamix.com
- Acon Digital Remix - acondigital.com/products/remix
- Audioshake - Audioshake.ai
- Cryo-Mix - Cryo-mix.com/separator
- Demixer - Demixer.com
- Heard Sounds - Heardsounds.com
- Lalal - Lalal.ai
- Moises - Moises.ai
- RipX Hitnmix - Hitnmix.com
- Sounds.studio - Sounds.studio
- Spleeter - www.deezer-techservices.com/solutions/spleeter/

Ai AUDIO PLUGINS

The idea behind Ai-enabled compressors, limiters, equalizers and reverbs is to take the work out of setting them up. While there are traditional manual methods for setup for all of these processors (see my Mixing Engineer's Handbook or Music Mixing Primer course for how that's done), it does take some time and know-how to do so. Using an Ai audio plugin means the setup is done for you without the guesswork if you don't know how to do it.

In most cases, setup couldn't be simpler. You select a *Profile* (kick, snare, guitar, bass, etc.), hit the *Learn* button, play about 8 seconds of the track, and you're good to go as the Ai selects what it believes to be the most appropriate settings based on its training. If you have an instrument that's not on the profile list, select the *Universal* profile and you're likely to get a setting that will work.

The Ai does this by first training on a dataset of samples of that particular instrument. The larger the dataset of really good sounding samples, the more likely it will automatically dial in a setting that works.

This automatic setup is great for fast mixes, but a pro mixer will take these automatic settings just as a starting point and tweak them as he or she listens to the track in the mix.

As of the writing of this book, there aren't many developers of Ai-enabled audio plugins, mostly because of the cost of the training and the expertise required to build the neural network is in short supply.

Ai Compressor Plugins

Ai audio compressor plugins are currently dominated by three developers; Sonbile, Focusrite and iZotope. Among these, iZotope probably has the most extensive experience in developing Ai-enabled plugins, although they don't always emphasize this fact in their marketing. Focusrite, on the other hand, uses the Sonible Ai engine but presents it with a distinct user interface.

Sonible has two product series that cover the needs of beginners to more advanced users; the *pure:* series and the *smart:* series. For example, the pure:comp has a limited number of user variable parameters, while its smart:comp is a full featured compressor that uses the Ai to get you in the ballpark so you can tweak it later yourself (see Figure 5.5). As a result, the pure:comp creates settings that are somewhat more noticeable since it's assumed that the user probably won't be tweaking it much.

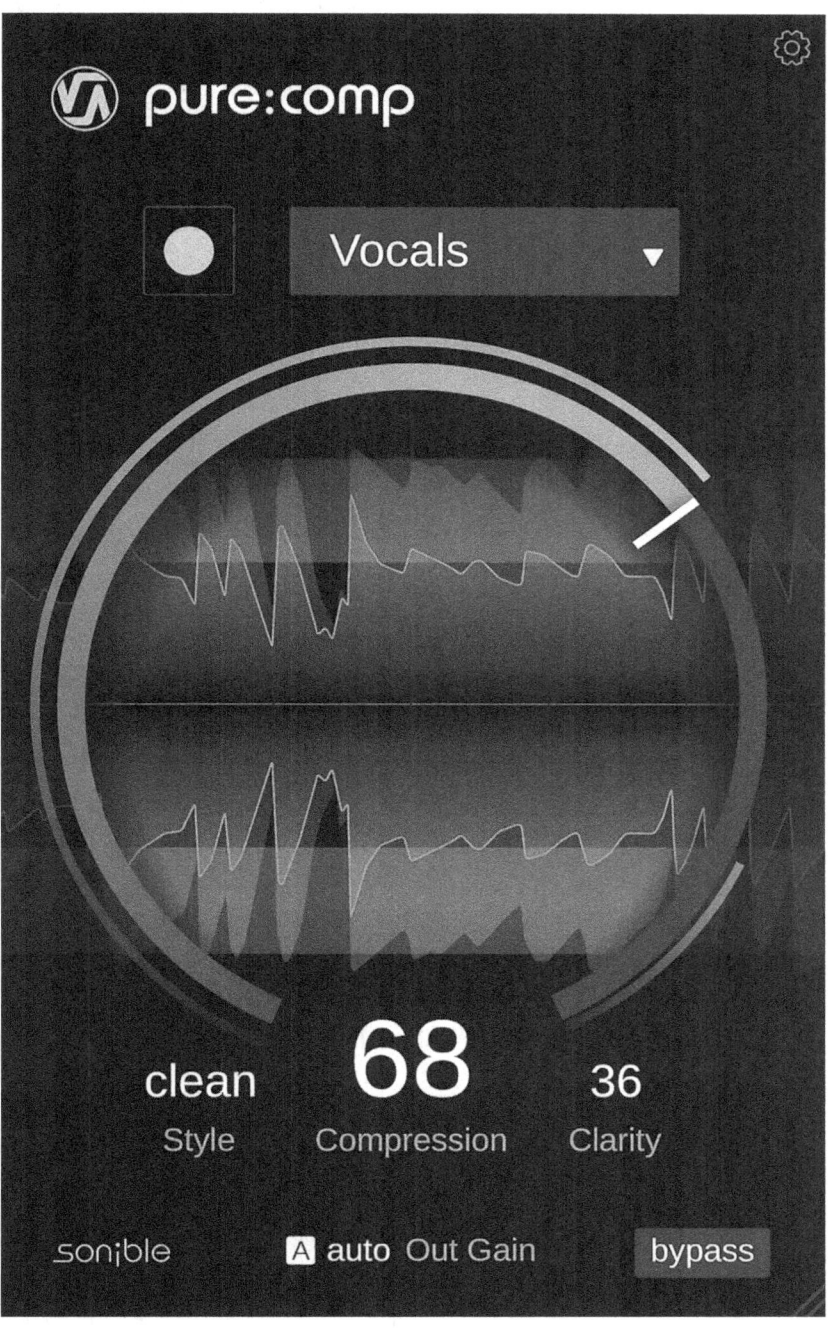

Figure 5.5: Sonible pure:comp plugin
Courtesy Sonible

As stated above, Focusrite's FAST series uses the Sonible Ai engine but with a different user interface. It's FAST Compressor falls somewhere in-between the Sonible *pure:* and *smart:* series in terms of complexity, but many users prefer its interface.

iZotope's Ai compressor is part of its multi-module Neutron and Ozone products, both of which contain just about any type of audio processor that you can imagine. It should be noted that Ozone is intended to be used on a mix buss for its mastering functions (see Chapter 7). As with the others, they're set up using iZotope's version of the *Learn* button called *Assistant* (see Figure 5.6).

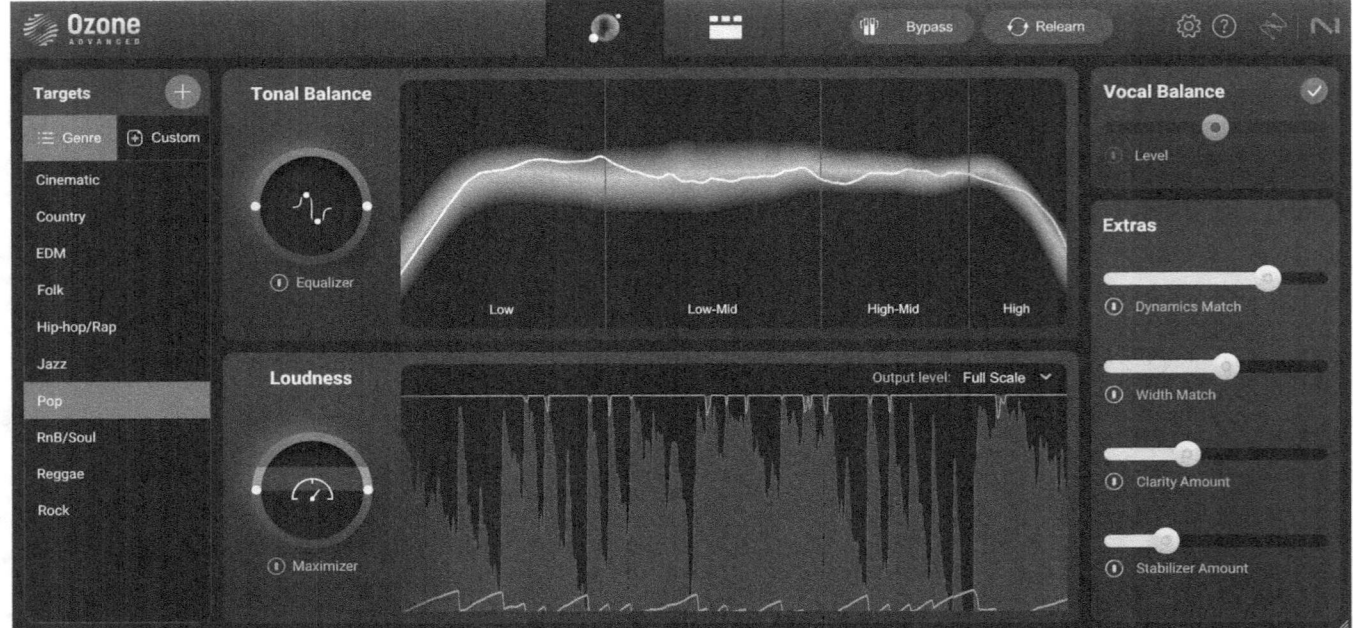

Figure 5.6: iZotope Ozone Master Assistant
Courtesy iZotope

Here's where you can find out more on the Ai compressors mentioned above:

- Focusrite FAST Compressor - collective.focusrite.com/products/fast-compressor
- iZotope Neutron - zotope.com/en/products/neutron.html
- iZotope Ozone - izotope.com/en/products/ozone.html
- Sonible pure:comp - Sonible.com/purecomp
- Sonible smart:comp - Sonible.com/smartcomp

Ai Limiter Plugins

While limiters are sometimes used on kick, snare and bass, they're more typically used on the mix buss for overload control and to increase the gain of the mix. The secret parameter in the modern limiter is its *Ceiling* control, which stops the signal from going beyond a certain pre-set level, usually set to somewhere between -1dB to -.1dBFS, but can be set an any other desired level as well.

Since Ai limiter plugins are intended to be used on the mix buss to process a full mix, their *Profile* section contains music genres like rock, hip-hop and jazz instead of instrument types.

As with Ai compressors, there are a limited number of Ai limiters available, again from Sonibile with pure:limit and smart:limit, Focusrite with FAST Limiter (see Figure 5.7), and iZotope Neutron. You can generally expect about 4 to 5dB of extra mix level from any of these plugins when used on the mix buss.

The Musician's Ai Handbook - 1st edition

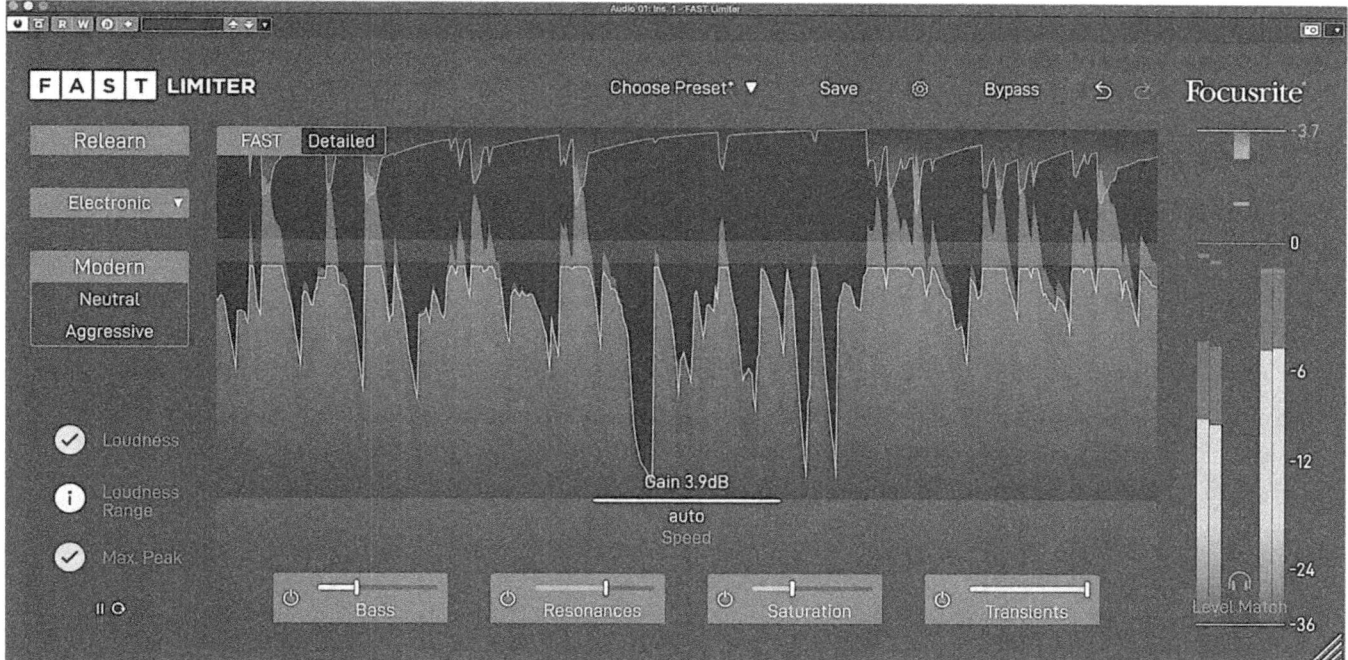

Figure 5.7: Focusrite FAST Limit
Courtesy Focusrite

- Focusrite FAST Limiter - collective.focusrite.com/products/fast-limiter
- iZotope Neutron - izotope.com/en/products/neutron.html
- Sonible pure:limit - Sonible.com/purelimit
- Sonible smart:limit - Sonible.com/smartlimit

Ai Equalizer Plugins

Ai equalizers are a bit tricky in that they will get you into the ballpark by using the same *Profile* and *Learn* process as above, but that doesn't necessarily mean that the equalization curve for the mix element will be a perfect fit for your mix.

The reason is because every song is different. At the very least, the arrangement, production, players/vocalists, sounds, ambience, and tempo are different, so the same EQ (or any processing for that matter) that worked brilliantly on a previous song may be less than stellar on the one you're working on now.

The Ai will use its capabilities to make that mix element (vocal, guitar, kick, piano, etc.) sound what it thinks should be ideal *on its own*, but that doesn't mean it will work when added to the full mix.

I can remember visiting an A-list mixer working on the mix for a major artist. He allowed me to solo each track to hear what it sounded like by itself. I was amazed at just how bad some of the tracks sounded on their own when soloed, yet when played back in the context of the mix they worked perfectly.

The guidance here is that you should still use an Ai equalizer to its fullest, but be prepared to tweak it more than you would with an Ai compressor or limiter.

Ai Equalizer Developers

Once gain, the players in this processor space include Sonible with pure:eq and smart:EQ, Focusrite with FAST Equaliser, and iZotope with its all-processors-in-one Neutron. There are some other developers who have excelled in this area as well.

For instance, Soundtheory's Gullfoss samples the audio program over 300 times a second, then uses its intelligence to tame, brighten, or restore frequencies across the frequency spectrum (see Figure 5.8), as does Accentize Spectral Balance. Oeksound Soothe 2 is a dynamic resonance suppressor designed specifically for removing unwanted, nasty-sounding frequencies from your audio.

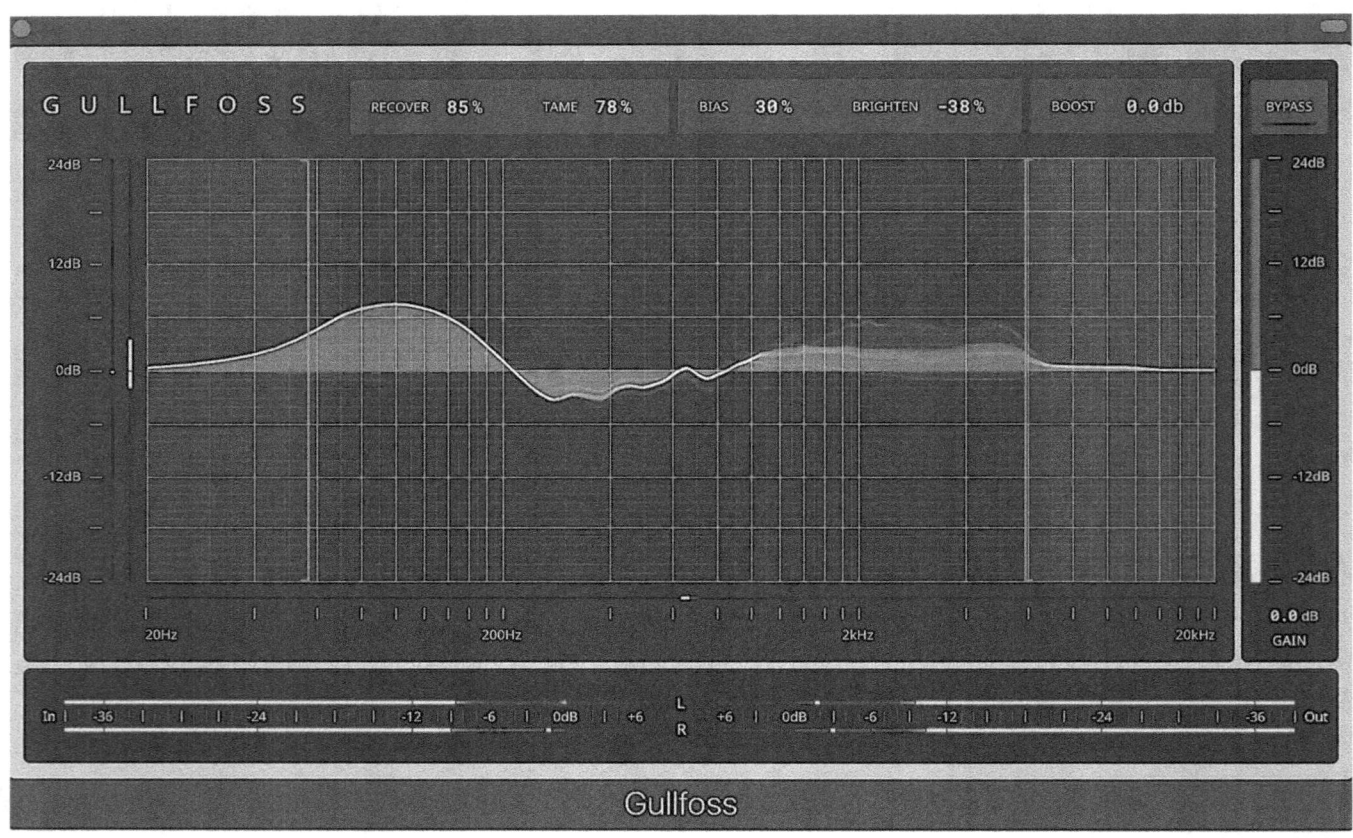

Figure 5.8: Soundtheory Gullfoss
Courtesy Soundtheory Ltd.

MeldaProduction MDrumStrip is a multi-module, smart multi-processor designed just for drums (see Figure 5.9). There's a separate module for each piece of the drum kit (kick, snare, toms, high hat, and overheads), as well as one for the drum buss and parallel compression. Each module not only shapes the equalization, but the compression, reverb and bleed suppression as well.

Figure 5.9: Melda Production MDrumStrip
Courtesy Melda Production

Ai Frequency Balancers

Another way to equalize a track is through the use of a frequency balancer like Focusrite FAST Balancer or iZotope's Neutron. A frequency balancer takes a slightly different approach to EQing.

As with other Ai-powered equalizers, you'll set a Profile for the mix element (drums, vocals, etc.), again hit the *Learn* button, and the plugin will compare your mix element against its dataset of similar sounds. At this point it will impose a frequency balance to make your track sound similar to what it considers is optimal for that kind of track. You'll then see a frequency spectrum display of the new frequency response.

With Neutron, you'll see the frequency that Assistant View recommends for your track (see Figure 5.10). As you get closer to the solid red center, you're getting closer to the ideal spectral curve. If your current track is outside of the red target area, you can manually use the controls in order to get closer to the center dark red area.

75 | Ai Audio Tools

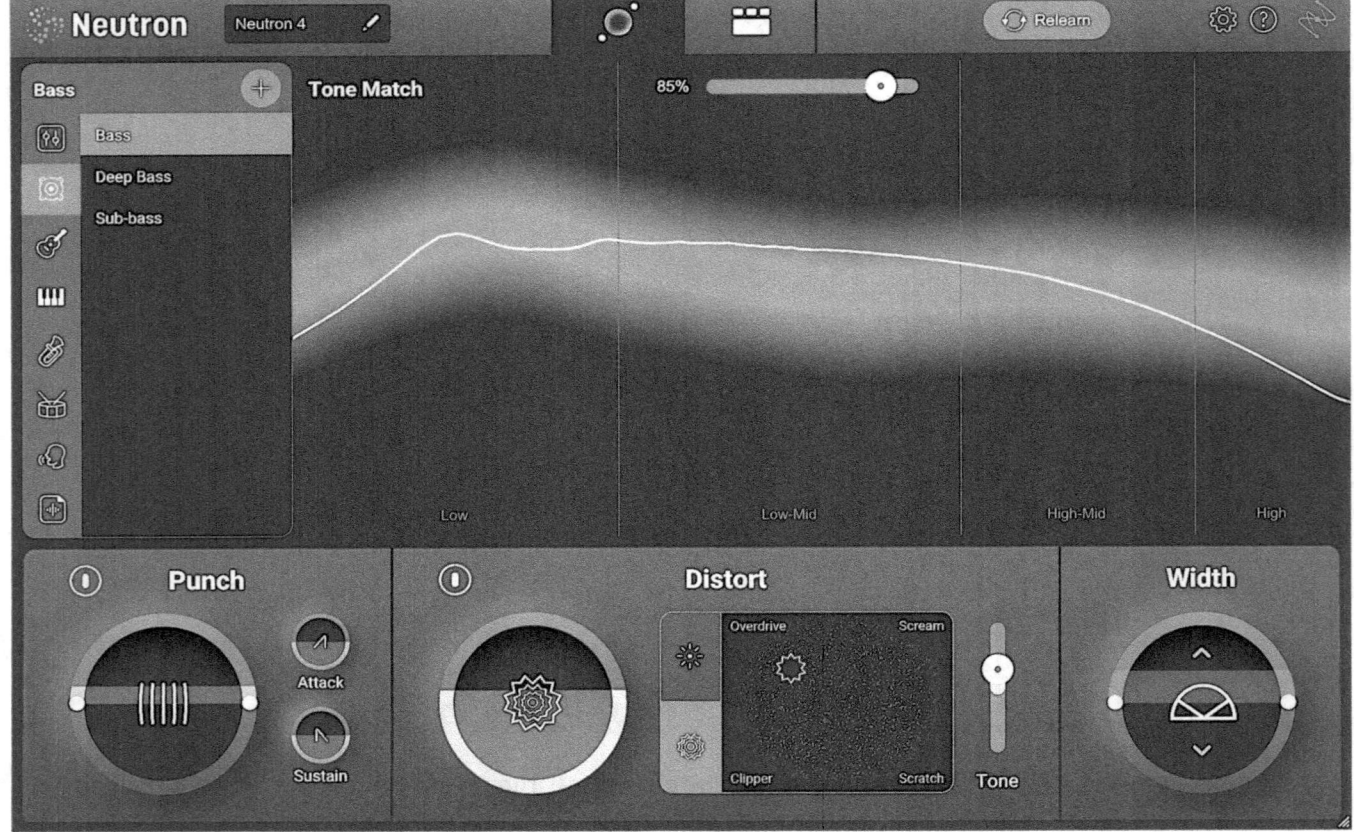

Figure 5.10: iZotope Neutron 4 Assistant View
Courtesy iZotope

Neutron also has a reference track feature which can be useful. This allows you to upload a track that you think sounds good so that you can match its frequency response. Neutron will copy the frequency response of the track and use that as the target response.

As with almost all equalizers, it's best to make any adjustments while listening to other tracks or the full mix as you can get fooled by just listening to a track by itself. After all, how it works in the mix is what ultimately counts.

Ai-Driven Modeling

Although many software developers have been successful at modeling a wide variety of analog gear, the process to do so is long and tedious. One of the overlooked features of Ai is that it can not only make the modeling process much faster, but do it with much more precision as well. That means that the Ai modeled processor will sound much closer to a particular vintage analog piece than ever before.

The developer can use a neural network to accurately interpret the sonic characteristics that make a piece of analog gear sound and behave in the way it does. This happens by feeding an algorithm various training data of dry vs. processed audio and teaching it to identify the exact characteristics that make up the difference. Once these differences have been learned by the AI, they can be applied to new audio.

Some good examples of this technique are the various plugins from Tone Empire. Plugins like their Neural Q (see Figure 5.11) have been modeled by its proprietary Ai-driven process to provide a more accurate digital version of the vintage analog device.

Figure 5.11: Tone Empire Neural Q
Courtesy Tone Empire

Although not specifically an equalizer, Baby Audio's TAIP is an Ai-powered tape saturator that once again, uses the Ai to model a 1970s Studer tape machine.

You'll notice that there's no user interface leading directly to the Ai in these examples and that there's no *Learn* button to sample the audio. That's because the Ai is only used to model the analog device and therefore does not automatically adjust processor parameters like in the other Ai plugins that we've looked at.

Here's a list of Ai equalizer plugins to check out:

- Accentize Spectral Balance - Accentize.com/spectralbalance
- Baby Audio TAIP - babyaud.io/taip-plugin
- Focusrite Fast Equaliser - collective.focusrite.com/products/fast-equaliser
- iZotope Neutron - izotope.com/en/products/neutron.html
- MeldaProduction MDrumStrip - Meldaproduction.com/MDrumStrip
- Oeksound Soothe 2 - Oeksound.com/plugins/soothe2
- Sonible pure:EQ - Sonible.com/pureeq
- Sonible smart:EQ - Sonible.com/smarteq3
- Soundtheory Gulfoss - Soundtheory.com
- Tone Empire Neural Q - Tone-empire.com

Ai Reverb Plugins

Like Ai-powered equalizers, Ai reverbs also tend to get you in the ballpark but still require some tweaking. These plugins will set up the type of reverb for the track (plate, hall, chamber, etc.), but mix engineers know that setting the predelay and decay times are a function of the tempo of the song (see The Mixing Engineer's Handbook for more details on how this is done manually).

Also, these reverb plugins will set up the parameters for a single mix element based on inserting it on to a vocal or guitar track, but most mix engineers will place the reverb on an aux track and send from multiple mix elements via an aux send.

That said, some Ai reverbs like Rivium (see Figure 5.12) adapt to your track in real time so it has just the right amount of decay at any given place in the song. Zynaptiq Adaptiverb is interesting in that it adds a synth-like drone quality to the reverb which is perfect for single instrument ambient washes, and Accentize Chameleon specializes in imitating any ambient or reverberated sound.

Figure 5.12: Rivium Reverb
Courtesy Rivium Ai

Here are some Ai reverb plugins to check out:

- Accentize Chameleon - Accentize.com/chameleon
- iZotope Neoverb - izotope.com/en/products/neoverb.html
- Focusrite FAST Reverb - collective.focusrite.com/products/fast-verb
- Rivium - Riviumsoftware.com
- Sonible pure:verb - Sonible.com/pureverb
- Sonible smart:reverb - Sonible.com/smartreverb

- Zynaptiq Adaptiverb - Zynaptiq.com/adaptiverb

Ai Gate Plugins

If ever there was an audio processor that was difficult to set up it's the noise gate. For those unfamiliar with the concept, a noise gate allows the signal to be heard only when it reaches a certain level. Below that level, it's attenuated so you don't hear it. Think of it like a garden gate for sound. When the audio is loud enough, the gate opens and lets the sound into the yard. When the sound is too quiet (below a certain threshold that you set), the gate closes and prevents any sound (or noise) from getting through.

Gates are very touchy to set up and if the input signal isn't steady the gate will open and close quickly causing what's known as "chattering." Luckily Ai comes to the rescue to help us.

Traditionally gates were mostly used on the drums to reduce leakage, although they can be used on any other mix elements that are noisy. That said, with today's advanced automation, DAW editing, and clip gain, noise is no longer the issue that it once was so gates aren't used as much anymore in the studio. When you need to use one though, you're better off using an Ai-powered gate because it just makes your mixing life so much easier when it comes to cleaning up noise and leakage on a track.

With Sonible's smart:gate, you set the *Target* for the sound you only want to hear (like a vocal or snare drum), and smart:gate will only let that through and eliminate the noise. This can also be used on a drum loop where you'd like to separate the different elements. For instance, if the loop has a kick, snare and hat sound, if we set the target for kick, that's all we'll hear, so if we set up three instances of the loop each with smart:gate, we can separate out the three different elements.

The Sonnox Oxford Drum Gate (see Figure 5.13) can do exactly the same thing, where you can teach it to differentiate between the different elements of a loop besides being able to attenuate leakage from other drums, even with a track with a lot of ghost notes.

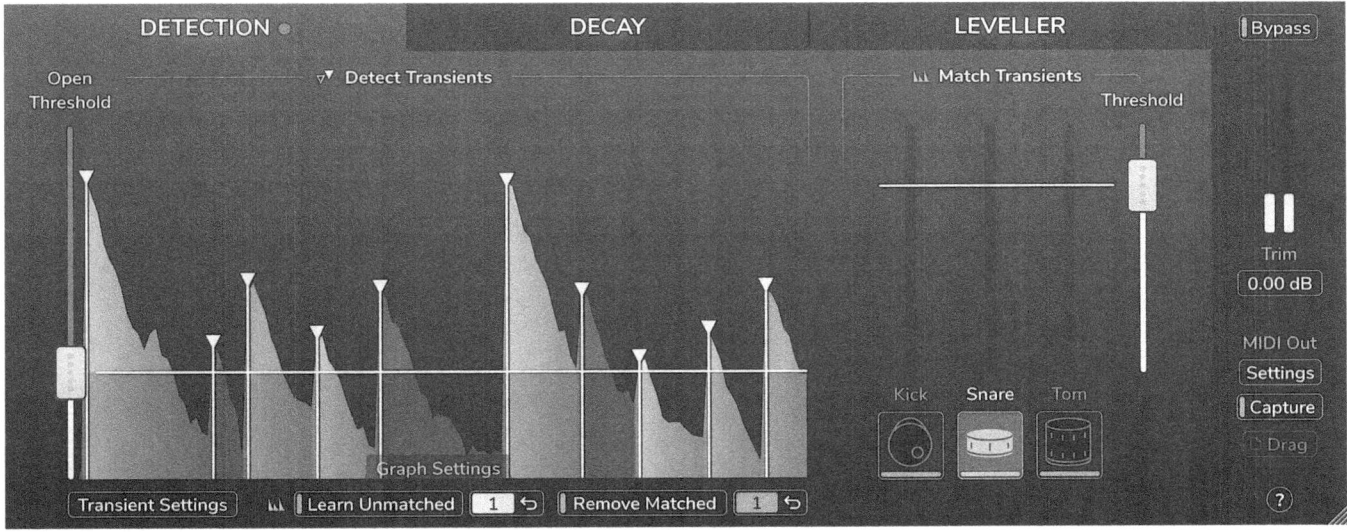

Figure 5.13: Sonnox Oxford Drum Gate
Courtesy Sonnox Ltd.

- Sonible smart:gate - Sonible.com/smartgate
- Sonnox Oxford Drum Gate - Sonnox.com/plugin/drumgate

How To Use

1. Place the Ai plugin at the appropriate insert point on the track channel (see Ai Signal Paths at the end of the chapter)
2. Click the *Learn* button on the plugin
3. Play approximately 8 seconds of music (usually the loudest section of the song)
4. Listen to the track in the mix and tweak as necessary

Ai NOISE REDUCTION TOOLS

Noise reduction tools have gotten better and better over the years, with the incorporation of Ai neural networks responsible for a giant leap in functionality over the last few years. Ai-powered noise reduction can now be found either as a standalone app, as a plugin, or even as a browser-based site. Many of them do their processing locally on your computer rather than in the cloud, and since that can take up a lot of computer processing power, that means fewer instances of the tool can be used at the same time.

Many of the tools are actually bundles of individual tools like Acon Restoration, iZotope RX and Zynaptiq Repair. The individual modules focus on a particular type of noise reduction like hum removal, transient repair, de-clipping, background noise removal and reverberation attenuation.

Examples include Hush by Ian Simpson, which is both a stand-alone app and a Pro Tools plugin that suppresses background noise and room reflections, along with Waves Clarity VX and VX deReverb, Supertone Voice Clarity (formerly Goyo), and Accentize dxRevive among others. Clarity VX and VX deReverb have two versions, a simple inexpensive option and a more sophisticated Pro option with an extra neural network. dxRevive is interesting in that not only does it attenuate or totally eliminate any kind of noise, but it also makes frequency corrections to restore frequencies that might have been absent in the original recording (see Figure 5.14).

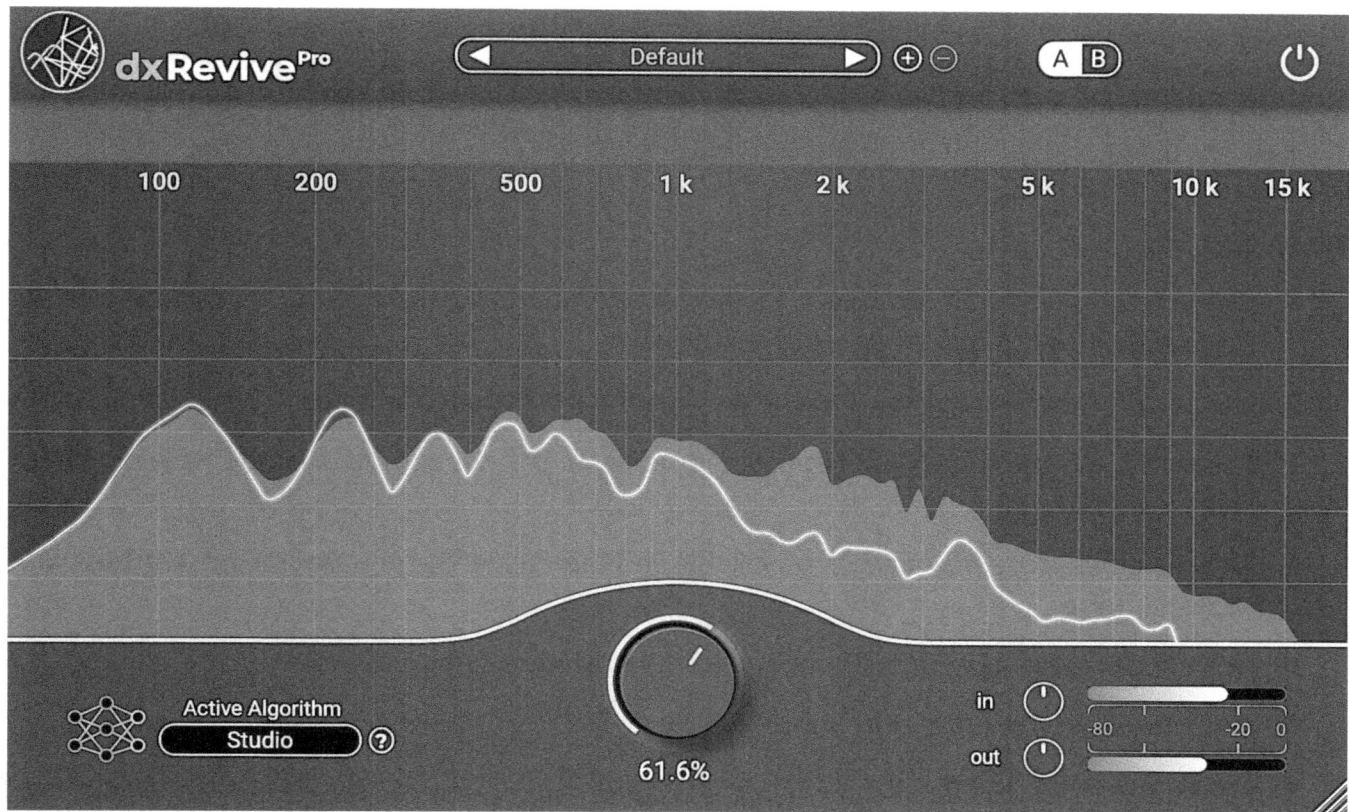

Figure 5.14: Accentize dxRevive
Courtesy Accentize GmbH

If guitar string squeaks are constantly bugging you, then it might be time to investigate iZotope RX for the Guitar De-Noise module (see Figure 5.15), or the more advanced Spectral Editor.

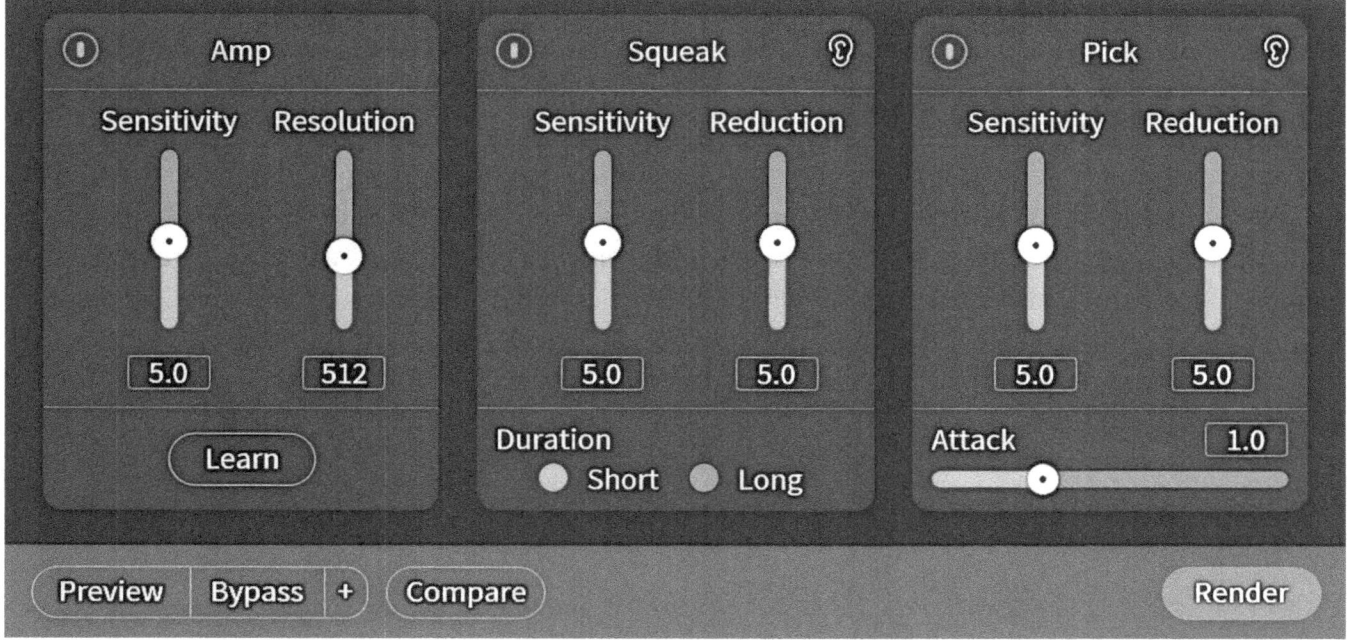

Figure 5.15: iZotope RX Guitar De-Noise
Courtesy iZotope

These tools are amazing not only in their results but also in their prices, which vary from around $30USD to more than $500 for full suites or bundles that are intended for professional post-production. The next time you run into a noise problem, it's worth taking one of these tools for a spin to see what it will do.

How To Use

1. Place the noise reduction plugin in the first or second slot of the noisy track's channel (see the next section on Ai Signal Path in the next section)
2. If available, click the *Learn* button and play the track for about 8 seconds
3. Raise the De-Noise control until the noise disappears, but not so much that the remaining track sounds altered
4. Select a different neural network if available and then select the one that sounds the best with the least noise

- Acon Restoration - acondigital.com/products/restoration-suite/
- Accentize dxRevive - Accentize.com/dxrevive
- Supertone Goyo - Goyo.app
- Hush - Hushaudioapp.com
- iZotope RX - izotope.com/en/products/rx.html
- Waves Clarity VX - Waves.com/plugins/clarity-vx
- Waves Clarity VX deReverb - Waves.com/plugins/clarity-vx-dereverb
- Zynaptiq Repair - Zynaptiq.com/repair

Ai SIGNAL PATHS

The place where an Ai audio plugin is inserted in the signal path makes a big difference to the overall sound of that track. In many cases, a multi-module Ai plugin like iZotope's Neutron 4 will take the place of the usual variety of compressors, EQs, saturators and exciters that are typically used on a particular channel during a mix, so it won't matter where in the signal path it's inserted. However, Ai plugins that do only one thing, like compressors, limiters, EQs and reverbs, are best inserted using the exact same signal path strategy as traditional plugins. Let's take a look at a typical signal path in a DAW (see Figure 5.16).

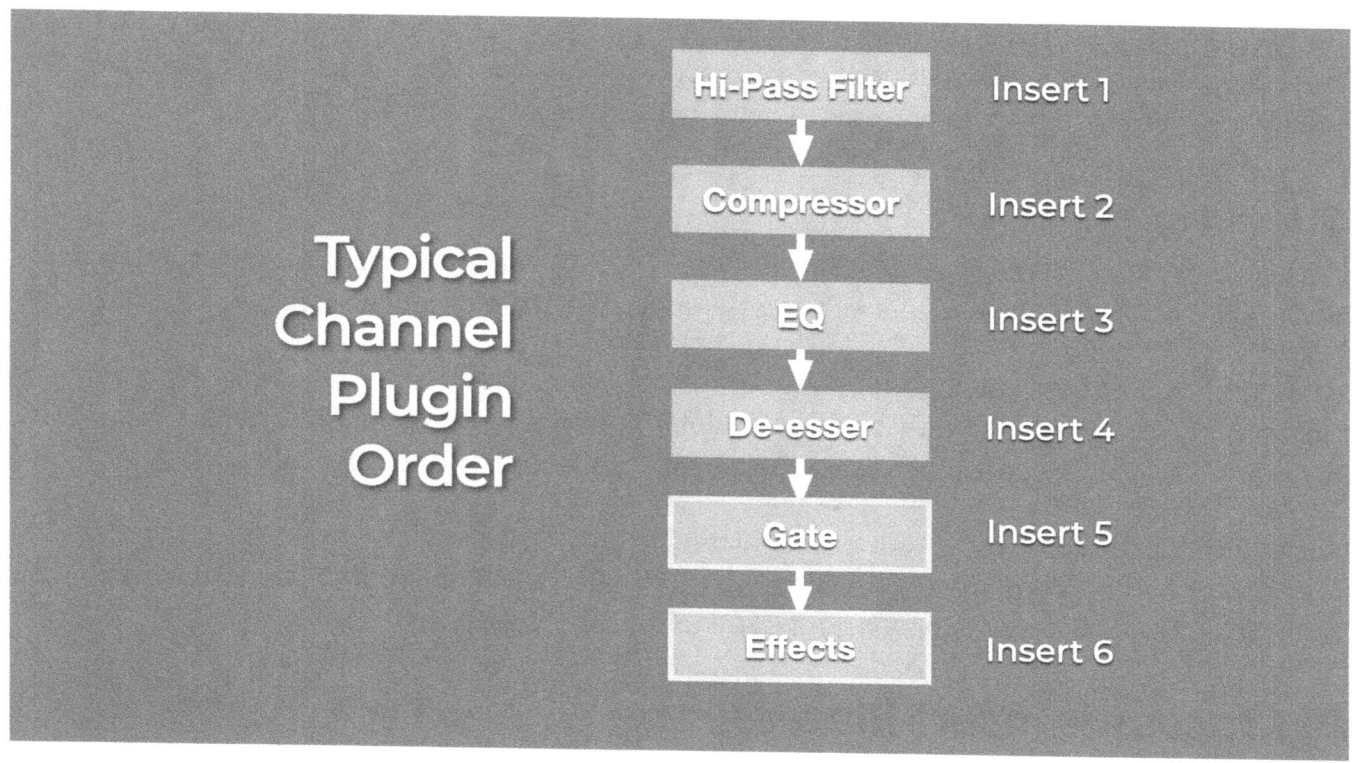

Figure 5.16: DAW typical signal path
© 2023 Bobby Owsinski

As you might imagine, there's a good reason why every flavor of plugin is selected for a particular insert slot. For instance, many mixers like to place a high-pass filter in the first slot on many of the tracks in order to filter out some of the low end that gets in the way of the bass and kick.

Compressor-EQ Placement

Next comes the compressor in the second slot, which is sometimes controversial because here it's inserted before the equalizer. Many mixing engineers advocate placing the EQ before the compressor but there are several good reasons for having the compressor come before the EQ instead.

First, when the EQ is placed before the compressor, if you were to boost your EQ 6dB at 5kHz, for example, the compressor would see that frequency as higher than the rest and start to compress it more than the other frequencies. That basically undoes what you're trying to add since that frequency is now being attenuated (how much depends on how you set the threshold and ratio controls).

Second, the compressor is usually set at the beginning of a mix and we don't normally have to tweak it much afterwards. On the other hand, the EQ is tweaked a lot during a session as you're constantly comparing one channel to another in order to make sure than neither one is being masked.

If the EQ is placed before the compressor, every time we tweaked the EQ, we would have to tweak the compressor as well. Placing the compressor first before the EQ saves you time since you usually don't have to worry about tweaking it later.

The exception to this (there's always at least one), is if you're using the equalizer strictly in cut mode. In other words, you're only attenuating the frequencies and not boosting them. In that case, a separate equalizer is placed after the compressor to only boost the frequencies that require it.

Other Plugins

Usually a de-esser comes next in the fourth insert slot. The tool is generally used on vocals but sometimes also on cymbals or other instruments with excessive upper-midrange frequencies in the 3k to 8kHz range.

Although not used very much these days because of clip gain and ease of automating most DAW functions, a gate will come after that in the fifth slot. This works well here since it's after the compressor so the level doesn't fluctuate much cause the gate to "chatter" (open and close too quickly).

Finally, any effects like delay, reverb or modulation usually come last, since we want the processing decisions to be already made before applying them. Effects like reverb also sound different when processed this way because of how the reverb algorithm is activated.

Ai Processor Insert Placement

As said before, if using an all-in-one processor like iZotope's Neutron, that usually means that you don't need any other processors on that channel, so you'd place it in the first slot. In the event that you feel that you need additional processing, it will probably work best placing it after Neutron in the signal path (see Figure 5.17).

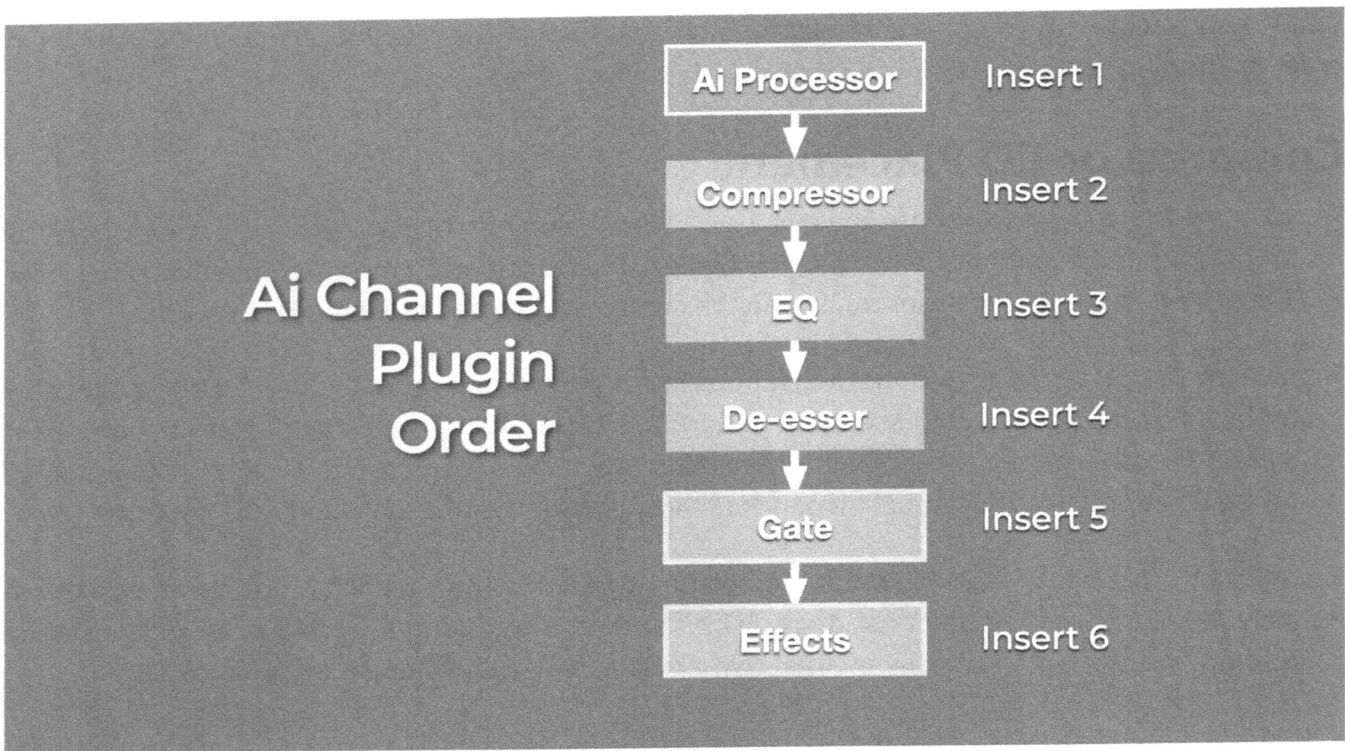

Figure 5.17: DAW Signal path with an Ai processor
© 2023 Bobby Owsinski

Dedicated compression or EQ processors like Sonible's pure:comp and smart:EQ will be assigned to the slots that their non-Ai cousins would normally go to. That means an Ai compressor would sit in the second insert slot while an Ai EQ would be inserted in the third slot (see Figure 5.18).

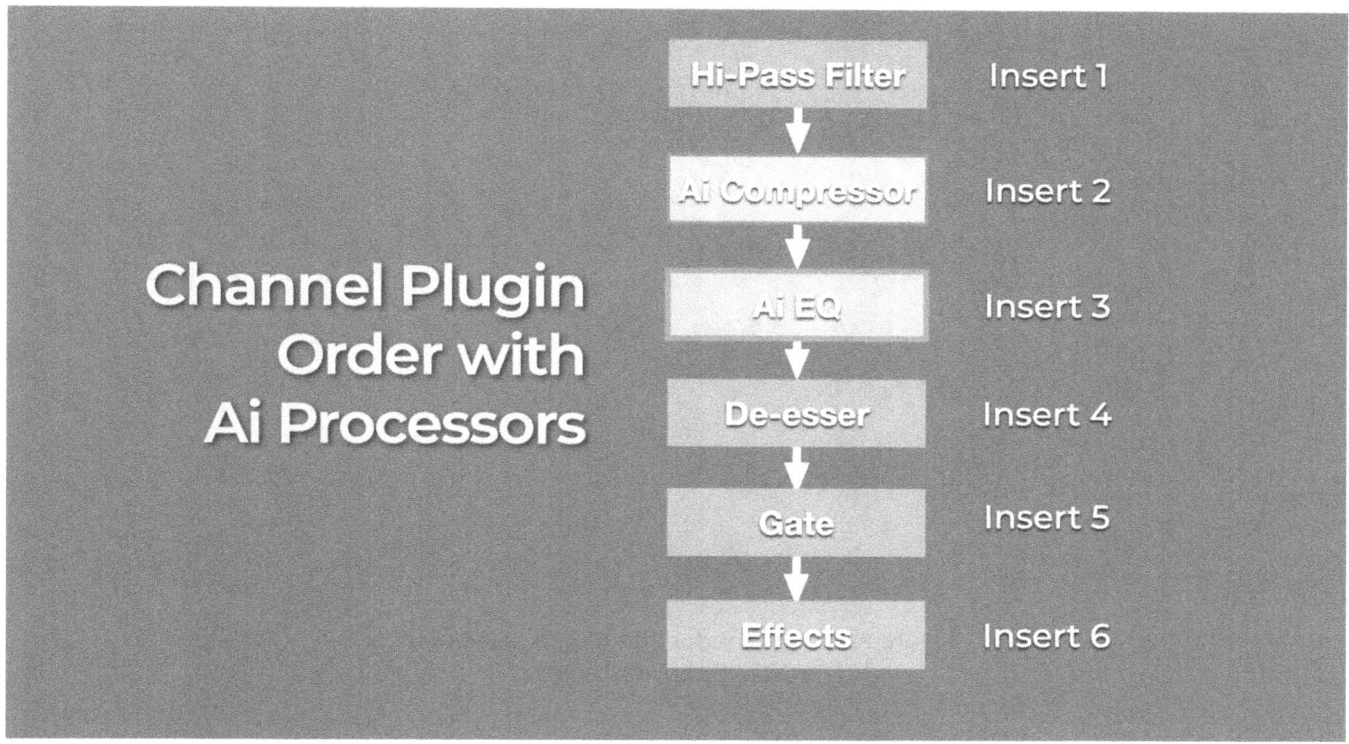

Figure 5.18: Channel plugin order with Ai processors
© 2023 Bobby Owsinski

Ai reverb processors like smart:reverb or Neoverb will still work best in the either last slot, or any slot after an all-in-one Ai processor like Neutron.

Ai Noise Reduction Processor Placement

Ai noise reduction processors are a special case. You usually want to treat the noise as early in the signal chain as possible so the noise isn't emphasized by any other processing. As a result, the processor is best placed in the first slot.

That said, there are times when the level of the sound being processed is uneven, sometimes dropping below the threshold of the noise reduction processor. In this situation, the noise reduction can be inconsistent, so it's then best to place it after a compressor to keep the level evened out before it hits the noise reduction processor (see Figure 5.19).

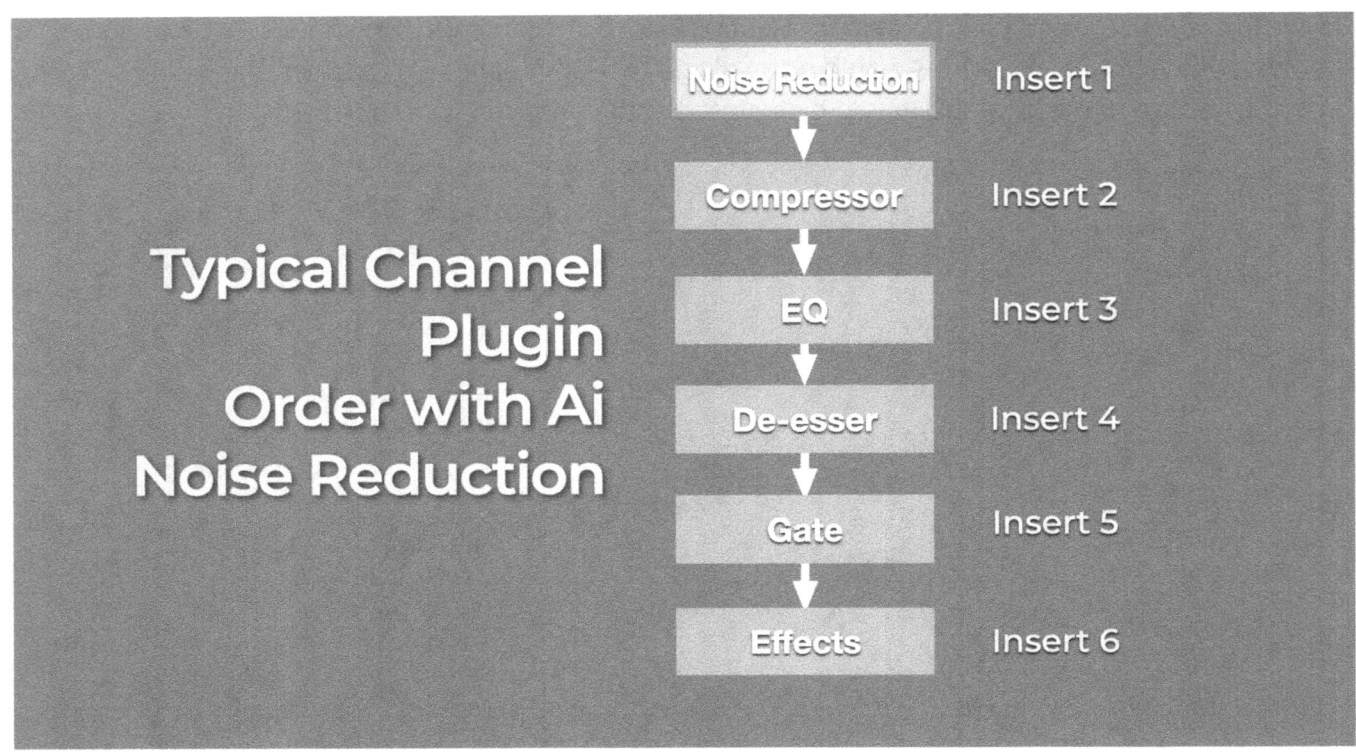

Figure 5.19: Noise reduction plugin placement
© 2023 Bobby Owsinski

Placement On The Mix Buss

Most mixers will use at least a compressor, EQ and limiter inserted on their mix buss these days (see Figure 5.20). The limiter is always inserted in the last slot and its ceiling control is set to anywhere from -1dB to -.1dBFS to make sure that no overloads occur.

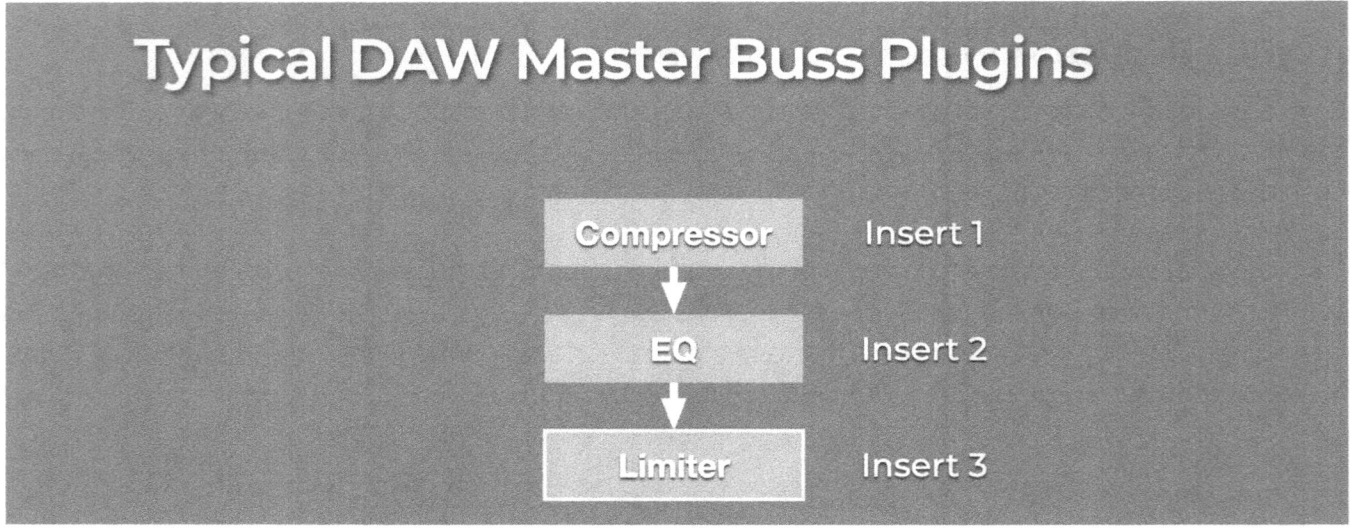

Figure 5.20: Typical Mix buss plugin placement
© 2023 Bobby Owsinski

If using an all-in-one processor like Ozone or Neutron on the mix buss, it will normally replace all of the previous processors, so it can go in any slot as a result (see Figure 5.21).

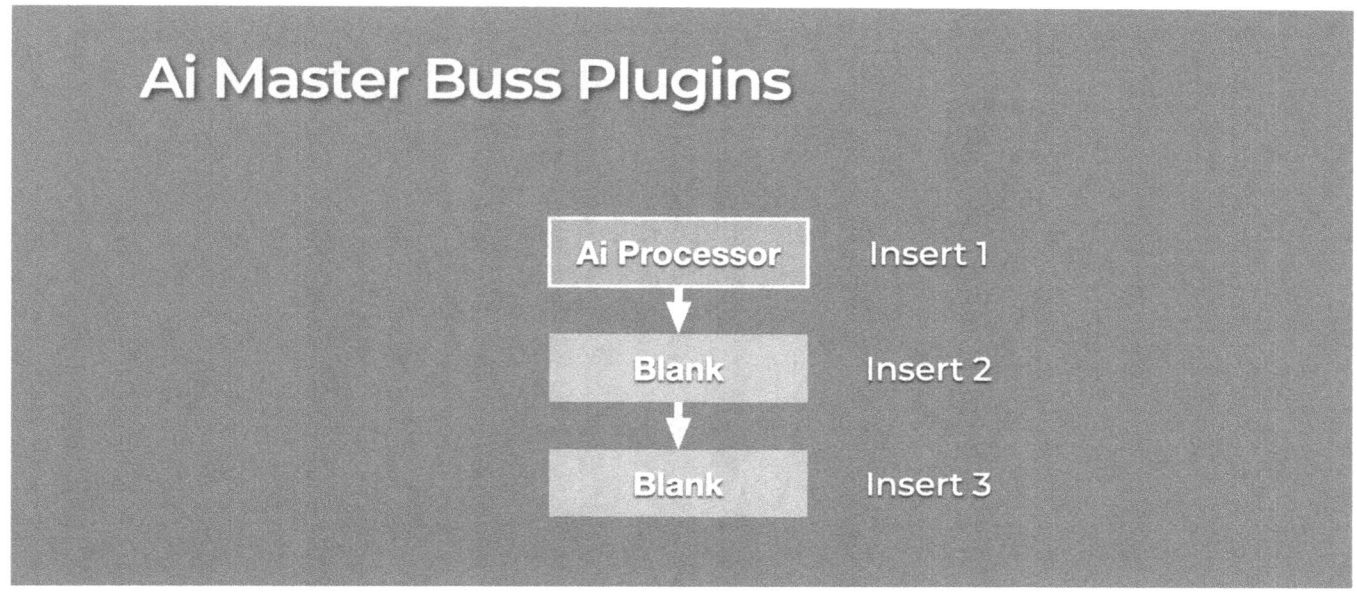

Figure 5.21: Master buss with Ai processor
© 2023 Bobby Owsinski

SUMMING IT UP

- Be sure to use the *Learn* button for the Ai to understand your track
- If an appropriate profile is not available, use *Universal* instead
- If available, use *Reference* to load in a track with the sound you like so the Ai can match it
- In some cases, the settings will probably need to be tweaked even after its learning cycle
- Where the Ai audio tool is placed in the signal path is critical to the final result
- Ai reverbs and noise reduction tools tend to use a lot of computer processing power, so you may not be able to run many instances simultaneously on a session
- Ai noise gates excel at extracting different drum tracks from a stereo loop
- Ai reverbs usually require additional setup after the processor finishes its learning cycle
- Ai neural networks are now being used to precisely model analog gear, but the user will have no interface with the Ai
- Some Ai processors feature individual modules for compression, limiting, noise reduction, equalization, and even reverb
- Track separation tools can extract anywhere from 2 to 10 individual mix elements
- Digital audio workstations that contain a generative Ai component become a new category called a GAW or Generative Audio Workstation

For The Best Manual Mix!

Add The Best Selling Book On Mixing Ever Written

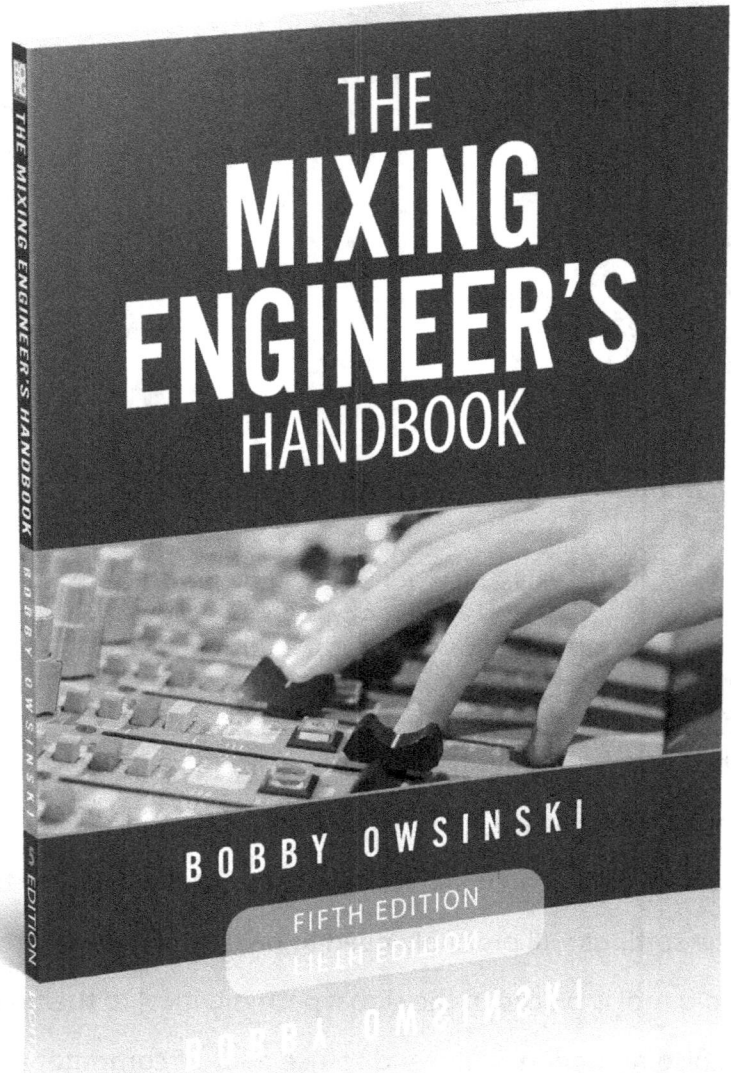

Get 14% off when you order it at bobbyowsinski.com/handbook

(Sorry, due to high shipping costs this offer is only available for customers in the United States, but you can still get it on Amazon)

Ai MIXING AND MASTERING

One would think that with the power of Ai we could have our mixing done for us by a nice robot, but unfortunately we're still a long way from that. Help is on the way in other ways though. You've seen how Ai plugins can take some of the guesswork out of equalizing, compressing and limiting, and it can make your mixing and mastering easier as well.

While Ai mixing lags behind somewhat, Ai online and self-mastering especially have greatly improved as both online services and mastering plugins have gained more real-world training. While using anything other than a human mastering engineer might not have been recommended five years ago because of the quality drop-off, Ai-powered mastering tools and platforms are now viable alternatives to using a mastering engineer in terms of speed and cost.

Ai MIXING AND BALANCE

If you're new to mixing, you might find balancing your tracks to be a challenge. Undoubtedly some mix elements are too loud while others are not loud enough. Typically the vocals may be either too loud versus the rest of the mix or low enough that you can barely hear them. Luckily we cover many of balance strategies in *The Mixing Engineer's Handbook* and my *Mixing Primer and Mixing Accelerator* online courses, but Ai can also help with that, although right now not as much as you might like.

I know what you're thinking, "If Ai is so great then why can't it blend together my 60 tracks so it sounds like an A-list mixer did it." Someday that might happen (I know of several developers who are working on it), but for now about the best it can do is work with a very limited number of tracks.

As of the writing of this book, Ai mixing either is commonly available for only two mix elements - vocals and music bed like with Cryo-Mix (see Figure 6.1). On the other hand, RoEx Automix (see Figure 6.2) can mix up to 8 stems.

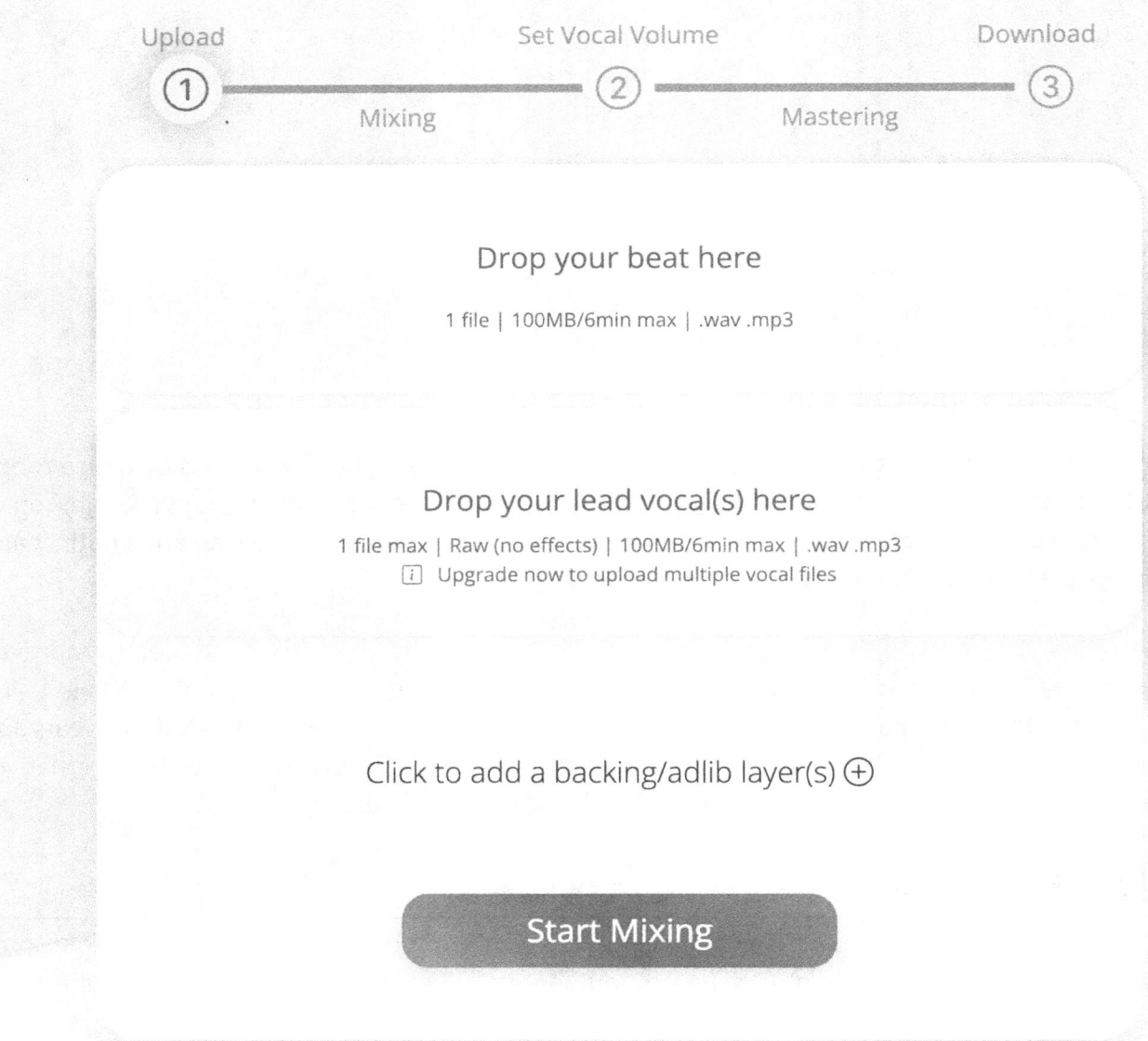

Figure 6.1: Cryo Mix separator
Courtesy of Cryo Mix

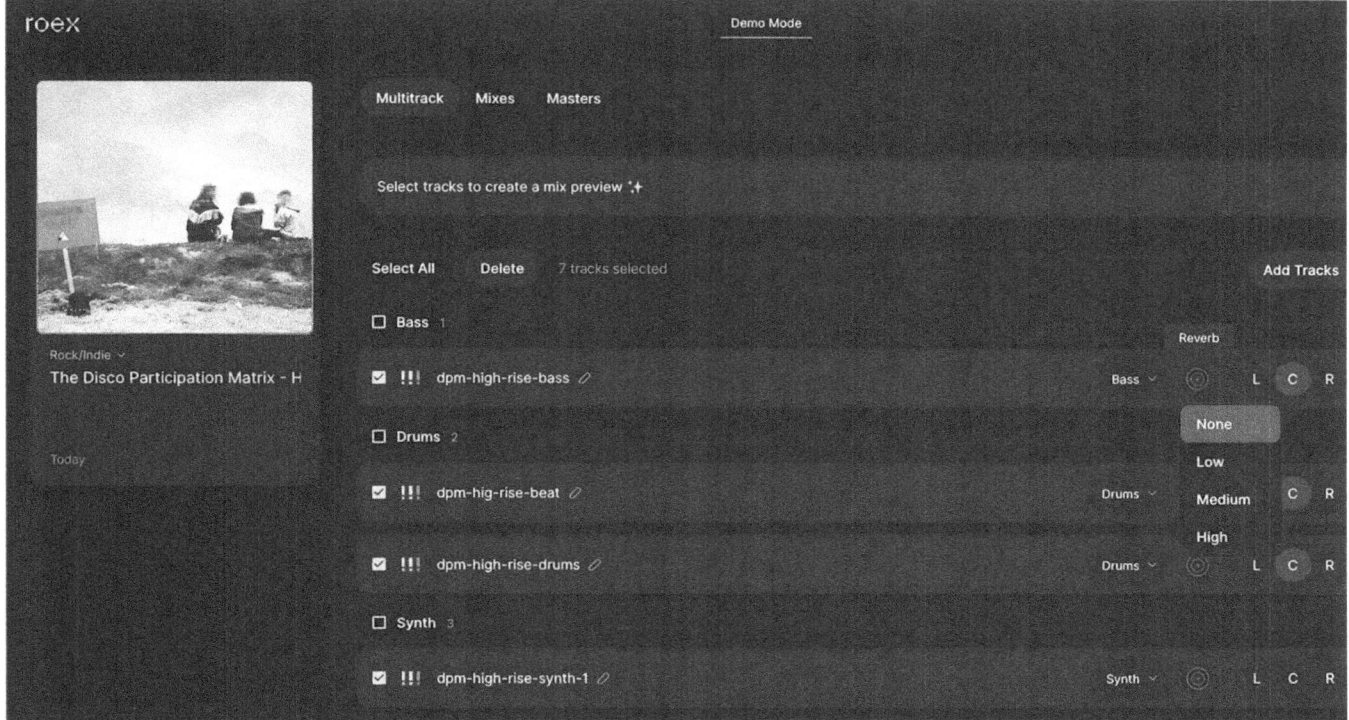

Figure 6.2: RoEx Automix
Courtesy of RoEx Audio

Tracks vs. Stems

Let's get the definition of "stems" out of the way since there's some confusion about the term. Many musicians and artists today refer to stems when they really mean tracks, which are all the individual instrument and vocal files that make up a mix. Stems are stereo groups of these tracks and they might include:

- Drums
- Bass
- Vocals
- Background Vocals
- Guitars
- Keyboards

Stems generally have all processing and effects already mixed into them. For instance, a vocal stem would have the appropriate panning, compression, EQ, pitch correction, reverb and delay already mixed together. The idea is that you could easily fix the balance of a mix by just adjusting the levels of the stems without redoing the entire mix (see Figure 6.3).

Figure 6.3: Stems mix with drums, bass, guitars, background vocals and vocal stems
© 2023 Bobby Owsinski

For the music score of a film, stems are commonly used to easily create the perfect balance so that the music doesn't get in the way of the dialog or effects. These might be vocals, bass, music bed and any mix element with an abundance of high frequency information.

While you'll see examples of where Automix mixes a song with 30 to 40 tracks, when you look closer you'll find that these tracks are first mixed down into 8 stereo stems, and then uploaded to Automix to do its thing. The problem here is that you still have to create the stems manually and the balance within the stem is just as critical as the stems mix that you'll be asking Automix to do. If you get the balance wrong when creating the stem, it will still be off in the final mix.

Another problem is that none of the various Ai mixing services can add effects to your mix at this time. Ask any mixing engineer and they'll tell you that effects (delay, reverb, flanging, etc.) processing and how they're set up are essential to how the final mix sounds. This is something that you still have to do manually. Even with only voice and music bed mix elements there's more to mixing than just setting the level, but again, these are techniques that an Ai could no doubt learn. As of the writing of this book, that's so far not the case.

Hardware Ai

There is another case of Ai mixing but this time it's actually on a Lawo broadcast console (see Figure 6.4). In this case they call it AutoMix (again) or A+. It's best use case is when multiple television studio

hosts or guests are present and their dialog levels need to be equal. A+ watches the master level and makes sure that all the other levels match it when a particular host or guest speaks. While not music mixing, it showcases a situation where Ai can do a rather mundane mixing task very well.

Figure 6.4: Lawo A+
Courtesy Lawo Inc.

Ai Unmasking

One of the key processes of mixing is making sure that you can hear each track clearly in the mix. While much of this is a product of the arrangement (a good arranger will avoid instruments that play in the same frequency range at the same time), a professional mixer will constantly compare tracks to one another to be sure that one track is not masking another frequency-wise. This means that a guitar and keyboard might be soloed and then EQed so that each can be clearly heard. The process continues with each mix element being compared to the others. This can be a long process and is one of the reasons why a mix can take 8 to 12 hours or more.

Ai can help eliminate much of this tedious work however. Thanks to unmasking plugins like Focusrite FAST Reveal (see Figure 6.5) or the Unmask module of iZotope Neutron, unmasking can be done fairly easily.

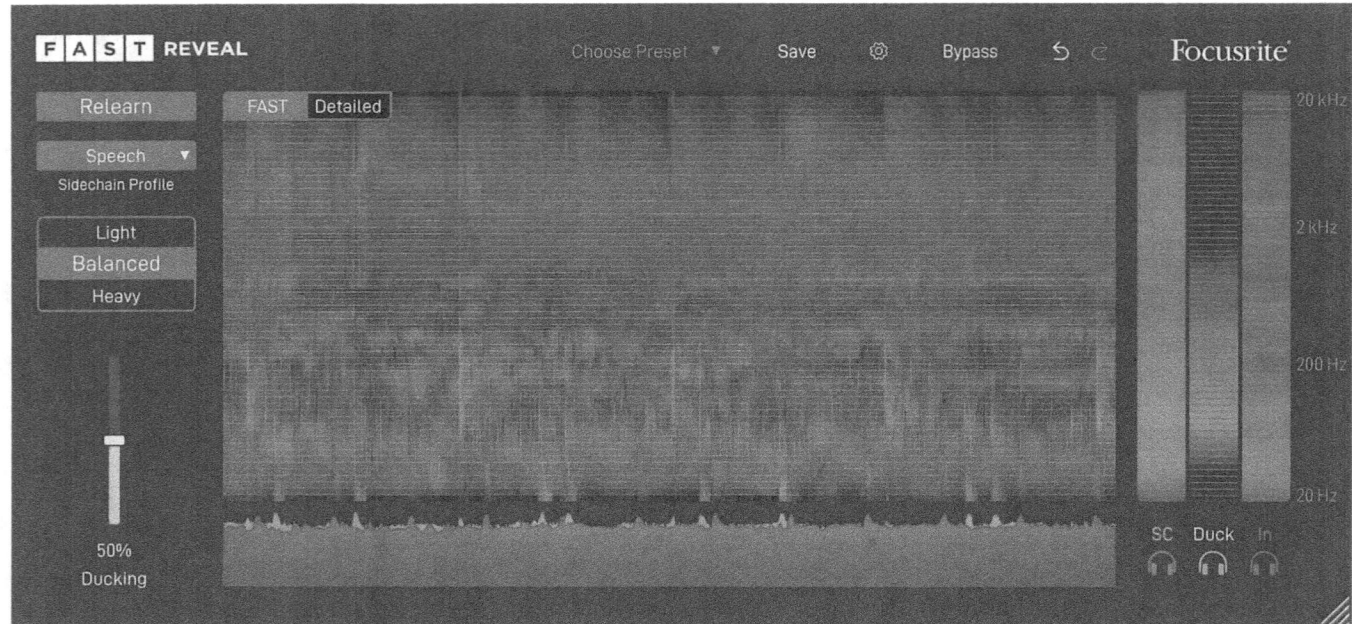

Figure 6.5: Focusrite FAST Reveal
Courtesy Focusrite

Unmasking works on the sidechain principle (see Figure 6.6). If we go back to our guitar and keyboard example where we feel that the guitar is clashing frequency-wise with the keyboard, we'd send the signal from the guitar to the sidechain of the unmasking plugin inserted on the keyboard track.

The signal from the guitar is sent via a buss, so we'd assign the guitar to an aux send (let's say buss 5), and then select buss 5 on the unmask plugin's sidechain. Then we'd hit the *Learn* button and have it listen to the guitar input for about 8 seconds, and the plugin would then determine what the frequency curve of the keyboard should be so that we can now hear both the guitar and keyboard clearly.

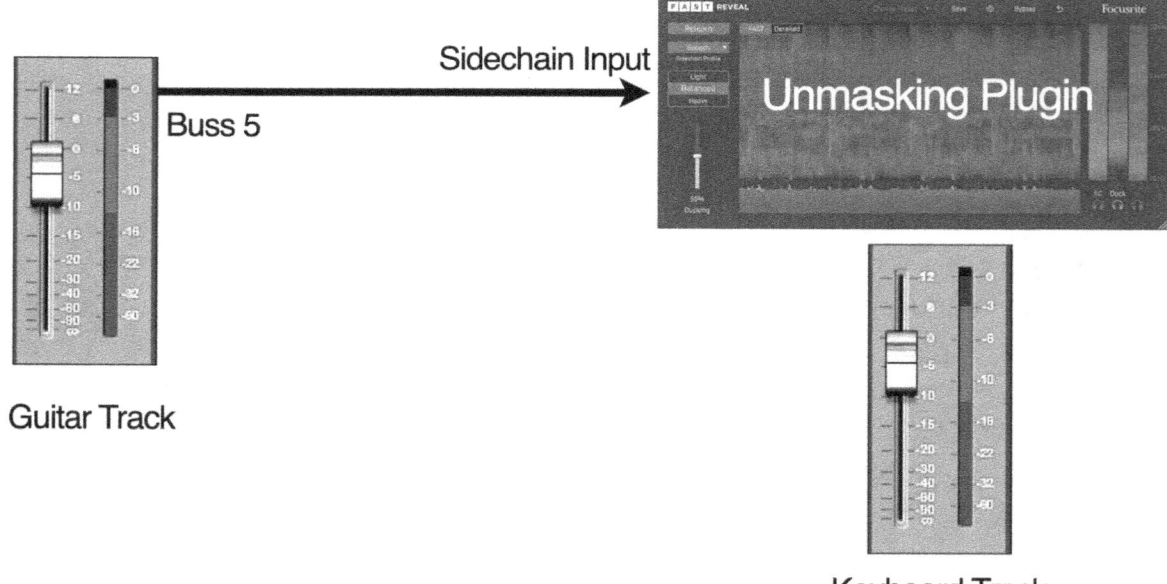

Figure 6.6: Unmasking plugin with sidechain input
© 2023 Bobby Owsinski

Mix Check

An interesting mixing service is RoEx Mix Check Studio, which doesn't actually change anything in your mix but provides suggestions on how to improve it. All you do is drag and drop your audio file into the browser page, indicate whether it's a mixed song or if it's been fully mastered already, then indicate the music genre of the song.

After Mix Check finishes analyzing the track, it will indicate the sample rate, bit depth, mono compatibility, loudness level, any phase or clipping issues present, and show a tonal profile (see Figure 6.7). It will also provide a list of suggestions on how to improve the mix, as well as an explanation of any of the techniques that it suggests.

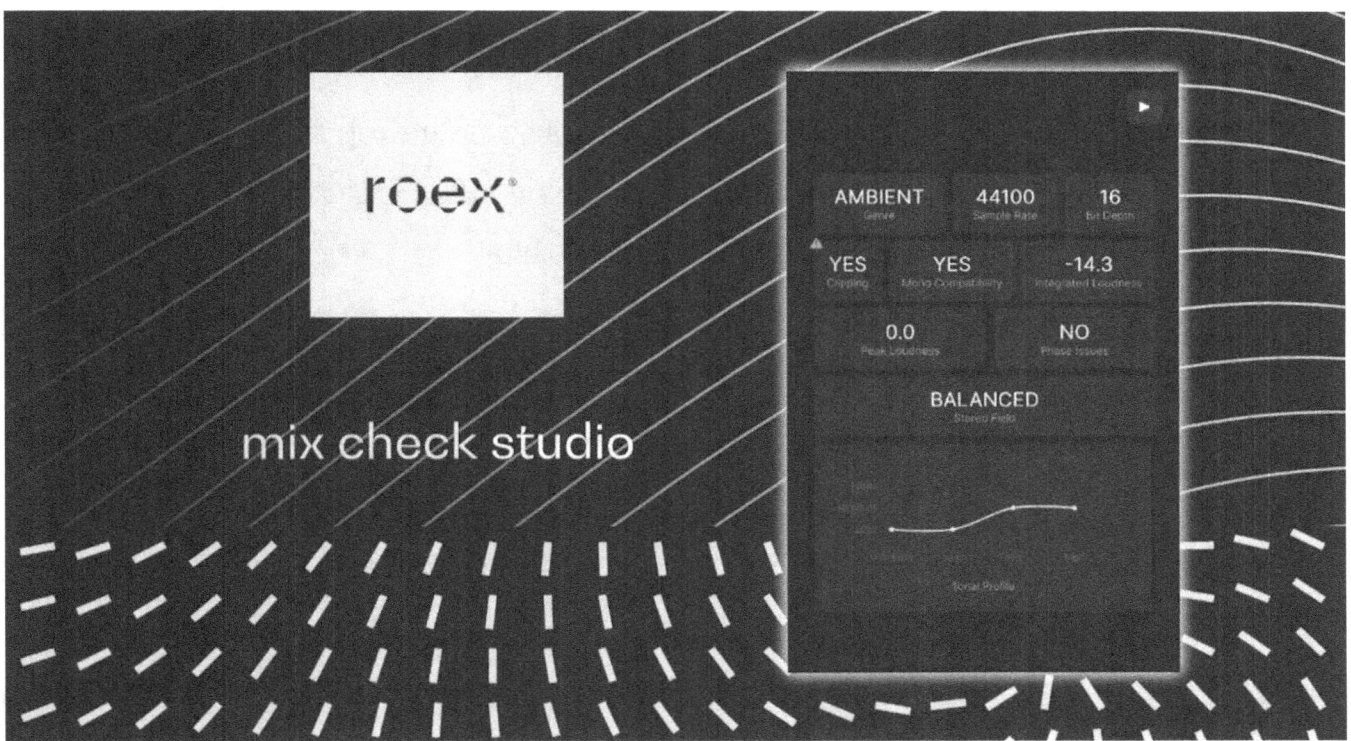

Figure 6.7: RoEx Mix Check
Courtesy RoEx Audio

I've fed Mix Check some #1 hit songs that were very well mixed and it still came back with some improvement suggestions. so this service probably won't be of too much help to mixing pros. If you're just starting and aren't sure about your mixes though, it can be a big help by showing you what can be improved and how to do it.

How to Use

1. Upload your individual tracks or stems to the Ai mix service.
2. Adjust available settings like song genre, instrument/stem profile, panning, reverb, mute, etc.

3. Create a preview.
4. Make any adjustments as needed.
5. Download your mix.

Here are some Ai mixing tools to check out:

- Cryo-mix - Cryo-mix.com
- Lawo Automix - Lawo.com/automix
- TrackSpacer - wavesfactory.com/audio-plugins/trackspacer/
- RoEx Automix - Roexaudio.com
- Mix Check - Mixcheck.studio
- Focusrite FAST Reveal - collective.focusrite.com/products/fast-reveal
- Focusrite FAST Balancer - collective.focusrite.com/products/fast-balancer
- iZotope Neutron - izotope.com/en/products/neutron.html

Ai MASTERING

As mentioned at the beginning of this chapter, Ai-driven mastering has gotten better and better thanks to at least five years of real-world training in a wide variety of genres and enhanced neural networks.

It should be noted that a top pro mastering engineer will beat Ai mastering almost every time (I've compared them), but will also cost you a lot more. While price is not a concern for an artist signed to a major label, it is for an indie artist or songwriter on a budget who wants to apply the finishing touches of a mastering engineer to their masters. On the other hand, Ai mastering fits any budget and can get professional-sounding results if you let it work its magic.

Ai mastering is especially attractive if you want to master entire albums, large groups of publishing demos, or submissions for television or film syncing at a very reasonable amount of money with very good results.

What Is Mastering?

Technically speaking, mastering is the intermediate step between taking a mix from the studio and preparing it for replication or distribution, but it's really much more. The old definition of mastering is *"The process of turning a collection of songs into an album by making them sound like they belong together in tone, volume, and timing (spacing between songs in physical mediums such as CD and vinyl)."*

The new definition applies more to the streaming world that we live in today. In this case it's *"The process of fine-tuning the level, frequency balance, and metadata of a track in preparation for distribution."*

Mastering is considered the final step in the creative process because it's the last chance to polish and fix a project. It's worth noting that almost all of the major record labels and most of the larger indie labels still choose to master all of their projects with a major mastering house (see Figure 6.8), even though extensive mastering resources are widely available to just about any engineer, artist and songwriting.

Figure 6.8: Oasis Mastering
Courtesy Oasis Mastering

A project that has been mastered (especially at a top-flight mastering house) simply sounds better. It sounds complete, polished, and finished because the mastering engineer has added judicious amounts of EQ and compression to make your project bigger, fatter, richer, and louder. He or she has matched the levels of each song of an album so every one has the same apparent level. They've fixed the fades so that they're smooth. They've inserted the spreads (the time between each song) so that the songs now flow seamlessly together on a CD or vinyl record. They've sequenced the songs so they fall in the correct order, and made all the songs blend together into a cohesive unit. They've proofed your physical master product before it goes to the replicator to make sure it's free of any glitches or noise, and made and stored a backup in case anything should happen to your cherished master. This process is executed so swiftly and smoothly that you may hardly notice it happening.

All that takes time and experience, which is why a pro mastering job costs what it does. If your songs need mastering but you're on a tight budget, luckily there are some Ai alternatives.

Online Mastering

Like mixing, mastering costs vary quite a bit. A job by an A-list mastering engineer can start anywhere from about $250 to more than $500 an hour. As a result, you can expect the overall price for mastering an album at a top facility to come in anywhere from around $2,000 to around $10,000 or more, especially if specialized masters for vinyl, CD or Apple Digital Masters are required.

There are now some very good alternatives to spending a lot of dough on mastering however. By far the cheapest is to use one of the automated online mastering services like Landr, eMastered or Cloudbounce. The prices of these services vary anywhere from as low as $4 a song to a monthly fee of around $100, where you can upload an unlimited number of songs.

Depending upon the quality of a mix (a better one will produce a better final product), the results can be surprisingly good. The Ai mastering service will usually allow you to try different mastering settings for just a single price. On some platforms you'll also be able to choose from multiple revisions without being charged again as well.

There are now many Ai mastering platforms available but Landr has been around the longest (see Figure 6.9). It was launched back in 2014 and has benefited from the most training, having created masters for over 5 million songs since them. As we know, training an Ai is all important and the larger the dataset the better job it does. Landr has certainly gotten better through the years and now approaches results that are not that far off from a human mastering engineer.

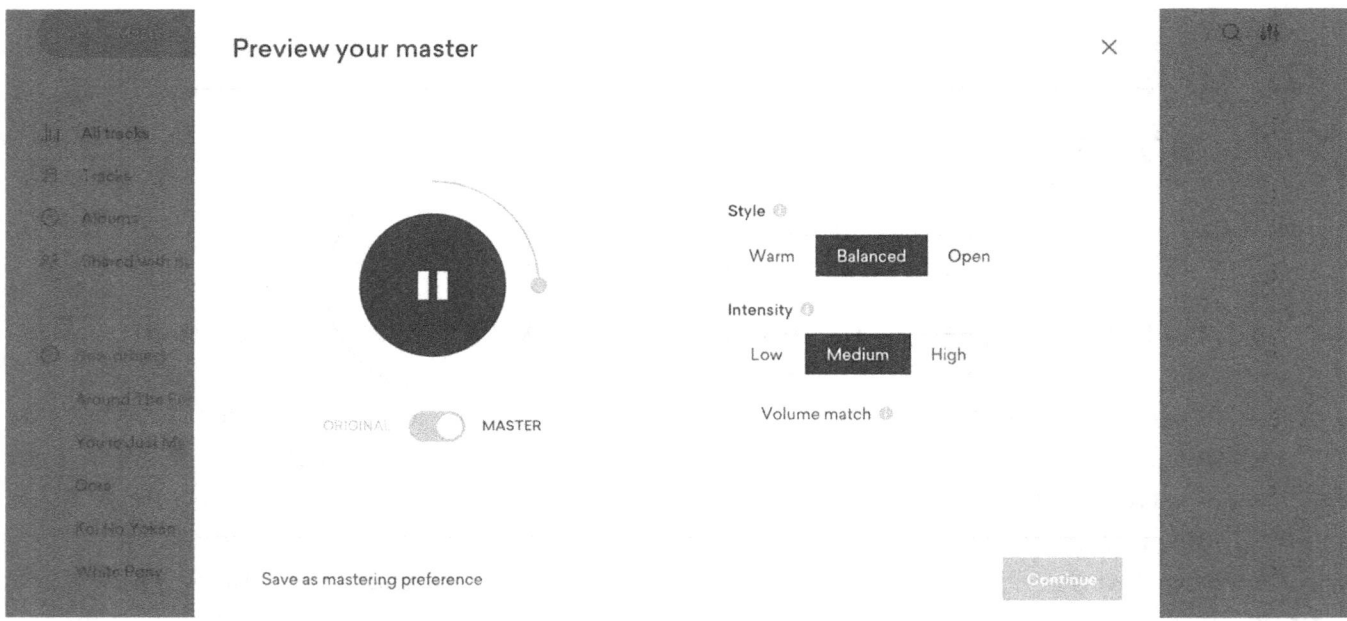

Figure 6.9: LANDR Mastering
Courtesy LANDR

There many other mastering platforms that have been released in the last few years. eMastered, Cloudbounce, Maaster, Songmastr, Soundborg, Master Channel and Bakauge are just a few that have vied for market share in this area. Plugin developers like Waves (Waves Mastering), Slate Digital (Virtu) and Plugin Alliance (mastering.studio) are among the manufacturers that have entered the online mastering market as well (see Figure 6.10).

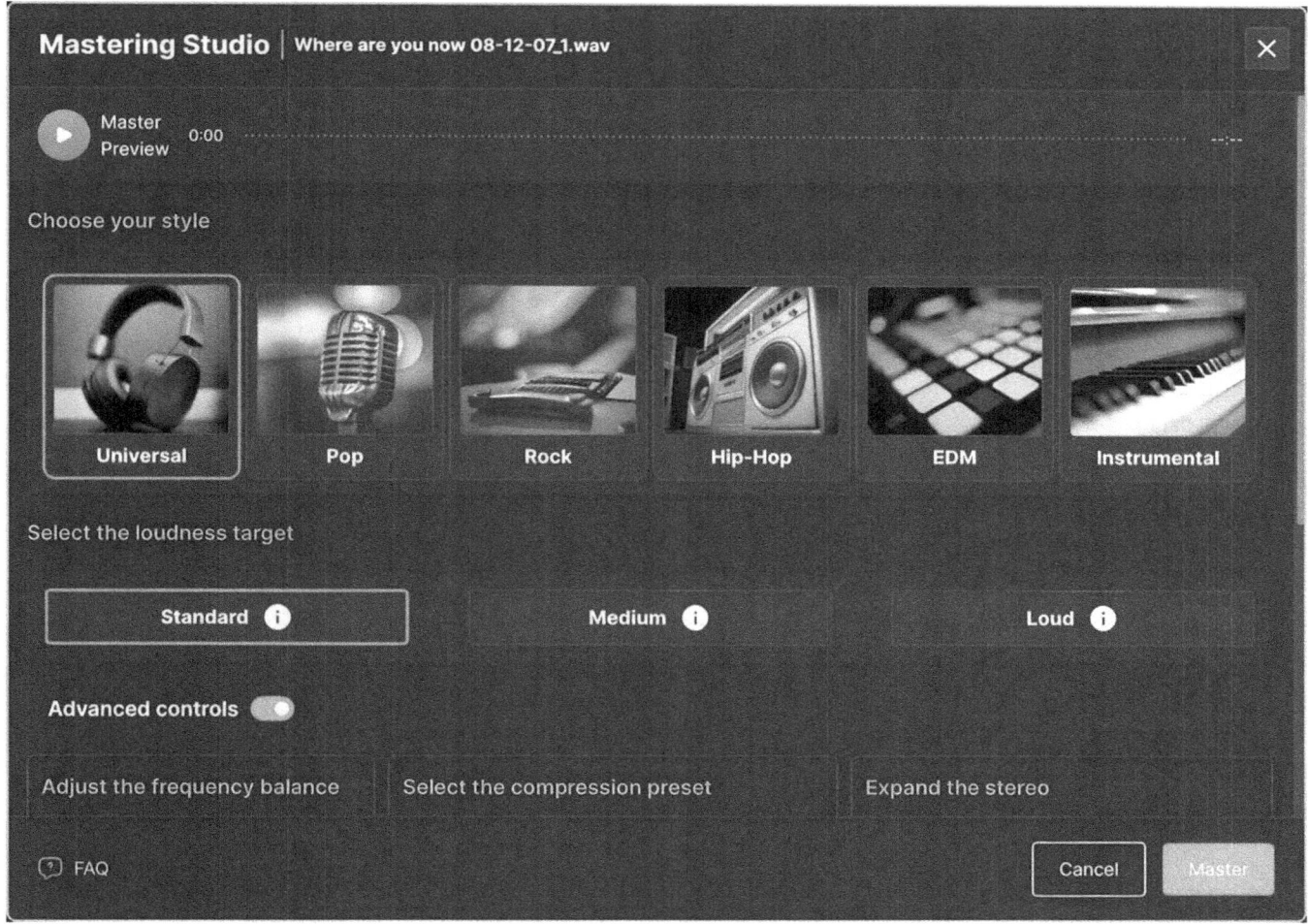

Figure 6.10: Slate Digital Virtu online mastering
Courtesy Slate Digital

Using A Reference Track

One of the keys to creating a great master when using an Ai mastering platform is to use a reference track. That means that you upload a finished song that you like the sound of to the mastering platform where it will analyze it and copy the EQ curve, dynamics and loudness. It will then apply those properties to your song file and create a master that sounds similar to your reference track.

One of the secrets to selecting a good reference track is to first choose something in your genre, and secondly, make sure its already a mastered file. It's okay if you copy a major label release track from a streaming service like Spotify, Apple Music, or a CD. The reference track isn't actually stored by the platform so you're not violating anyone's copyright - only its parameters are temporarily copied and applied to your master.

You can experiment by uploading your song to Landr, Cloudbounce, Maaster, Songmastr, or any of the popular mastering platforms, then have it create a master track without using a reference track. Now upload a reference track and create another master and compare the two. Most likely you'll be a lot happier with the master that was created as a result of using the reference track.

Limitations To Be Aware Of

While online mastering can produce surprisingly good results, there are also some caveats to be aware of. Some platforms are not equipped to master an entire album, so you have to master each song by itself. The downside to this is that all the songs can have a slightly different sound and level as a result. This is one area where mastering engineers are particularly good at what they do and it's hard for a mastering Ai to beat them at making a group of songs sound similar with similar levels.

Even the Ai mastering services that will master an album in its entirety will not creatively insert spreads (the time in between songs) and fades in between songs. The timing of the spreads can make a difference in how the songs flow from one another, and so far there's not an online mastering platform that will do crossfades between songs. Of course, this is only important for physical products like vinyl and CDs and and doesn't apply to songs that are intended only for streaming.

Another thing to keep in mind is that many Ai mastering platforms have a maximum resolution of 44.1kHz/16 bit. While that works fine for a CD or for submission to a streaming distributor, it may not satisfy the needs of a record label or high-resolution distributor like Apple Music or Tidal, who require at least 24 bit files with a sampling rate at 96kHz or higher. (NOTE: If you originally recorded your tracks at 44.1k or 48kHz, you gain nothing by exporting to a higher sample rate.)

In fact, Apple Music has a special high-resolution program called Apple Digital Masters, which requires an Apple-certified mastering engineer for submission to the platform.

Yet another potential downside is if you're planning on pressing vinyl. A mastering engineer will normally create a separate master that's not as loud and not as bass heavy to ensure that the disc cutting goes well. As of now, Ai mastering platforms do not have this feature, although you can experiment with alternative settings to obtain a separate master that will work for vinyl.

How To Use

1. Upload your song to the online mastering service
2. Select the appropriate settings for your song
3. Upload a reference track (optional)
4. Select *Create Master*
5. Preview the track and make revisions if necessary
6. Download

Here are the online Ai mastering platforms mentioned above:

- Bakauge - Bakauge.com
- Cloudbounce - Cloudbounce.com
- eMastered - eMastered.com
- LANDR - LANDR.com
- Maastr - Maastr.com
- Masterchannel - Masterchannel.ai
- Songmastr - Songmastr.com
- Mastering.studio - Mastering.studio
- Soundborg - mrmastering.com/soundborg
- Virtu - Slatedigital.com/virtu
- Waves Mastering - Waves.com/online-mastering

Ai Mastering Plugins

Mastering plugins can be a boon or a bust, depending upon how they're used. By far the oldest entry in this category is iZotope's Ozone, which was released way back in 2001. In 2017 the plugin displayed its machine learning abilities with a module called Tonal Balance (which is also available as an individual plugin), and in 2019 it unleashed its latest Ai with it Master Assistant feature (see Figure 6.11).

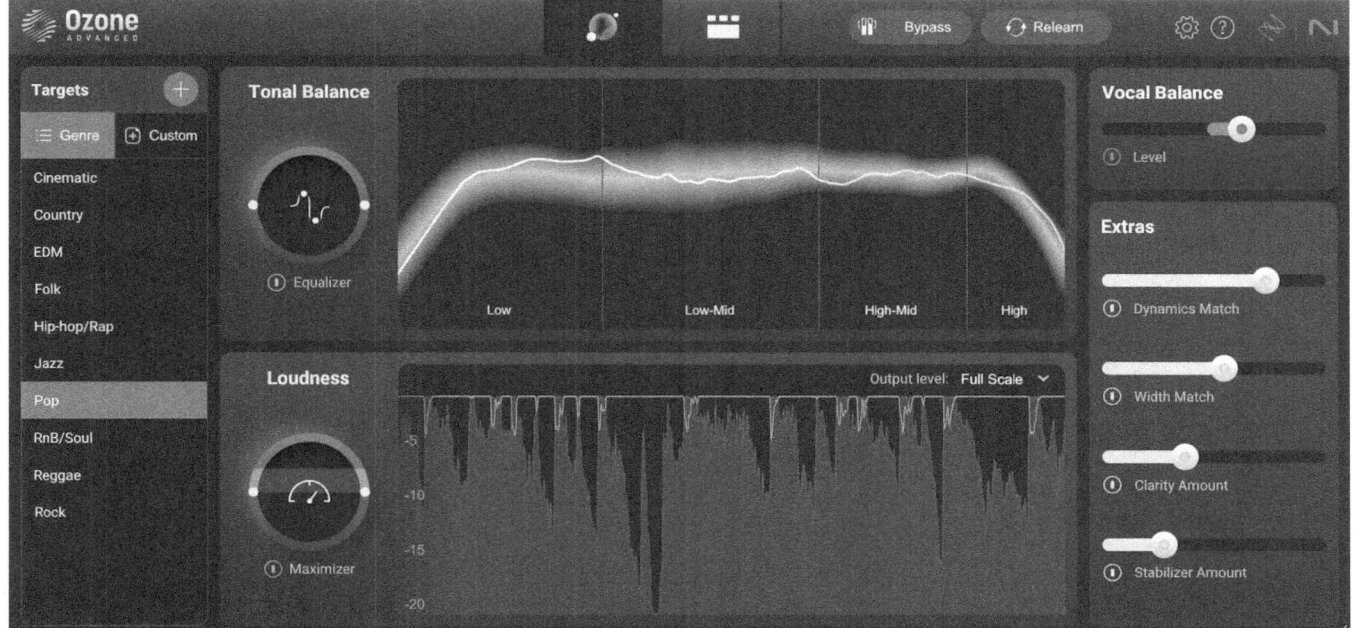

Figure 6.11: iZotope Ozone
Courtesy iZotope

Ozone is incredibly powerful thanks to its 11 modules (Clarity, Maximizer, Equalizer, Impact, Stabilizer, Imager, Low End Focus, Master Rebalance, Spectral Shaper, Dynamic EQ, Exciter, Dynamics, and Match EQ), but as Spider Man says, "With Great Power Comes Great Responsibility!"

This potent plugin has so many powerful features that a user could easily do damage to a song rather than help it if not careful.

Where the Ai comes in is with its Master Assistant, which is where Ozone's potential really lies. As with other audio plugins and their *Learn* buttons, pressing the *Master Assistant* button will engage the Ai and you can then play the track. *It's best to play the loudest place in the song for about 30 seconds for best results.* What's brilliant is that there's no need to select a profile as Master Assistant automatically recognizes the genre. If you think it got it wrong, you can always select a new target genre from the list on the left that pops up.

Master Assistant will then automatically select the processing modules needed and set their parameters as well. You can always manually make changes but this is where users frequently get in trouble by trying to outthink the Ai and make the song "sound better."

As with the online Ai mastering services, it's best to upload a reference track into Ozone so it can copy its settings and apply it to your master. From there, *trust the Ai!*

Unless you have an excellent playback system with an acoustically-treated room to match, it's unlikely that you'll make the song sound any better, and you run the danger of making it sound worse.

One of the cooler features of Ozone is Tonal Balance, which allows you to look at the curves of typical mastered songs in your genre so you can try to match the frequency response. You'll notice that Ozone will have done a pretty good job of this already so it won't need much tweaking.

A helpful free add-on tool for Ozone and Neutron is Audiolens (see Figure 6.12), which gives you the ability to load up multiple reference tracks and instantly call them up from within Ozone. This saves a lot of time as you won't have to find and load the appropriate track every time. The perfect reference is only a click away.

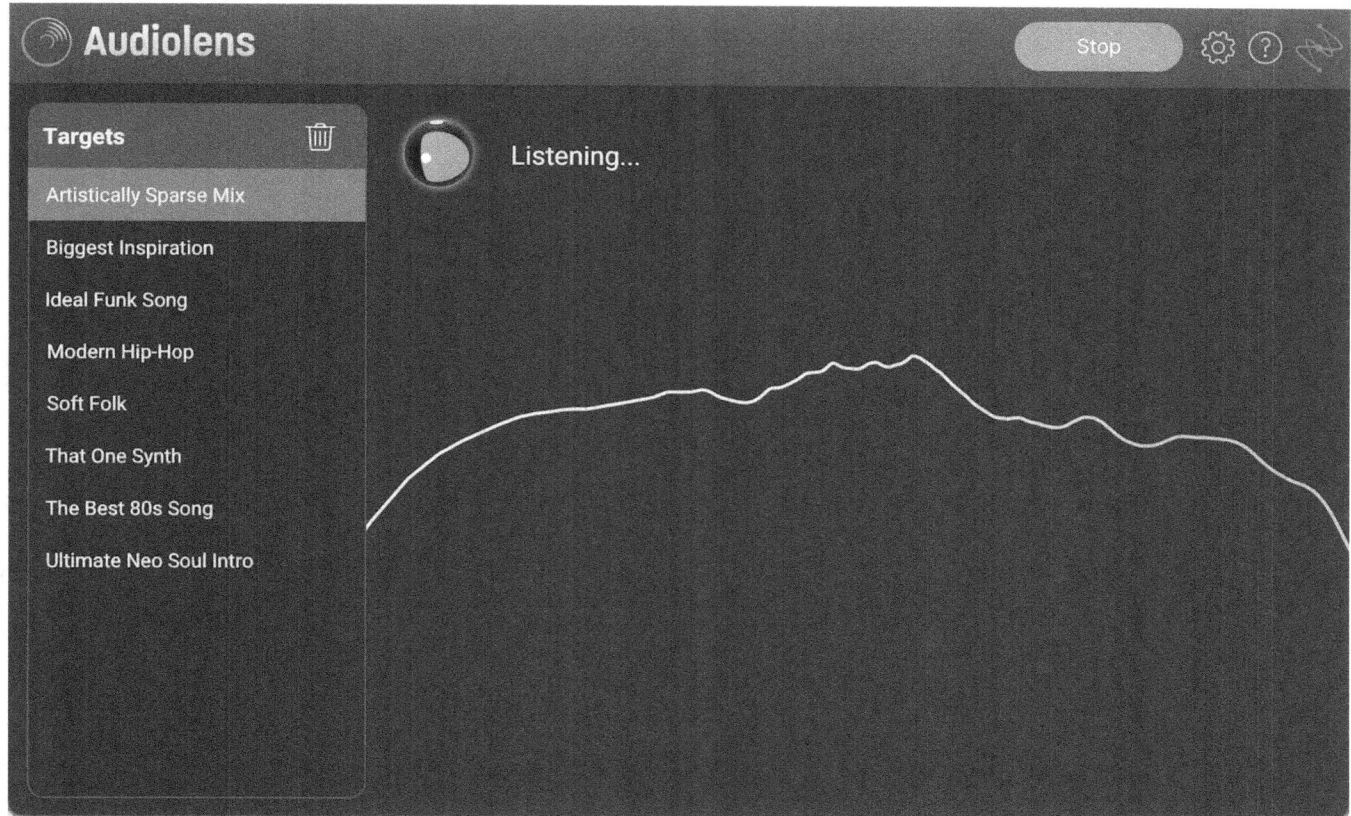

Figure 6.12: iZotope Audiolens
Courtesy iZotope

Another Ai mastering plugin is Exonic Ai Master. While Ai Master will enhance and optimize the dynamic range, spectral balance, stereo field and overall level of your song, it offers no manual parameter controls or even genre selection.

Where To Insert

Any self-mastering tool will take the place of any and all individual compression, limiting and EQ plugins that you might be using. It's best to remove them from the stereo buss and leave the Ai master plugin do all the work. As a result, it doesn't matter which insert slot it takes if it's the only plugin that's being used on the master buss.

If you choose to use other plugins in conjunction with your Ai mastering plugin, place the mastering plugin last in the signal chain. That way you'll be sure that there are no overloads and the output level stays exactly where it needs to be.

- Exonic AI Master - Exonicuk.com/product-page/ai-master
- iZotope Audio Lens - izotope.com/en/products/audiolens.html
- iZotope Ozone - izotope.com/en/products/ozone.html
- iZotope Tonal Balance - izotope.com/en/products/tonal-balance-control-2.html

How To Use

- Click the *Master Assistant* or *Learn* button in the header area to open the Master Assistant panel.
- Adjust the settings to suit your desired output.
- Upload an appropriate reference track
- Click Next to proceed to the Master Assistant analysis step.
- Playback your track for at least 30 seconds so that Master Assistant has enough time to analyze the input audio. Make sure to play the loudest portion of your track to achieve the best results. Enable loop playback in your DAW if you are analyzing a selection that is less than 30 seconds long.
- When Master Assistant is finished working, you can either Accept or Cancel the changes.

SUMMING IT UP

- For now, Ai mixing is limited to 8 tracks or stems
- Stems are submixes of track groups. Tracks are individual mix elements.
- At this time, Ai mixing won't add audio processing, panning and effects
- Masking means that one track is covering up another in the same frequency band
- Ai unmasking tools automatically adjust the EQ frequencies so that each track is heard clearly
- Mastering is the process of fine-tuning the level, frequency balance, and metadata of a track in preparation for distribution
- Online Ai mastering has gotten better thanks to the many years of training
- Use a mastered reference track of the same music genre to get the best results
- The highest audio resolution offered by most mastering services is only 44.1kHz/16bit
- Many online mastering services cannot do full albums
- Even the ones that do full albums cannot perform nuances like custom track spreads (time between songs), crossfades, Apple Digital Masters, and vinyl masters
- Mastering DAW plugins are extremely powerful and can do more harm than good if not used properly
- Other plugins on the master buss are not needed if an Ai mastering plugin is used
- Use the plugin's Ai assistant and trust the results
- Use a reference track for the best results

You Qualify For A Big Discount!

This online program includes these 4 modules:

- **Module 1 - Balance and Levels**: Discover the correct levels to use and a quick way to get the perfect mix balance every time

- **Module 2 - Using Compression:** The time-tested way to get the compressors to breathe with the track for greater punch and power

- **Module 3 - Using EQ:** How to tweak the EQ for more mix clarity and fullness

- **Module 4 - Using Effects:** The secret tweaks of hit maker mixers for smooth sounding reverb and delay that doesn't wash out a mix

Find out more at BobbyOwsinskiCourses.com/mixingprimer or use the QR code below

PART 3

Ai MUSIC MARKETING

Musicians love to create music but generally hate the idea of trying to sell it after it's complete. That's one of the reasons why every artist wants a manager, so the burden of everyday business is lifted off their plate. There aren't enough good managers available however, so artists are forced to consider hiring graphic artists, video makers, and digital marketers to help distribute and promote their music, but that cost can be way out of their budget. Enter Ai, your helpful online friend who can assume many of the music business tasks that we hate for a fraction of the cost of hiring a pro.

Let me be clear that a real professional in music marketing is worth their weight in gold just for the experience they bring. They're always the go-to alternative if you can afford it. For most indie musicians and artists that isn't the case though, and having an Ai guide you in the many marketing tasks required of today's musician, artist and songwriter is so much better than running in circles if you don't know what to do.

I've divided Ai music marketing into three chapters - Ai Graphics, Ai Videos, and Ai Marketing. Each chapter will take a deep dive into that particular marketing area and help get you up and running fast.

Ai GRAPHICS PLATFORMS

For anyone having trouble drawing a straight line (like yours truly) or if you're already artfully oriented, you'll find that the various Ai graphics platforms can generate everything you need, from album covers to social media graphics to logos to branding art.

I've broken down this music marketing category into 5 sub-categories:

- **Ai text-to-image platforms** - The most popular way to generate Ai artwork.
- **Ai stock images** - If you don't want to generate your own graphics, use some that were previously generated.
- **Ai photo tools** - If you have a great photo that needs to be edited, transformed or fixed, there's an Ai or two for that.
- **Ai art platforms** - If photorealistic graphics are not your thing, there are dedicated Ai platforms just to create illustrations and computer art.
- **Ai branding platforms** - Excellent for generating logos and product shots for merch.

Prompting is the most crucial task in graphics generation, so you'll also discover the best way to create prompts that will help get what you want.

Ai TEXT-TO-IMAGE PLATFORMS

Probably the easiest way to generate graphics is by using a text-to-image Ai. This category is dominated by three platforms - Open Ai's DALL-E, Midjourney, and Stability Ai's Stable Diffusion. All of these platforms are very young, bursting onto the public in 2022 and becoming popularized in 2023.

If you're wondering why each of these platforms generate different results, it's because each of them utilizes a particular way of image generation. Although all three use deep learning to generate images, DALL-E makes use of a collection of text-image pairs. It then learns to associate visual cues with the meaning of text instructions (see Figure 7.1).

Figure 7.1: Prompt result from DALL-E 3
© 2023 Bobby Owsinski

On the other hand, Stable Diffusion uses what's known as a latent diffusion neural network, a type of mathematical model that can be used to generate realistic images from low-resolution inputs (see Figure 7.2). This works by starting with a random image and gradually adding details until the desired output is reached. Although there are few public details, many computer scientists think that Midjourney also uses this model as well (see Figure 7.3).

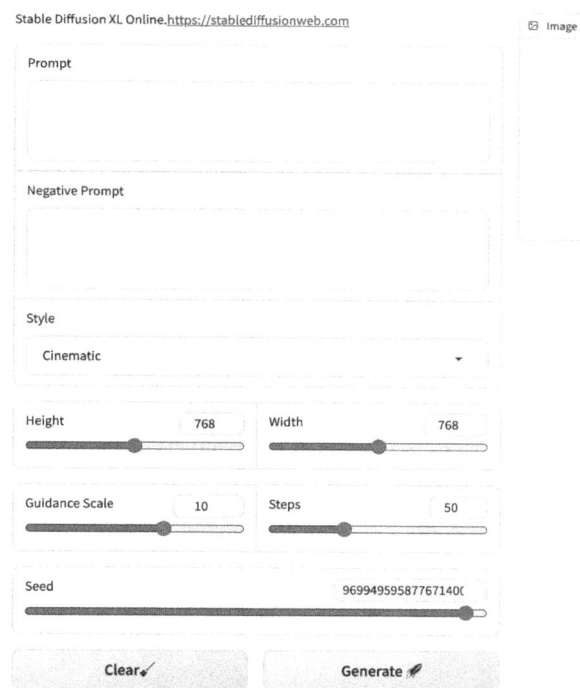

Figure 7.2: Stable Diffusion XL prompt interface
© 2023 Bobby Owsinski

Figure 7.3: A robot singing into a microphone generated by Midjourney
© 2023 Bobby Owsinski

While DALL-E and Stable Diffusion are accessed through a web browser, Midjourney is accessed via a Discord account, which means that setup can be confusing and there are many more steps required to generate an image than with the other two.

The pricing structure is also different between the three. While Stable Diffusion is free (at least for now), DALL-E works on a system where you buy credits, which are used to pay for generating images through a text prompt, an edit request, or a variation request. Midjourney has four subscription tiers that vary by the number of jobs (images) that you can concurrently generate, and how fast they'll generate.

It should be noted that each of these platforms is now way beyond their original versions so they're much better than when they were first released. In fact, DALL-E 3 takes Ai image generation to another level as it's now integrated into ChatGPT. That means that your prompt doesn't have to be nearly as precise as these platforms usually require to get a great result (see the section on Image Prompts below) since ChatGPT is much better at recognizing natural language.

Platforms That Use The Big 2

There are a number of platforms that use either the DALL-E or Stable Diffusion algorithm (among others) along with a more user friendly interface to generate images.

One is Nightcafe, which allows you to access both Stable Diffusion XL and DALL-E along with Neural Style Transfer, VQGAN+CLIP, and CLIP-Guided Diffusion algorithms (see Figure 7.4). Each of these specialize in a different technique to generate an image so if one algorithm doesn't provide what you want, it's very easy to try another.

For instance, if you want to create images that look like an old artwork, you can choose Style Transfer. If you want images that look like art, you can pick CLIP-Guided Diffusion, while VQGAN+CLIP can be used to generate lush landscapes.

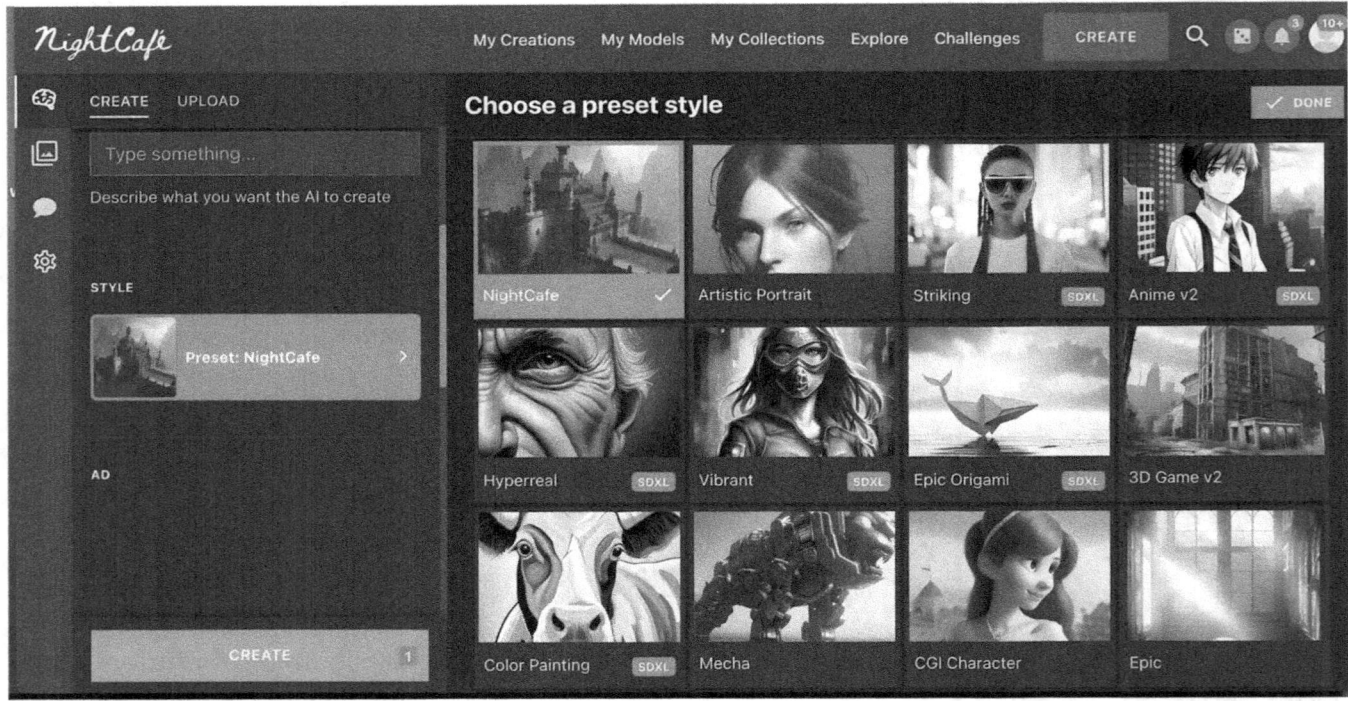

Figure 7.4: Nightcafe presets interface
© 2023 Bobby Owsinski

Nightcafe also works on a credit system but it provides you credits for free when you sign up, log in every day, and like or share images from the platform.

Other platforms include Dreamstudio, which uses the Stable Diffusion image generation engine, while Bing Image Creator uses DALL-E. Bing Image Creator is free but it's a little tricky to get to since you must use the Microsoft Edge browser. When you go to Bing.com or click on the icon on the top right, you'll get to the prompt window. Select Chat and start the prompt with "create an image" then click on the *Create* button. Bing Image Creator is also free, but it lacks ways to vary the image and the image resolution and size is rather low as compared to the other platforms.

Other Ai Image Generators

There is no shortage of text-to-image generators, and some of the most popular include Leonardo, Craiyon and Adobe Firefly. Leonardo was created to generate game assets like environments, buildings, items, helmets, and more (see Figure 7.5). It's also excellent at rendering faces, especially the eyes, which other image Ai's find difficult.

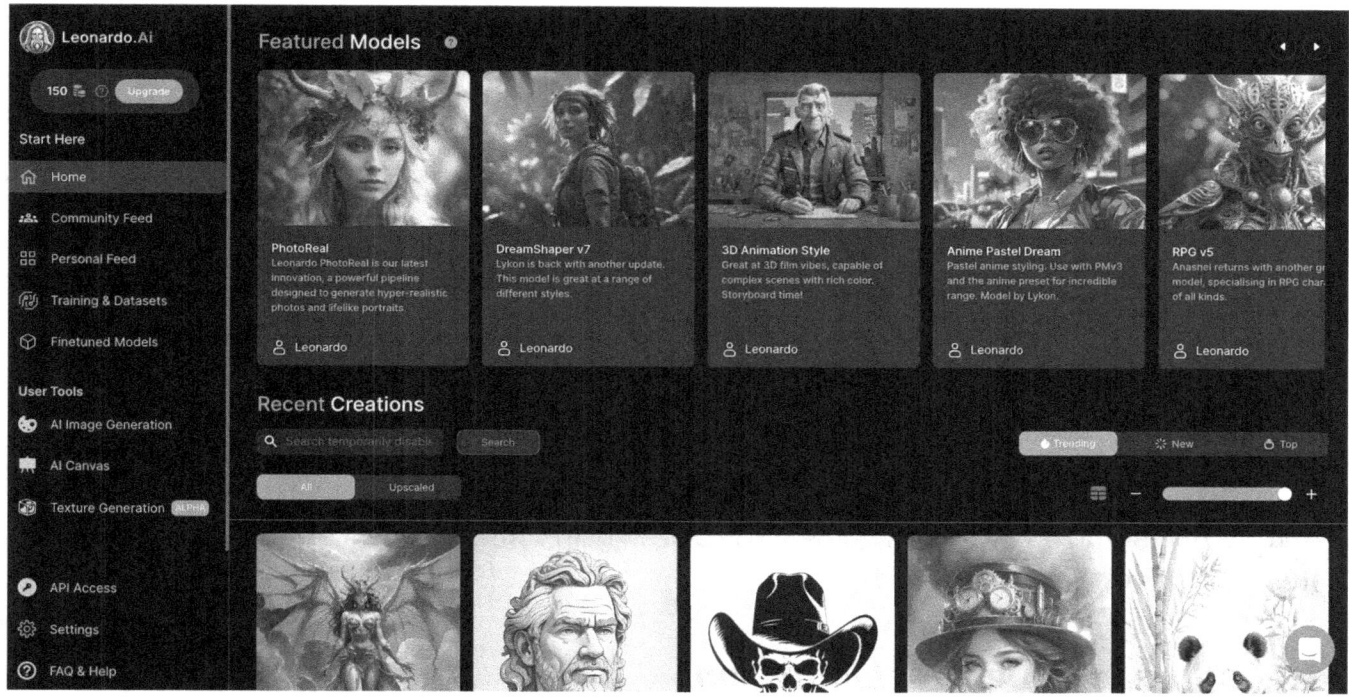

Figure 7.5: Leonardo interface
© 2023 Bobby Owsinski

Craiyon used to be known as DALL-E Mini, but since it had nothing to do with DALL-E or OpenAi, it was asked to change its name. It's a free platform with advertising, but with a subscription you can eliminate the advertising and speed up the rendering process. There's also an Android app for use on your phone or tablet.

Adobe Firefly is also a free (for now) platform as it's still a work in progress (see Figure 7.6). Besides text-to-image generation, it also uses its photo enhancement power for things like image expansion, vector recoloring, text effects, inpainting, sketch-to-image, and much more (see the Ai photo enhancement section later in the chapter for more on this).

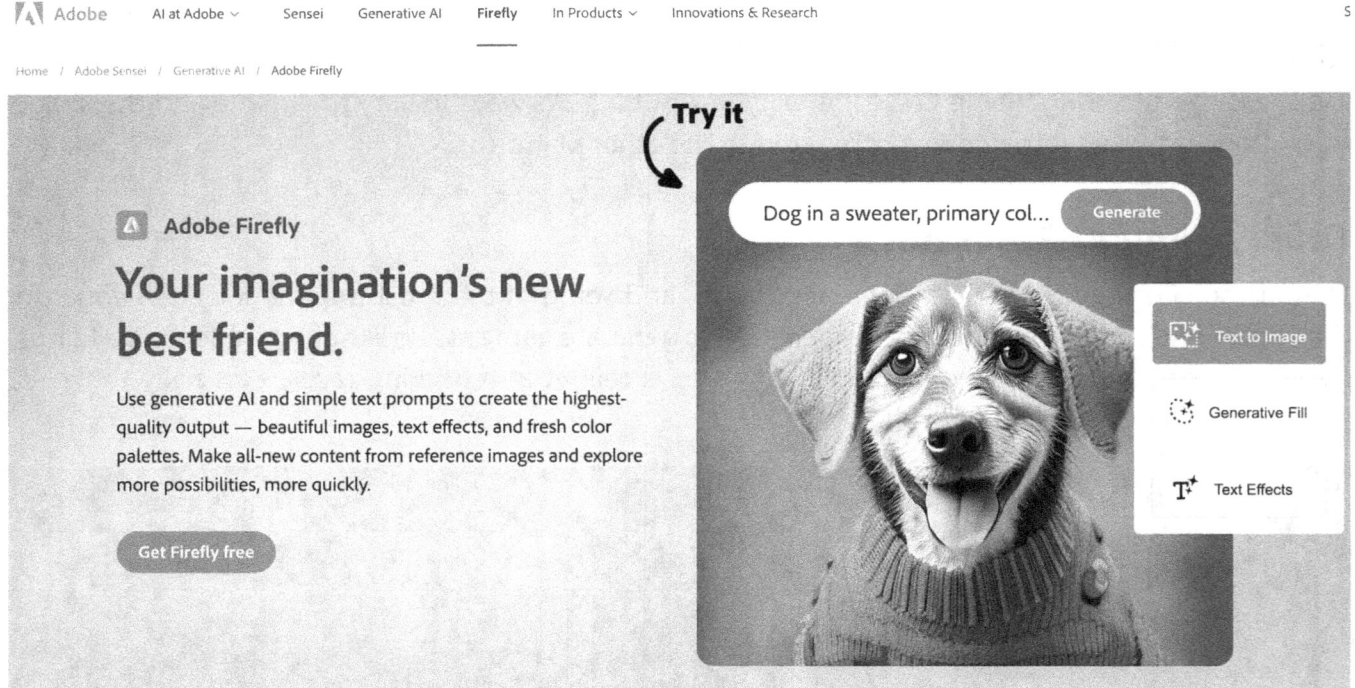

Figure 7.6: Adobe Firefly

There are plenty of other Ai image generators that all do about the same thing. The main differences between them are the user interface, their speed, and how much they cost. As we've seen, many are built on either DALL-E or Stable Diffusion or both, while some use their own algorithm.

It's easy to be overwhelmed by the number of graphic Ai's available, which is why it might be a good idea to start with the ones mentioned here so you can gain some experience and understand which features might best serve your needs.

Text-To-Image Generator Limitations

Ai text-to-image generators have some limitations that you should be aware of. It's easy to get caught up in the fun of it all only to have a cold case of reality slap you later. Consider the following when using anything from this Ai category:

Image Irregularities

There are a number of ways to spot an Ai image at this time after you know what to look for. For instance, image generators tend to have trouble with hands, and you'll frequently see hands missing fingers or going in directions that aren't normal. Also, one hand might look normal while the other might not.

Irregular eyes is another glitch to look for. Ai image generators tend to create eyes that don't match, with one sometimes looking one way while the other is looking in a different direction. Also, one eye may be perfect for the image while the other won't match in color or expression.

I like to use a prompt that includes an electric guitar, especially a Fender Stratocaster. My favorite is "Create a photorealistic image of a blue Fender Stratocaster on a bed of orange flames." Some Ai image generators have trouble with parallel lines, especially like the strings of a guitar (see Figure 7.7). A few strings look like they're loosened near the bridge. Also, the pickups won't be identical, almost like the eye problem from the previous paragraph, and the neck and frets will be imperfect.

Figure 7.7: Blue Fender Stratocaster on a bed of orange flames from Stable Diffusion XL
© 2023 Bobby Owsinski

Copyright

As with music Ai's, it pays to read the Terms and Conditions of each Ai image generator since the copyright information is different for them all. In some cases it's very clear who the copyright owner is (usually the user), while in others it's a bit nebulous.

Some platforms claim to own the copyright and will license the image to you to use depending on how much you're paying. Others set no such limitations whatsoever.

One thing that you'll see on most of them though, is that you give the platform the right to use and store your content to "improve their services." In some cases you actually give them the right for non-exclusive use of your images as well.

It shouldn't need to be stated that generating images that are considered violent, hateful, exploitive, and generally offensive are prohibited on most Ai graphics platforms.

Once again, **READ THE TERMS OF SERVICE** so you don't have any surprises later.

Creating Art from Photographs

One of the coolest features offered by many Ai image generators is the ability to create new images from an image that you upload. You can ask for it to be turned into an illustration, a sketch in the style of Andy Warhol, or a superhero character from a video game.

Usually there will be a parameter that will allow you to fine tune how much of the uploaded photo to reference to. In other words, you can get a much more abstract image by dialing the sensitivity back, or something that's true to the image by cranking it up.

Some artists like this effect so much that they've chosen to use this kind of generated art as an album cover (see Figure 7.8).

Figure 7.8: Album cover by Diamond Jim Hewitt created in DALL-E
Courtesy Diamond Jim Hewitt

Here are some text-to-image generators worth checking out:

- Adobe Firefly - firefly.adobe.com
- Bing Image Creator - Bing.com/create
- Craiyon - Craiyon.com

- DALL-E 3 - openai.com/dall-e-3
- Dreamstudio - Dreamstudio.ai
- Fotor Album Cover Generator - fotor.com/features/ai-album-cover-generator/
- IMGCreator - IMGCreator.zmo.ai
- Leonardo - Leonardo.ai
- Midjourney - Midjourney.com
- Nightcafe - creator.ightcafe.studio
- Stable Diffusion XL - stablediffusionweb.com/StableDiffusionXL

Ai Image Prompt Guide

Apart from DALL-E 3, just about all other Ai image generators work via prompts. In other words, you type a text string describing the image that you want and in theory the Ai will create it for you. "In theory" is the key phrase here, because the more descriptive the prompt, the closer the Ai will get to the image that you imagined.

Although all Ai image generators will create something from a simple prompt like "Draw an image of a dog, (see Figure 7.9)" you'll get a much better image if you instead type something like, "Create an 8k photorealistic image using a wide shot of a yellow cocker spaniel romping in a green field of clover with blue mountains in the background (see Figure 7.10)." Detailed prompts generally use the structure below.

Figure 7.9: The result of a simple dog image prompt with DALL-E 3
© 2023 Bobby Owsinski

Figure 7.10: The result of a more extensive prompt with DALL-E 3
© 2023 Bobby Owsinski

The Structure Of An Ai Image Prompt

To be sure that the Ai generator knows what to search for in its databases, it's best to provide as much information as possible when creating an Ai image prompt. The following are just a few of the parameters that you can include.

1. **Describe the style of the image** like:

- A photograph of…
- A 3D rendering of…
- A charcoal sketch of…
- An illustration of…
- A cartoon of…
- A poster of…
- Digital art of…
- A film still of…
- A sculpture of…

2. Then **describe the subject or content of the image**:

- Actions that the subject is doing (looking up, running)
- How they're doing these actions (joyfully, boldly)
- The mood of the image (ominous, nostalgic)

3. **Add details about the form and style of the image** like:

- Collage
- Street art
- Textile art
- Installation art
- Ceramic art
- Lithography
- Abstract
- Minimalist
- Surreal
- In the style of…

For references to the styles of the great classic and modern artists, check out this excellent post from Shelly Palmer - shellypalmer.com/midjourney-reference-art.

4. **Describe the framing** using film direction terms that might include:

- Extreme wide shot
- Long Shot
- Wide Shot
- Medium Shot
- Close Up
- Establishing Shot

Go here for a reference to camera framing terms - studiobinder.com/blog/ultimate-guide-to-camera-shots.

5. Describe the lighting using film direction terms that might include:

- Soft light
- Hard light
- Dramatic lighting
- Or times of day - morning, sunset, golden hour

Go here for a reference of film lighting terms - academy.wedio.com/film-lighting-terms.

6. Describe the color scheme - Describing the lighting already introduces color, but you can also try adjusting the color schemes of objects, light, or the entire image look and feel.

7. Describe the level of detail and realism - Prompts like "4k" or "8k" tell the Ai to increase the level of detail in the image, although it doesn't increase the actual resolution of the image output.

If your photos aren't looking believable enough, try adding "realistic" or "ultrarealistic" to your prompt. You can also use the "Unreal Engine" prompt to get the feel of images rendered by a gaming engine.

Some Ai's only want a text string while others want you to separate each part of the description with commas as you add more elements to your prompt, like this:

"Create an image of a yellow cocker spaniel, romping on a field of green clover, photorealistic, 8k (the number of pixels as in an 8k television - 4k works as well), early morning as the sun comes up, orange hue, wide shot"

As with all prompts, this will probably not get you exactly what you want on the first try, but continue to tweak the prompt until you get closer to what you imagined.

Additional Ai Graphics Prompt Tips

- Don't use uncommon words to describe the image. Except for DALL-E 3 and ChatGPT, the image Ai's neural network was built for images and not text so there are words that it might not be able to understand.

- Keep your prompts brief and to the point (some say that the lowest number of words should be around 7), but don't be afraid to use as many as you need to describe your image. That said, too many words might not give you much of an advantage.

- Use a variety of adjectives to help describe your art's subject, style, and composition.

- Don't use words that have conflicting meanings. That means avoiding something like using both "realistic" and "abstract" in the same prompt to describe the style that you're looking for.

- Ai copywriting tools like ChatGPT can generate excellent Ai image prompts. Type the prompt that you used for the Ai image generator, then ask the chatbot to improve it.

- Remember that Ai image generators like Midjourney, DALL-E, and Bing Image Creator all work differently, so look at some images with their corresponding prompts first to see what works.

Ai STOCK IMAGES

If all this prompting strategy is just too much for you, there is an alternative. There are now websites that offer Ai-generated stock images, and all you have to do is search to find what you want.

For instance, Stock Ai features thousands of free Ai images created by Stable Diffusion and DALL-E. They're broken down into easy-to-use categories like artistic, nature, anime, space, painting, robot, fashion, animals, food and many more.

Not only that, each image also has the prompt that was used to create it attached, so it's a great way to learn what prompting works well to generate certain kinds of images (see Figure 7.11). Remember that many images have flaws (like the eyes and hands talked about above) so be sure to carefully look over the image before you decide to use it. Also, the downloadable sizes may be limited, but there are many upscalers available online (see the next section).

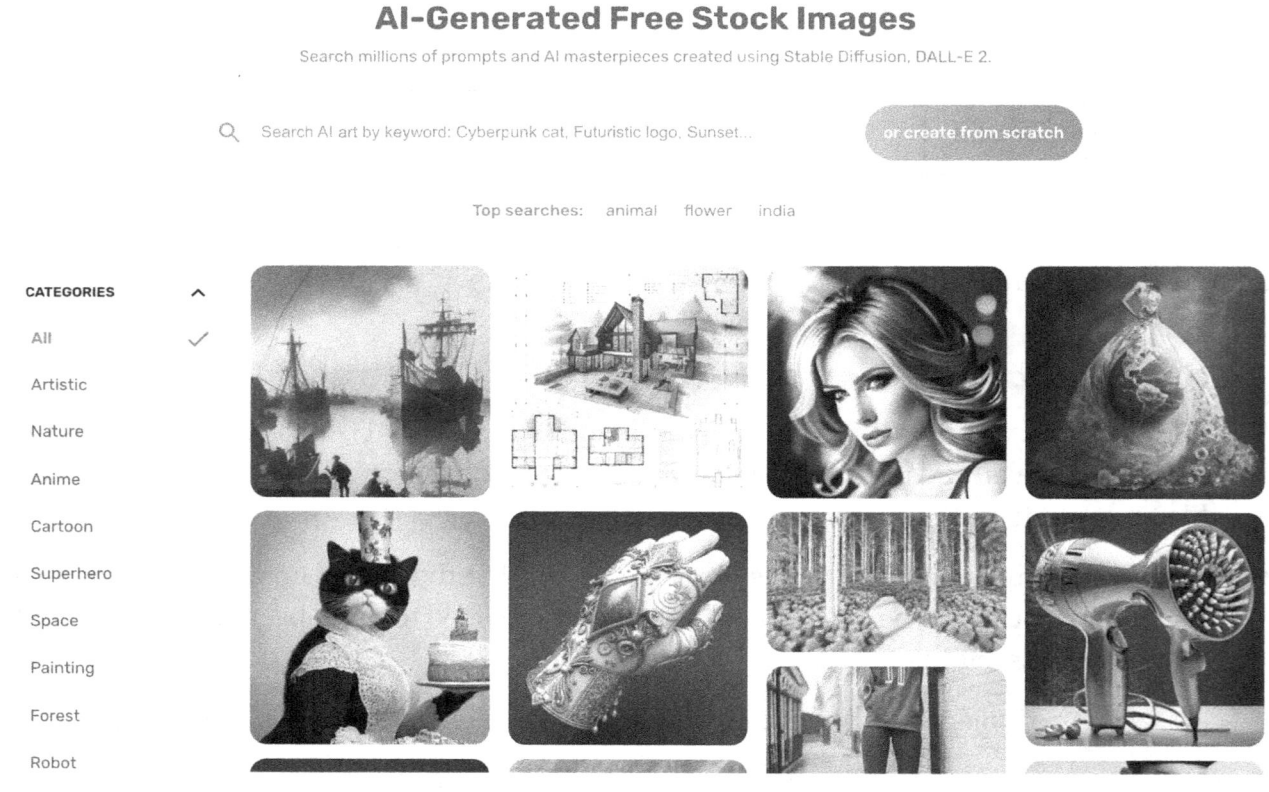

Figure 7.11: Stock Ai interface

Stock Image Ai also has similar features, although it can also generate images as well. The categories from Stock Ai are broader, but different. They include wallpaper, stock image, logo, poster, illustration, book and web UI.

Finally, Civitai is a platform where creators can seamlessly share their creations. The platform offers a collection of thousands of models from a growing number of creators. In this case, a model refers to a machine learning algorithm that's been trained to generate art or media in a specific style. Users can upload and share models and also browse and download models created by other users.

- Civit Ai - <u>Civitai.com</u>
- Stock Ai - <u>Stockai.com</u>
- Stock Image Ai - <u>Stockimage.com</u>

Ai PHOTO TOOLS

Ai photo enhancement tools are especially enticing since they allow photos to be changed in ways that were once unimaginable or required a skilled graphics artist just a few years ago. Although clone stamp tools have been available in platforms like Photoshop and Pixelmator for a long time, they weren't able to match the quickness and ease of use of some of the online Ai photo enhancement tools (this is changing soon). These Ai tools go way beyond cloning as a retouch technology known as inpainting is now widely available.

Inpainting can be used to remove unwanted objects in a photo (such as a person or a telephone pole) and paint over it with an area that matches the background so you never know the object was there (see Figure 7.12). Even better, some platforms even allow you to use Ai to generate a different object to replace the one you didn't like (see Figure 7.13). Some examples of this are Cleanup and Photoroom.

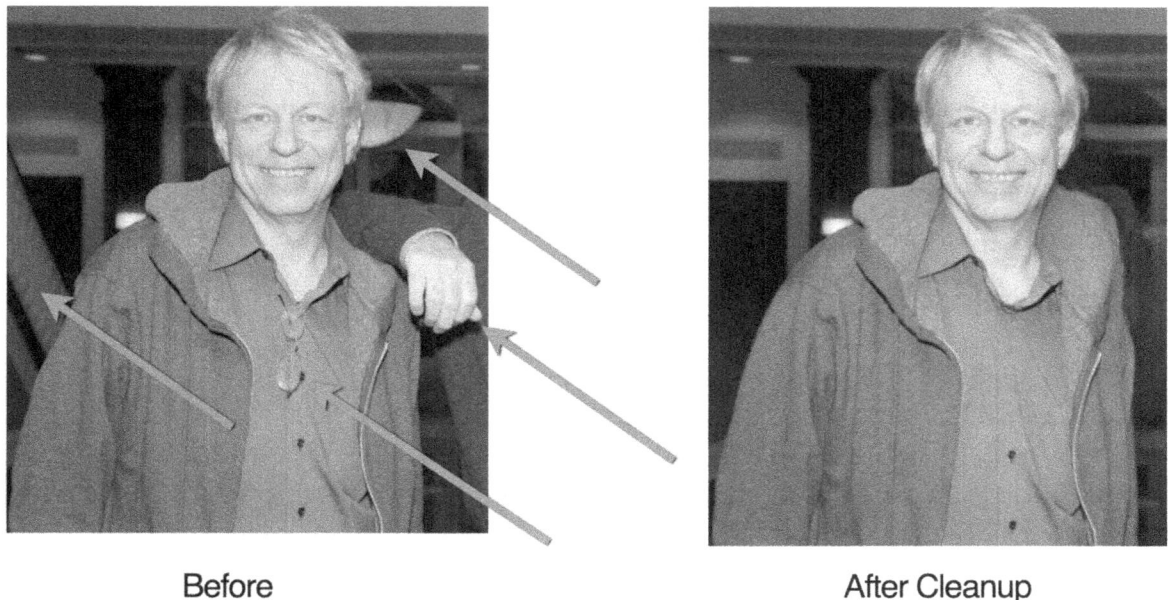

Before   After Cleanup

Figure 7.12: Photo alteration with Cleanup.pictures

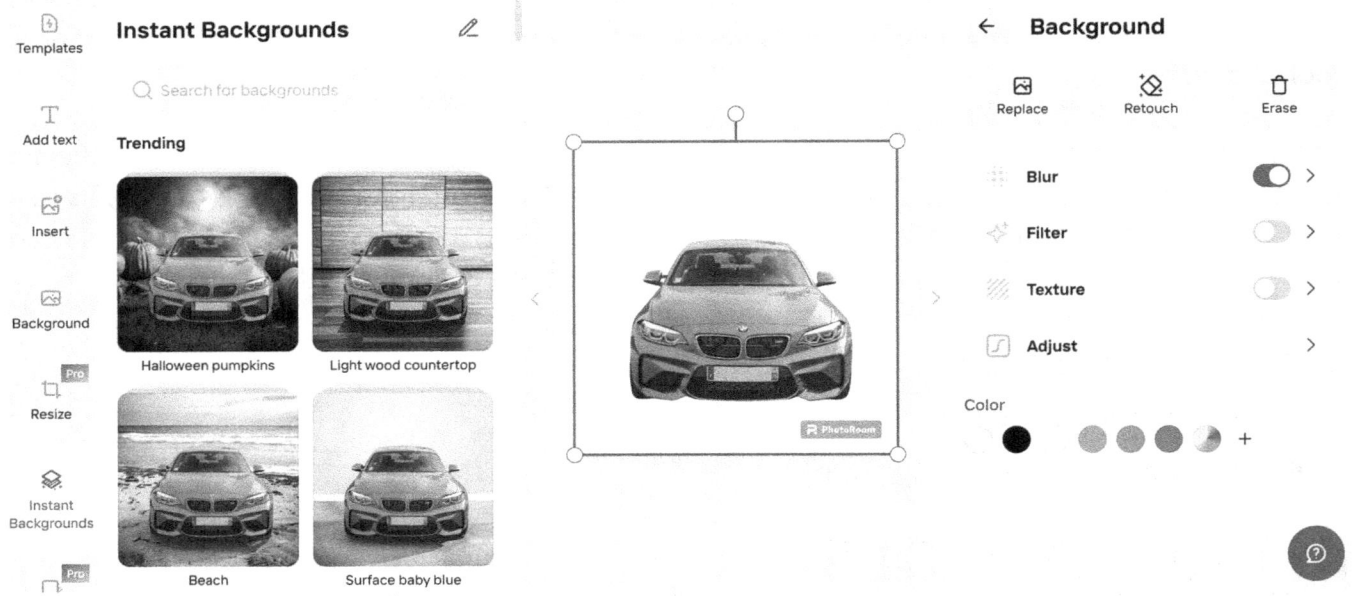

© 2023 Bobby Owsinski
Figure 7.13: Instant backgrounds from Photoroom

Some Ai photo enhancement tools allow you to remove the background completely, replace it with another background, change the background's color, or enhance the color and detail of a photo. But that's not all. You can also blur the background, perform a variety of crops, add text or a border, or turn the photo into a cartoon. Some, like Fotor or Pixelcut are able to take a photo with a small size and upscale it to a higher resolution.

As with most Ai platforms, there are usually at least two subscription tiers. A free tier lets you perform a variety of photo editing tasks, but not all, and the export of the result will be limited to a low 720px resolution. The premium or professional tier usually has no limits on the size or the number of features that you can use.

- Cleanup - Cleanup.pictures
- Fotor - Fotor.com
- Photoroom - Photoroom.com
- Pixelcut - Pixelcut.ai

Ai ART PLATFORMS

Ai art platforms are different from the typical text-to-image platform in that the look and the use of the generated output is different. This can be broken down into illustration platforms like Illustroke, and art platforms like Lexica Art.

Illustration Platforms

Illustration platforms specialize in creating vector images in the SVG file format. Vector images are perfect for logos and icons in that they maintain their resolution regardless of how large or small you make them. Vector files are built from a complex mathematical network of lines, dots, shapes, and algorithms, but because they don't contain any pixels, SVGs will never lose resolution and will always render to pixel-perfection even on newer display technologies.

SVGs are also a good choice for web design because search engines like Google can read their XML programming language. This helps with SEO and website rankings, and their smaller file sizes mean that images will load faster.

In platforms like Illustroke and neoSVG, you input a text prompt, select a style, select from the choices provided, then modify your vector image as necessary.

On the other hand you may have a normal image like a jpg or png that you'd like to turn into a vector image. In that case, a platform like Vectorizer Ai can do the job (see Figure 7.14).

Figure 7.14: Making a vector image from a jpg with Vectorizer

Ai Illustration Limitations

Just as some Ai image generators have trouble with hands and eyes, Ai illustration platforms have some of the same quirks. Look carefully at the curves to see if they're smooth, and zoom in to make sure that the corners are clean.

Art Platforms

As opposed to some Ai image generators that try to make photorealistic images, art generators make images that look like art that you'd hang on the wall. There's zero attempt to look real.

While most text-to-image platforms will have this feature, there are some Ai's like Hotpot, Artguru and Lexica Art that specialize in this area. Not only will these generate art-like images from your text prompt, but also from your photos as well.

For instance, if you want an avatar or portrait of yourself, simply upload your image and choose from a wide range of art styles, including different styles of paintings, anime, cyberpunk, 3D, and more (see Figure 7.15).

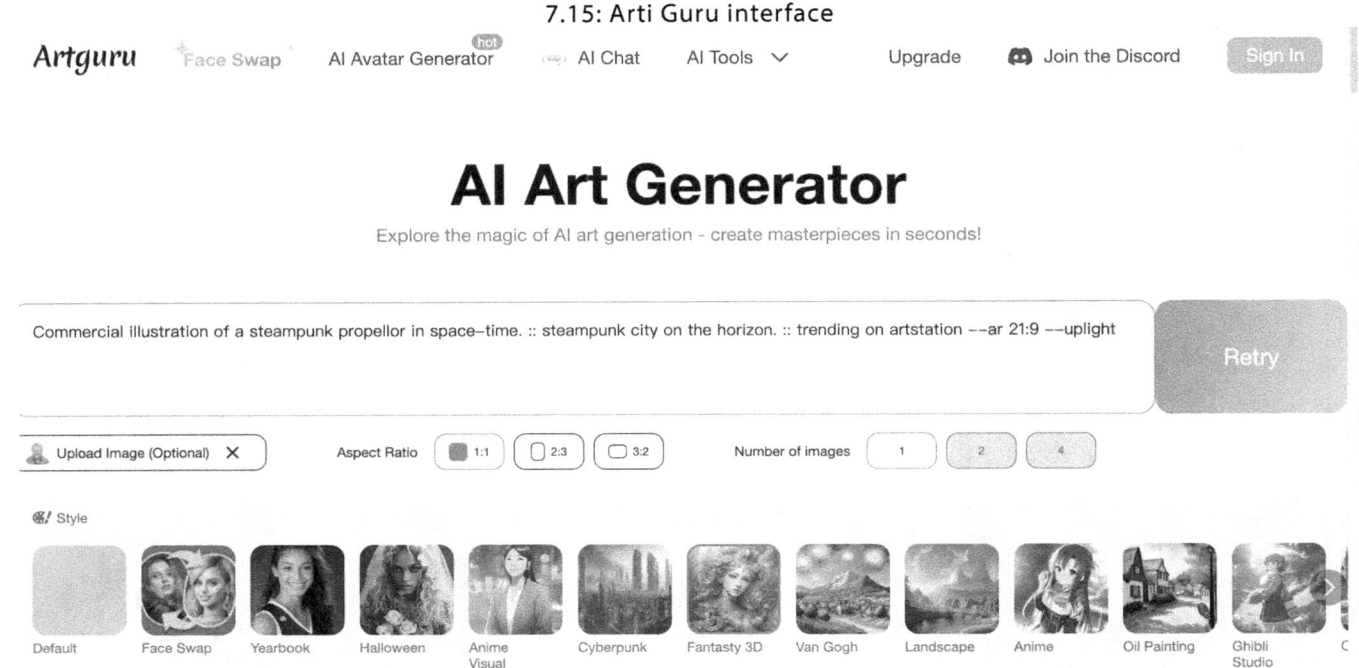

7.15: Arti Guru interface

Most Ai art platforms also have a gallery where you can show off your creation, or view others and learn from them. In many cases, the prompt used to generate the images is also displayed.

- Artguru - Artguru.ai
- Hotpot - Hotpot.ai
- Illustroke - Illustroke.com
- Lexica Art - Lexica.art
- neoSVG - neosvg.com
- Vectorizer Ai - Vectorizer.ai

Ai BRANDING PLATFORMS

One of the biggest components of branding is a consistent look across all media, both online and physical. Ai branding generators make it easier than ever to come up with both a professional look and the corresponding graphics assets.

While most of the platforms discussed above are multi-dimensional in terms of features, sometimes you need one that's focused on a specific task. Generating branding elements is one of those tasks.

Branding platforms are not only good at designing logos (the first thing you usually think of when branding is brought up), but also designing graphics for merch and generating excellent merch scenes that imitate a photoshoot.

Product photoshoots are highly specialized and typically cost in the thousands or tens of thousands of dollars. For a small fraction of that, you can get a fashion photoshoot for your merch that will make it look like a million bucks.

A platform like Flair Ai makes all this especially easy since all you have to do is upload an image of your merch. You can clean up the image by eliminating the background, then select the scene that you'd like to see it placed in. This means a variety of backgrounds from plain to exotic to different places like the ocean, woods or mountains. Then select if you want the merch to sit on a pedestal, select from a variety of styles and you'll be amazed how professional your merch shot looks (see Figure 7.16).

Figure 7.16: Flair Ai

A platform like Looka gives you the ability to design a logo from hundreds of templates, generate a brand kit to add your design to your email, flyers and posters, and customize your profile covers in social media. In a few hours you can look as professional as if you hired a dedicated branding company to develop your brand.

Finally, there are platforms that just focus on background patterns like Patterned Ai (see Figure 7.17). Eye-catching patterns can help in branding, but can be a pain to generate manually. Some pattern generators allow you to create patterns from scratch, while others let you customize existing patterns. You can also choose from a variety of different styles, including geometric, floral, and abstract patterns. In many cases you can upload a favorite image and generate a pattern from that.

Figure 7.17: Patterned Ai

- Flair Ai - Flair.ai
- Looka - Looka.com
- Patterned Ai - Patterned.ai

SUMMING IT UP

- DALL-E, Stable Diffusion, and Midjourney are the most popular Ai image generators.
- Many Ai image generators are just different user interfaces for either the DALL-E or Stable Diffusion algorithms.
- Most Ai image generators depend on a text prompt to describe the graphic that it should generate.
- A good form for a graphics prompt is: image style, subject or content, details of form or style, framing, lighting, color scheme, level of detail and realism.
- Some Ai text-to-image generators require a comma after each prompt element.
- Try using ChatGPT or other chatbot to generate an improved image prompt.
- You can spot Ai image imperfections by looking at the hands, eyes and parallel straight lines.
- As with music Ai's, copyright for images may be nebulous. Check the terms and conditions to understand who actually owns the copyright, if you're being granted a license, or if the generated image is in public domain.
- While some Ai image generators are free (at least for now), most work on a monthly subscription basis with multiple tiers.
- Many Ai image generators work on a credits system, where credits are used as you generate or change an image.
- Ai stock image platforms can be a quick alternative to generating an image.
- Ai branding platforms are very specific in that they generate professional-looking assets like logos, merch designs, and photorealistic merch presentation images.
- Ai photo enhancement platforms can perform tasks like upsampling, removing or replacing objects or the background, changing the color of the background, or enhancing the color and detail of a photo.
- Some Ai image generators can create a portrait or cartoon image from an uploaded photo.
- Ai illustration platforms can generate new vector images or convert existing images to vector files.

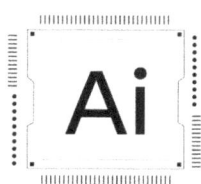

Ai VIDEO PLATFORMS

It wasn't that long ago that if you wanted a music video, you had to hire a director, crew, and an editor, and the whole process from conception to finished product could take weeks to finish. Flash forward to today, we have Ai video generators that can make all the different types of videos that musicians need at a tiny fraction of the cost and time.

Today an artist has many video requirements. While a full music video intended for YouTube might be less important than it once was, it's still needed to extract shorter clips for TikTok, Shorts, Reels and many other social platforms at the very least.

Lyric videos were once a relatively inexpensive substitute for a full production music video because of their short turnaround time and low cost to produce, plus they would draw just about the same number of views as the full production video.

However, there still was a cost, since at the very least you'd have to hire an editor to create one if your budget could afford it. Many artists with limited budgets learned how to edit their own videos, but at the expense of a steep learning curve and, as a result, less time for creating music.

These are all good reasons why Ai video generation has taken off. It's very inexpensive, can produce surprisingly good results, and you're able to create a video in an hour or so after you learn the platform.

Keep in mind that there are dozens of other great Ai video platforms than the ones mentioned below, but most of them don't directly apply to music and instead specialize in industrial applications using avatars for customer service, sales pitch or spokesperson videos. Many feature hundreds of different male and female avatars able to speak all different languages. Although one of these could well be used in an application where you might want a narrator for your video, they're not really oriented towards music applications. That said, platforms add new features all the time so don't be surprised if one or more these suddenly add music video features. Let's take a look.

Ai MUSIC VIDEO CREATION

Just like music and graphic Ai's, videos can be generated in several ways: text-to-video, graphics-to-video, and video-to-video. Although most video generation platforms focus on text-to-video operation, many will also do graphics-to-video as a secondary feature.

While text-to-video uses a text prompt to instruct the video what to create, graphics-to-video starts with a graphic or graphics that the Ai uses as a prompt instead. Depending upon the parameters that you select, the graphic can morph into different variations of the same image, or it can use it as a basis to create new images. Sometimes it will only use the colors of the image as basic information and change the image completely. Either way, you're in control of the creation and you can guide it through its various parameters.

Video-to-video generation is much the same as graphics-to-video, but uses a video that you upload instead of a graphic. Again, you can guide it through its various parameters.

In my experience, musicians make the best video editors because they can feel the pulse of the video just like they can with music. You'd think that a platform that would automatically generate a music video would lack this basic requirement, but the fact is that those platforms that have a music video option perform this function fairly well. They understand the rhythm of the song and make the video edits based on that pulse, just as a good editor would.

Of course if your music genre is Ambient, Space Music, or some forms of New Age music, there's not an obvious pulse to cut to. Don't worry, the video generator will usually have a style or template that fits this music genre.

Most Ai video platforms being their operation in one of two ways - by the user choosing a template or by choosing a style and clips.

Template-Based Video Generators

Platforms like Videobolt and Flexclip use templates as a way to speed video creation. The process is fairly straight forward. You select an appropriate template for creating a music video, upload your music to the platform, and tweak the template's parameters as needed (see Figure 8.1). This is designed to get you up and running quickly, but at the expense of flexibility.

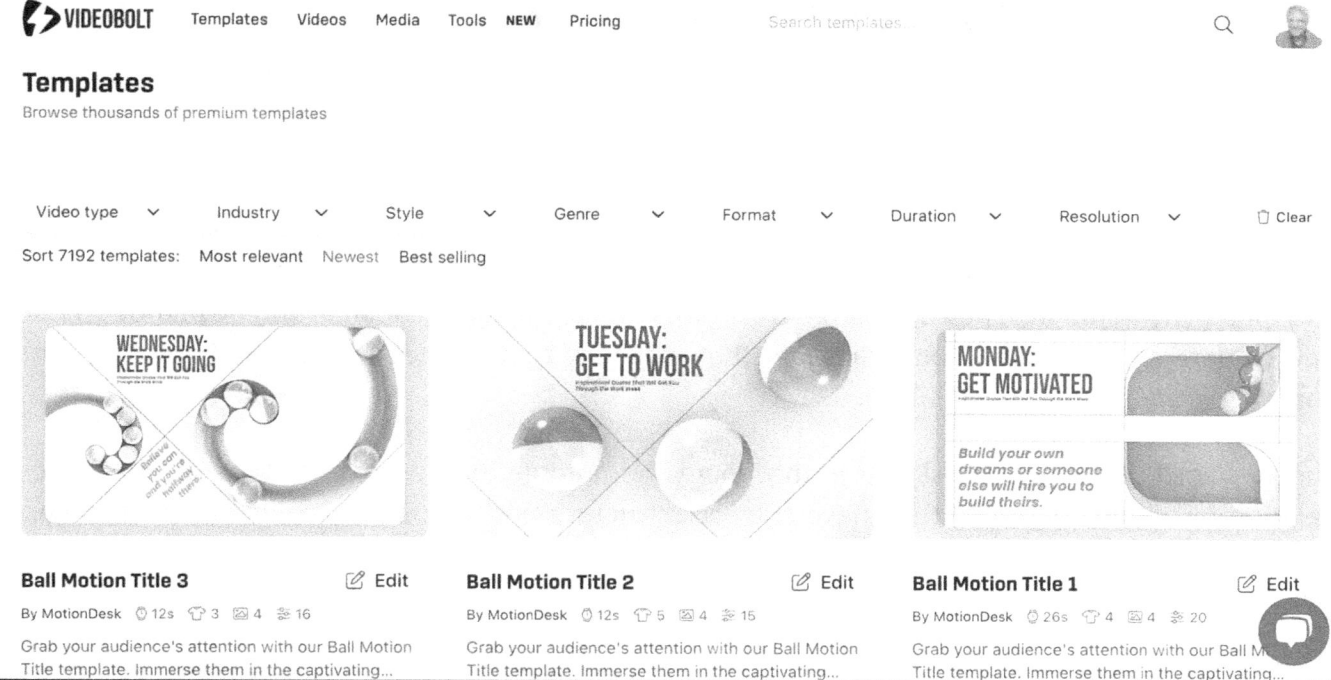

Figure 8.1: Videobolt templates

Your template should include elements such as background images or videos, transitions, effects, filters, colors and more. Thanks to all these options, you can personalize the video to more closely match the mood of the video or your brand.

You can design your own template as well, but it does require knowing exactly what you want to achieve and have the time to sit down and go through all the possibilities that the platform offers.

Many platforms also give you the ability to upload your own images and videos for inclusion in the video. This makes the generated video much more personal as it now revolves around the artist or band instead of a series of abstract images or video clips. Your uploaded videos don't have to be long (anything that's 3 seconds or longer will work) and the frame size usually won't matter as the platform will conform it to the size of the generated video.

A critical step in the process is selecting a frame size, since that dictates the resolution and where the video can be used. This can be anywhere from a low 720x480 to a full 1440P or 2k resolution (see the section on video resolution below).

Also be aware that most video generation platforms will only accept Wav or MP3 audio files. In most cases the common Mac Aiff audio format won't be accepted, so if a Mac DAW is your audio platform of choice, be sure to export a Wav file to be sure that it can be used by the video generation platform.

Theme-Based Video Generators

Theme- or Style-based video generators like Rotor or FlexClip are different from template-based in that there's generally a bit more leeway for your creativity, but that also means a lot more choices, and therefore more work required to generate a video.

Template-based generators are normally more structured as the template or style was constructed for a specific purpose, like music videos, lyric videos, sales videos, pitch videos, customer service videos, and more. The templates may be created by professionals in a particular area, and even though there may be different ones in the same category, they may tend to have the same feel to them unless their parameters are adjusted by the user.

Theme-based generators are similar in that there are multiple themes for each type of video (music video, sales video, etc.), but they have a looser structure and require the user to select multiple parameters and images before the generation process is even started (see Figure 8.2). As a result, there's less similarity between videos since the variety of assets are different.

Figure 8.2: WZRD themes

After logging in, you select from a variety of themes or styles, then add some images or short video clips from either stock images or footages from a library. You're usually able to select at least five of these, but the more you choose, the more interesting your video will look as it won't repeat scenes as much.

As with the template-based generators, the more you can personalize your video with short videos and images of your own, the better. Also, be aware that you'll probably need multiple video sizes for

YouTube, TikTok, Shorts and Reels, and some platforms will charge extra for this, while multiple sizes will be part of the subscription tier or credits sale for others.

Ai Generation For Film Makers

Runway is a special case as it caters to film and video professionals, and in fact, is used by some Hollywood film makers (see Figure 8.3). It has beautifully detailed images and custom video lengths that are longer than what most music videos require.

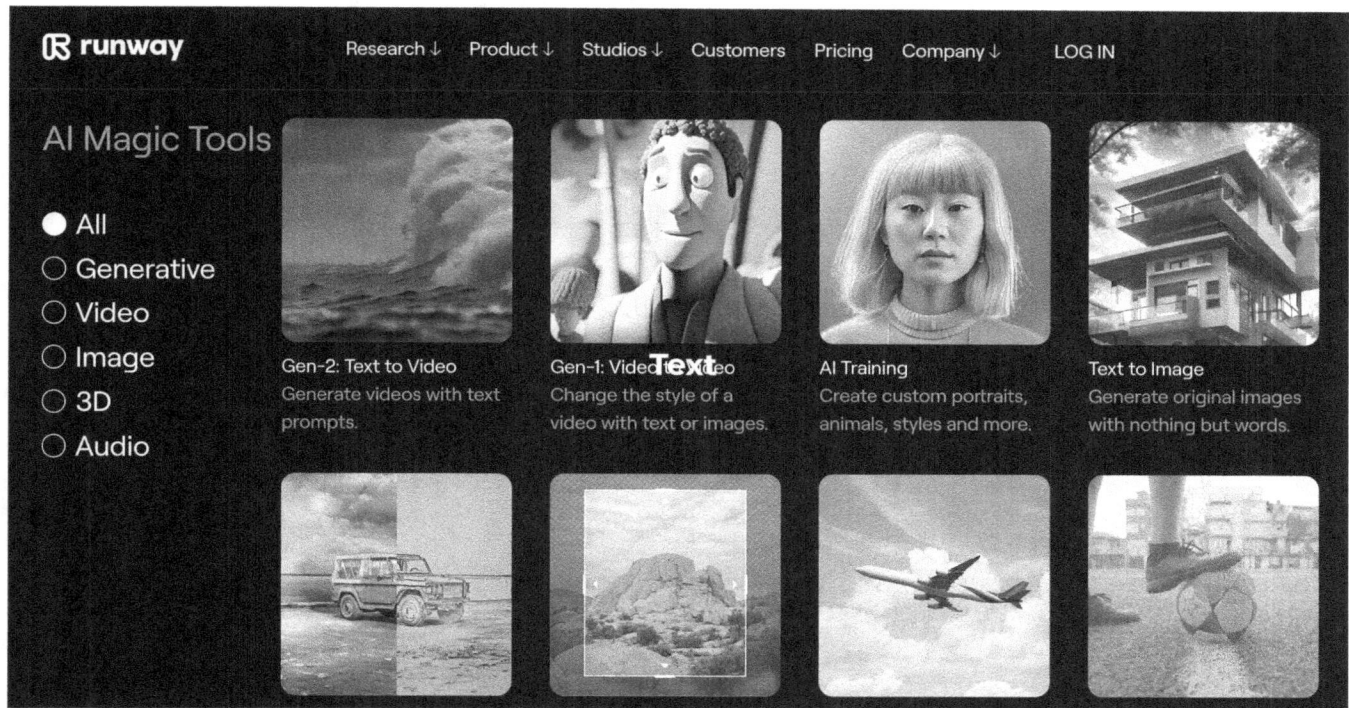

Figure 8.3: Runway tools

Runway is also rich in all the parameters that film makers or video directors might require. It has text-to-video, image-to-image, 3D texture, image variation, super slow motion, blur faces, depth of field, and many more tools that are useful for generating videos and images.

Going a step further, Runway Studios is the entertainment and production division of Runway and serves as a production partner and platform for the next generation of storytellers. There you'll find more advanced tools that provide additional control over video generation with options like duration, scene breaks, and camera angles, which makes it ideal for storyboarding a full music video.

Visualizer Videos

Visualizer or Artwork videos are a rather new but exciting concept. They're a way to make album or song artwork come to life by giving them some motion as a snippet of the song plays in the background (see Figure 8.4). This way you can maintain your branding as you show your viewers a short sample of your work.

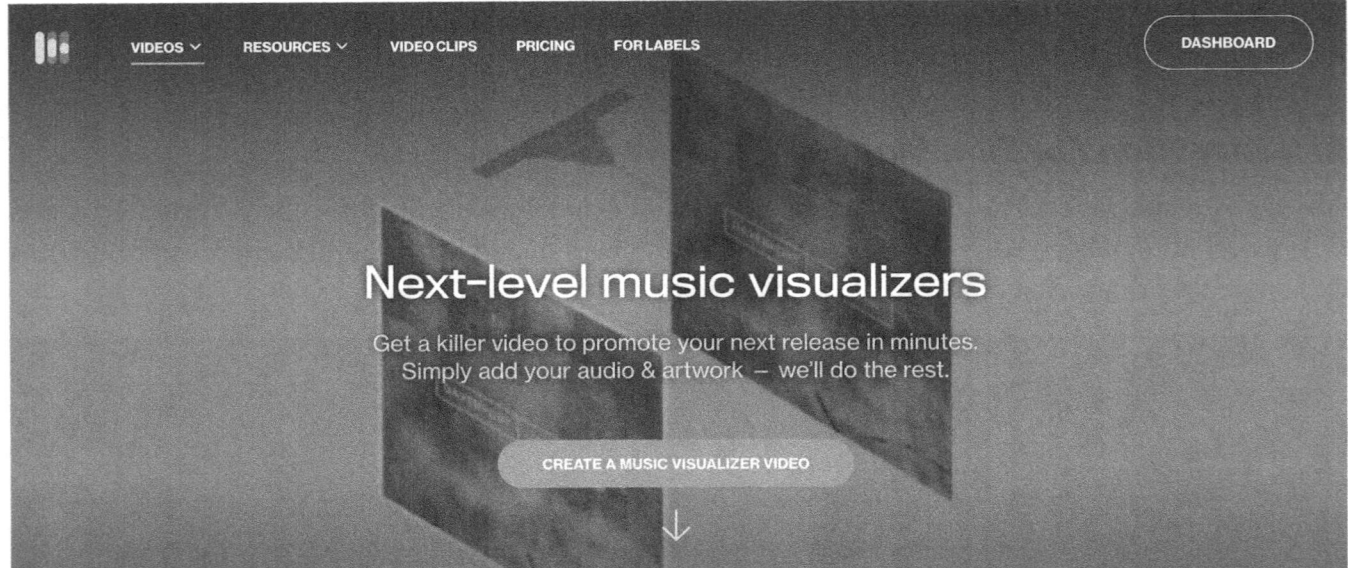

Figure 8.4: Rotar Video visualizer

On platforms that provide this feature like Rotor Video and WZRD, you'll first upload your music file, then your album or song artwork. From there you'll select at least one style (some platforms let you select several so you can see how each one looks), then add any additional text (maybe something like "Go to mysite.com to hear more") as required.

Visualizer videos can be used on your website or in social media posts and are just another way of promoting your release, but in a much tastier way than just a straight image post.

Video Formats Explained

Sometimes the abbreviations for video sizes can be confusing. Even if you know what they mean you can't always be sure of where they're applied. The following chart should help explain the various sizes.

VIDEO SIZE	RESOLUTION	USAGE
SD (Standard Definition)	640x480	Older TVs, DVDs, and social media videos
HD Ready (720p)	1280x720	Most modern TVs and Blu-ray discs
Full HD (1080p)	1920x1080	High-definition TVs, Blu-ray discs, and streaming video services
2K	2048x1080 or 2560x1440	High-resolution TVs, computer monitors, and streaming video services

VIDEO SIZE	RESOLUTION	USAGE
4K	3840x2160	Ultra-high-resolution TVs, computer monitors, and streaming video services
8K	7680x4320	High-end TVs, computer monitors, and streaming video services

The optimal video sizes and resolutions for social media platforms can vary based on the platform's guidelines and the intent of the content (e.g., stories, feed posts, ads).

Here's a breakdown of common video resolutions for some of the major social media platforms:

- **Facebook:**

    Feed Videos: 1280 x 720 (recommended)
    Stories: 1080 x 1920
    Carousel: 1080 x 1080
    360 Videos: 2:1 ratio (e.g., 4096 x 2048)

- **Instagram:**

    Feed Videos: 1080 x 1080 (square), 1080 x 1350 (portrait), 1080 x 566 (landscape)
    Stories & Reels: 1080 x 1920

- **X** (formerly known as Twitter):

    Feed Videos: 1280 x 720 (landscape), 720 x 1280 (portrait), 720 x 720 (square)

- **LinkedIn:**

    Feed Videos: 1920 x 1080 (recommended)

- **Pinterest:**

    Standard Pins: 1000 x 1500 (2:3 aspect ratio)
    Video Pins: 1000 x 1500 (vertical), 1000 x 1000 (square)

- **Snapchat:**

    Snap Ads & Stories: 1080 x 1920

- **TikTok:**

    Videos: 1080 x 1920

- **YouTube**:

    Standard Videos: 1920 x 1080 (recommended for HD), but it supports resolutions up to 8K (7680 x 4320)
    Stories: 1080 x 1920

These are just general guidelines as each platform's specific requirements or recommendations change from time to time. It's always best to refer to the service's official guidelines for the most up-to-date and detailed information.

It is also important to note that video size is not the only factor that affects video quality. Other factors, such as the video codec and bitrate, also play a role.

Video Script Generators

As with music and graphics, the secret to a great text-to-video result is a great prompt. That said, many of the more sophisticated video generators have the ability to accept a script and then generate the video from that.

Writing a script, even a short one, is not something that most musicians know how to do. Scripts have their own language, indicating a bit of the backstory of each character, when and where a character speaks, scene setup, lighting and camera direction, and more. Luckily, there's an Ai for that too.

Ai script generators can save users time and effort by automating the script-writing process. They can also help users come up with fresh and unique ideas.

Here are some Ai script generators:

- ToolBaz - (toolbaz.com/writer/ai-script-generator)
- Vondy - (vondy.com)
- DeepStory Ai - (deepstory.ai)

Of course don't over look the various chatbots like ChatGPT, Bing Ai and Bard as they're all capable of generating a usable script. If you decided to go this route, it's a good idea to ask for a script from more than one, as it's difficult to know in advance which one might respond the best to your initial prompt. Also be sure to regenerate your answer at least once and take pieces from each that work best for your purposes.

Ai-Generated Video Copyright

Like with music and graphics, it's prudent to be aware of any potential copyright issues that might come with an Ai-generated video. As with other platforms, the terms and conditions regarding copyright are all over the place.

In some cases, the platform claims that it owns the copyright and will grant you a license to use the video depending upon the subscription tier or number of credits that you pay. As with music, it's somewhat debatable whether the platform actually owns the copyright in the first place and has the ability to grant you a license, but that's still to be worked out by either the courts or the Copyright Office.

Other platforms like Neural Frames and Kaliber (in the paid tier) make no claims to the copyright and make it clear that the user that inputs the prompts to generate the video owns the copyright outright. As always, read the terms and conditions before generating something that you may not be able to use in the way you want because of copyright or licensing restrictions.

Steps To Create An Ai Music Video

1. **Choose one of the many video generators online.** Although there are many to choose from, not all have a music video option as some are aimed at industrial marketing applications only.

2. **Upload your Wav audio file** - Use the highest resolution Wav audio file (that's what most platforms want) allowed by the service. Just like uploading to any digital distributor, it will be encoded so the sound quality might be degraded, although some services use better encoders than others.

3. **Choose or upload a graphic(s)** - Upload your own graphic(s) to personalize the video, or choose one or more from the stock library offered by the service.

4. **Choose or upload a video clip** - Upload your own short video clip to personalize the video, or choose one or more from the stock library offered by the service.

5. **Pick an editing style or template.** Most services now offer many styles to choose from, so it might take some time to discover the best one for your project.

6. **Regenerate if necessary.** If you're not satisfied with the results, regenerate using a new style.

7. **Choose a video size and resolution.** Most video generation services offer a variety of video sizes and resolutions to choose from that range from full HD to sizes for TikTok, Shorts and other social media. Be sure to download at least one at 1080P HD.

8. **Download or share your music video.** You can either download your music video as an MP4 file or share it directly to social media platforms such as YouTube, Facebook, Instagram, etc.

9. **Be wary of any copyright restrictions.** Along with video size and resolution, most services have restrictions on use and monetization based on how much you pay. Many require the purchase of credits (more credits = higher resolution) while some require a purchase of a premium monthly tier to access the best quality video download.

Ai Music Video Editing Tips

I recently watched a music video that was obviously Ai-generated. It consisted of a morphing object that was constantly moving and changing in color. It was interesting for about 30 seconds, then despite its constant transformation, it became boring, and that's the thing that you have to try to avoid not only in Ai-generated music videos, but all music videos.

Just like a great well-produced song that constantly adds and subtracts mix elements from section to section, so should a music video develop over its course to keep our attention piqued. Here are a few suggestions on how to do that.

- **Don't rely on a single scene or clip.** Like my example above, no matter how much a scene morphs and changes during the course of a song, it will get boring sooner or later. You need multiple scenes or clips to keep the interest high. Many Ai video generators require that you select at least five before it will generate a video, and that's a good number to start with.

- **Don't use images that don't move.** This usually isn't a problem with an Ai-generated clip, but if you were to insert a logo that didn't have movement, it would get boring very fast. Use the Ai to give it some movement.

- **Cut on the action.** The golden rule of editing is to cut on the action to the next clip which already has action. That means that if there was a clip of the frontman waving his arms to the right, that would ideally cut to the next clip that had complementary motion also going to the right.

- **The 4 second rule.** Back in the beginning of film, it was noted that it was rare for a scene to go for more than 9 seconds before a cut to another scene. Today that's been reduced to 4 seconds because of our decreased attention spans. That means that ideally a particular scene should not last for more than 4 seconds, especially with B-roll (see the next point).

- **Use your B-roll in 3's**. B-roll is secondary footage that's not directly part of the main action. For instance, if the main action is a vocalist singing, then the B-roll could be clips from members of the band, the vocalist's hands in action, or the audience. Most ace Hollywood editors like to use B-roll in 3's - in other words, 3 short secondary clips in a row (each no more than 4 seconds long), before returning to the primary footage.

Most Ai video generators have an editor that allows you to tweak the video manually after it's been generated. That's where you'll put the above points into action. The Ai might already do most of this, but if it doesn't, you can always help it a bit by your own hand.

Ai LYRIC VIDEO CREATION

Anyone that's ever created a lyric video in the traditional way knows that it takes some time matching the lyrics on the screen to the lyrics in the song. Ai video creation platforms can make this a lot easier.

First of all, lyric creation templates can be found on many Ai video generation platforms. In most cases the process is similar to music video creation in that you upload your music and lyrics text, then select a template. Among the parameters to set is the type of font, size, color and how it will scroll onto the screen (see Figure 8.5).

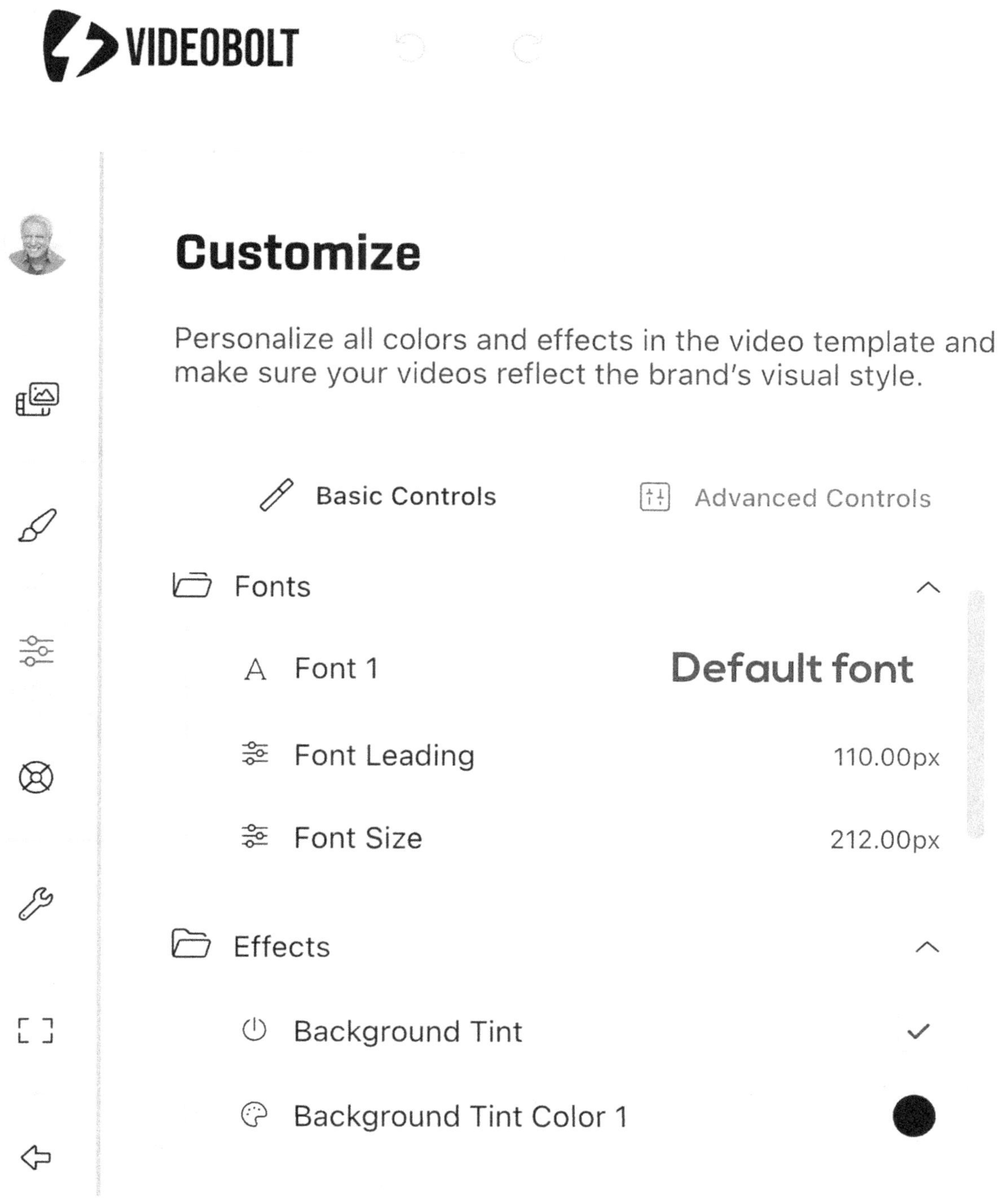

Customize

Personalize all colors and effects in the video template and make sure your videos reflect the brand's visual style.

| ✏️ Basic Controls | ⊟ Advanced Controls |

📁 Fonts ∧

A Font 1   **Default font**

≈ Font Leading   110.00px

≈ Font Size   212.00px

📁 Effects ∧

⏻ Background Tint   ✓

🎨 Background Tint Color 1   ●

Figure 8.5: Lyric customizer in Videobolt

On most platforms you then have to conform the lyrics to the music on a timeline. In other words, you place the lyrics text at the place where the lyrics are being sung in the song. This takes a little time but not as long as you might think, as typically after you place the lyrics on the timeline you're just sliding them around to begin and end at the right spots during the video (see Figure 8.6).

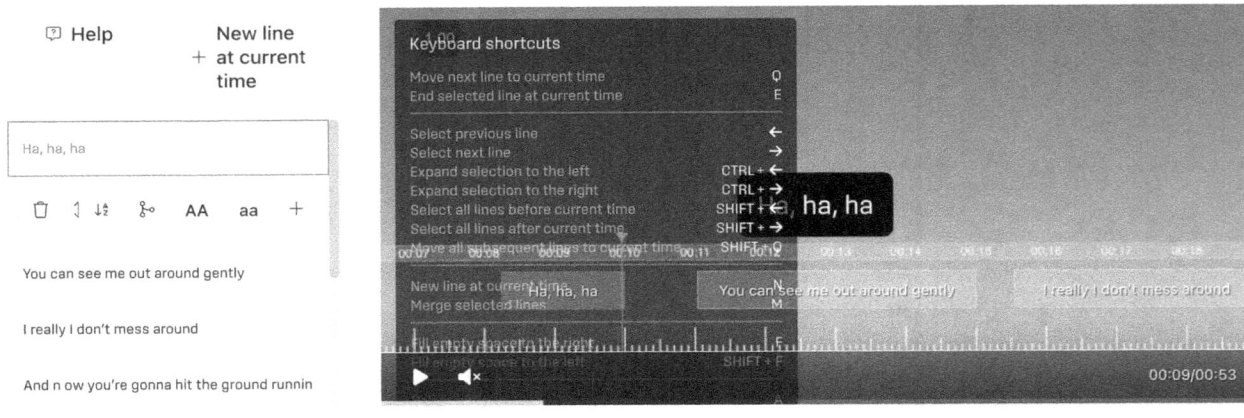

Figure 8.6: Editing the time of lyrics

There are some platforms where the Ai detects the words and automatically places the lyrics on the screen at the right time. You still have to tweak the timing of the lyrics but this does save you a step.

While lyric videos don't have much of a life outside of YouTube and Shorts, they still are a massive draw, and in many cases outpace traditional music videos in total views. Many artists now release both a music video and a lyric video simultaneously, although it used to be more common to release a lyric video first because of its quicker turn around time.

Thanks to Ai generated videos, this is no longer the case as both types of videos take about the same amount of time to create.

Steps To Create An Ai Music Lyric Video

1. **Choose a music video generator with a lyric function.** Although there are many music video generators to choose from, not all have a music video option and not all have lyric capabilities.

2. **Upload your audio file.** Use the highest resolution Wav audio file allowed by the service. Just like uploading to any digital distributor, it will be encoded and the audio will be degraded as a result, although some services use better encoders than others.

3. **Upload your lyric text file.** Be aware of the file type that the service uses. You may have the ability to type in the lyrics manually as well.

4. **Upload a video clip or image.** You many have the ability to upload a personalized image or video clip to build the video around.

5. **Pick an editing style.** Most services now offer many styles to choose from so it might take some time to pick one that you like.

6. **Choose a text style.** You'll have the ability to choose the font, its size, and any stylization to make your lyrics stand out. *Also choose where you want the lyrics to appear on the screen.*

7. **Place the lyrics in time with the music.** In most cases this must be manually done or tweaked.

8. **Chose the video size and resolution**. Most video generation services offer a variety of video sizes and resolutions to choose from that range from full on HD to sizes for TikTok and Shorts. *Be sure to download at least one at 1080P HD.*

9. **Download or share your music video.** You can either download your music video as an MP4 file or share it directly to social media platforms such as YouTube, Facebook, Instagram, etc.

10. **Be wary of any copyright restrictions.** Along with video size and resolution, most services have restrictions on use and monetization based on how much you pay. Many require the purchase of credits (more credits = higher resolution) while some require a purchase of a premium monthly tier.

LIMITATIONS OF Ai VIDEO GENERATORS

Ai text-to-video generators are still in their infancy, so there are limitations to be aware of.

- Many Ai text-to-video generators can't use the most current stock photos/videos because the services use libraries like Shutterstock or Splash, which aren't updated on a daily basis.

- There may be an audio file upload issue. At this time, most video generation platforms require an MP3 or Wav file only. That means an AIFF (if you work on a Mac) won't work, although almost all workstations are capable of exporting Wav files as well.

- There may be a frame-rate issue. Many video generators are able to create smooth 30fps videos, but many can't, so the video has a jerky feel instead. Again, this can be alleviated if you pay for a higher subscription tier or more credits.

- There may be graphics quality issues. Artifacts like pixelation, warped reflections, distorted images and emotionless images might detract from what you're trying to achieve, or maybe enhance it.

- There may be copyright issues. Be sure you know who owns the copyright and understand if you have a license to distribute and monetize the video.

- Be sure to check the video duration. Some platforms are limited to short durations of 3 to 30 seconds, which means that you'll have to generate several then edit them together to cover an entire song.

Here are just a few Ai video generators to look into:

- Flexclip - <u>Flexclip</u>
- Kaliber - <u>Kaliber</u>
- Invideo - <u>Invideo</u>
- Make A Video - <u>Make A Video</u>
- Neural Frames - <u>Neural Frames</u>
- Pika Art - <u>Pika Art</u>
- Runway - <u>Runway</u>
- Rotor Videos - <u>Rotor Videos</u>
- WZRD Ai - <u>WZRD Ai</u>
- Videobolt (lyric videos) - <u>Videobolt (lyric videos)</u>

SUMMING IT UP

- Text-to-video generators use a text prompt or script in order to generate a video.
- Graphic-to-video and video-to-video generators use a graphic or video instead of a prompt to generate a new video.
- Be aware whether the platform claims that it owns the copyright to the video or if it says you own it outright.
- Be aware if you're being granted a license to use the video and if certain platforms or monetization are restricted.
- Music video generation may be a primary feature of a platform, or it may be just one of many video features that are offered.
- Lyric video generation is usually just a feature on a video generation platform and may not be apparent unless you search the menus.
- Be aware of the frame rate, frame size, and resolution of the video you're creating. Can you download multiple sizes for social media?
- Most music video generation platforms require either a Wav or MP3 audio file and will not accept an Aiff sound file.
- A dedicated script generator that generates a script-style prompt may be helpful when using a sophisticated video platform.
- An artwork visualizer video adds motion to album or song artwork so that it's more eye catching.
- Some video generators are not capable of generating videos long enough for a typical song length. If that's the case, several videos must be generated then edited together, or use another platform.

9
Ai MARKETING PLATFORMS

Ai marketing platforms consist of mainly chatbots, which as you remember from the first chapter, are a computer program that mimics human conversation allowing humans to interact with software as if they were communicating with an actual person. Probably the highest profile examples at the moment include OpenAi's ChatGPT, Microsoft's Bing Ai, Google's Bard, and to a lesser degree, Anthrophic's Claude. Of course there are dozens of other chatbots available, although many are actually just a different user interface based on ChatGPT.

Artists and bands generally hate marketing their music and would much rather have a management team or record label take over those tasks, but if you don't happen to have either one, and don't have the budget to hire a group of music marketing consultants and PR people, then a chatbot can at least point you in the right direction.

Among the music business functions that you can ask it to do include:

- Make suggestions about the kind of merch to sell to make the most money
- Write your bio or bio outline
- Write a series of social media posts appropriate for each platform that you're on
- Create a survey for your followers to determine what kind of merch they like the best, or a cover song that they'd like you to do
- Developing a marketing plan for your next music or video release
- Make suggestions for the best tour route
- Plan a record release party
- and much more.

As with music prompts, chatbot prompts require some precision to get the types of results you're looking for, which we'll cover later in the chapter.

THE BIG 3 CHATBOTS

The three chatbots that have received the most press include OpenAi's ChatGPT, Microsoft's Bing Ai, and Google's Bard, and they have leapfrogged each other for the dominant marketshare position during 2023. By far, ChatGPT has had the most visibility and there's reason to believe that it actually started the popular Ai revolution by making the chatbot concept user friendly.

ChatGPT

There are two versions of ChatGPT - the free ChatGPT 3.5 and the $20 per month subscription ChatGPT 4.0. Although ChatGPT 3.5 is very powerful, it does have limitations. For one thing, it's not connected to the internet and its training stops at September 2021.That means that while it will work well for many general purpose queries, anything that requires up-to-date information won't get an answer.

ChatGPT 4.0, on the other hand, is connected to the internet via a number of user accessible plugins, is much faster, and stores all of your queries and answers after the fact so that you can review them at a later time (see Figure 9.1).

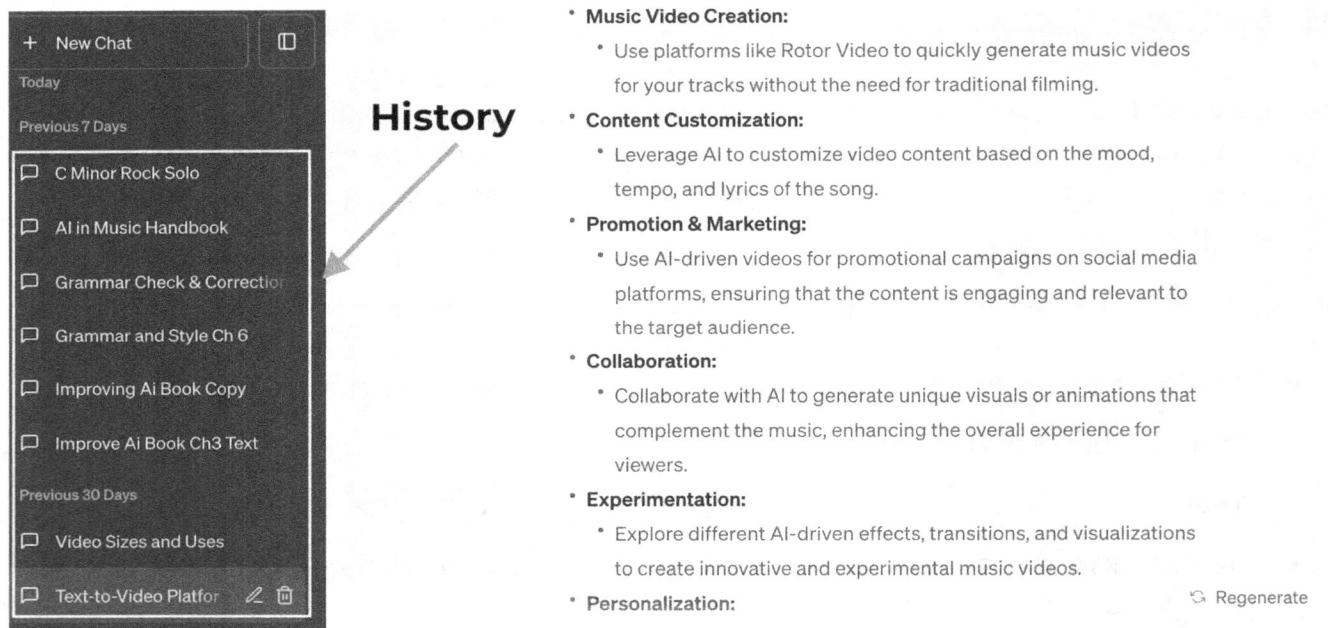

Figure 9.1: ChatGPT user history
© 2023 Bobby Owsinski

ChatGPT 4 is now also linked to OpenAi's DALL-E 3 (since they're both products of the same developer). The advantage is that ChatGPT is able to take a plain language prompt and turn it into an image without having to resort to the more strict framework of a typical DALL-E prompt (see Chapter 7).

Google Bard

Google's Bard provides much the same functions as ChatGPT 4, except that it can be connected to not only Google Search, but the Google Workspace (formerly called G Suite) as well. That means that you can access it from within Google Docs, Google Sheets, Google Forms and all other Workspace components.

Google Search with Bard is interesting in that it takes search to a new level. As you know, a typical Google search turns up pages of links to sites that may provide you an answer to your question. With Bard connected to Google Search, a combination of text and graphic answers appears at the top of the page along with reference links to where the info came from, as well as the typical site links to follow (see Figure 9.2).

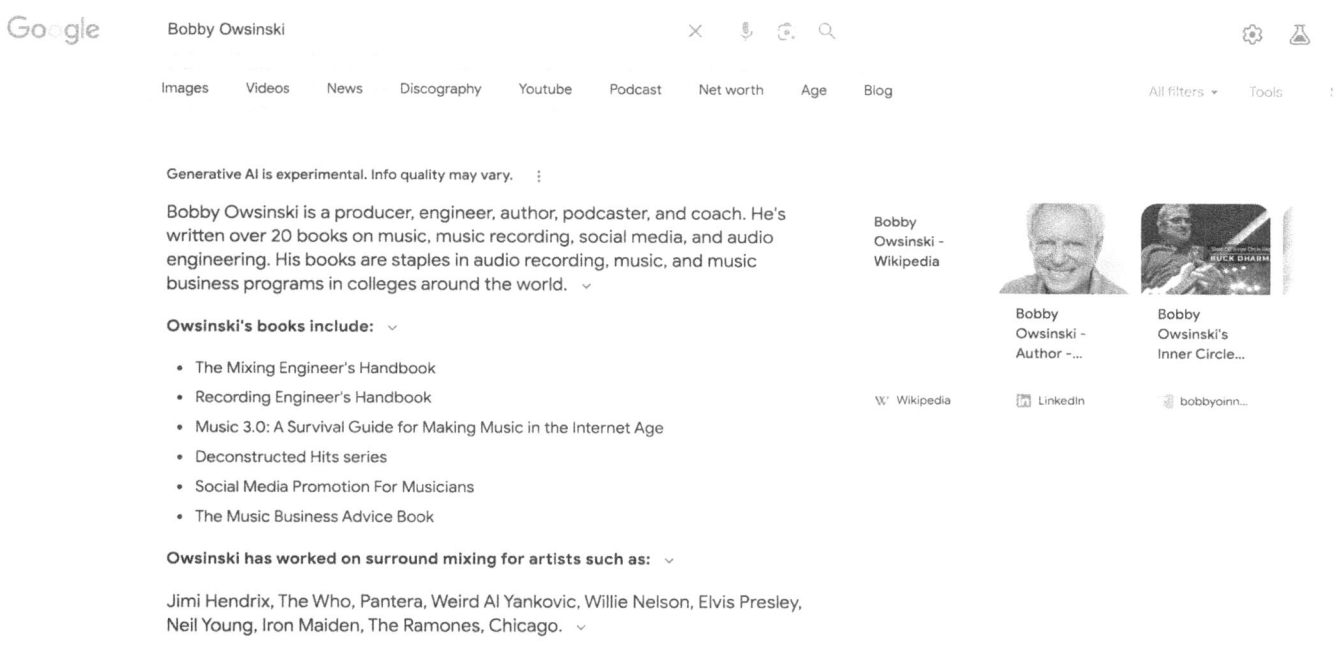

Figure 9.2: Google Ai-augmented search for Bobby Owsinski
© 2023 Bobby Owsinski

Bing Ai

Bing Ai is a bit different in that the only way it can be accessed is through Microsoft's Edge browser. That said, it's a bit more flexible in that it has multiple operating modes - Chat, Compose and Insights.

Chat is the normal chatbot interface but it has three conversation types - Creative, Balanced, and Precise. These determine the style of the language that the prompt result creates, from a normal easy chat to a very formal reply that might be used for a scientific paper or book.

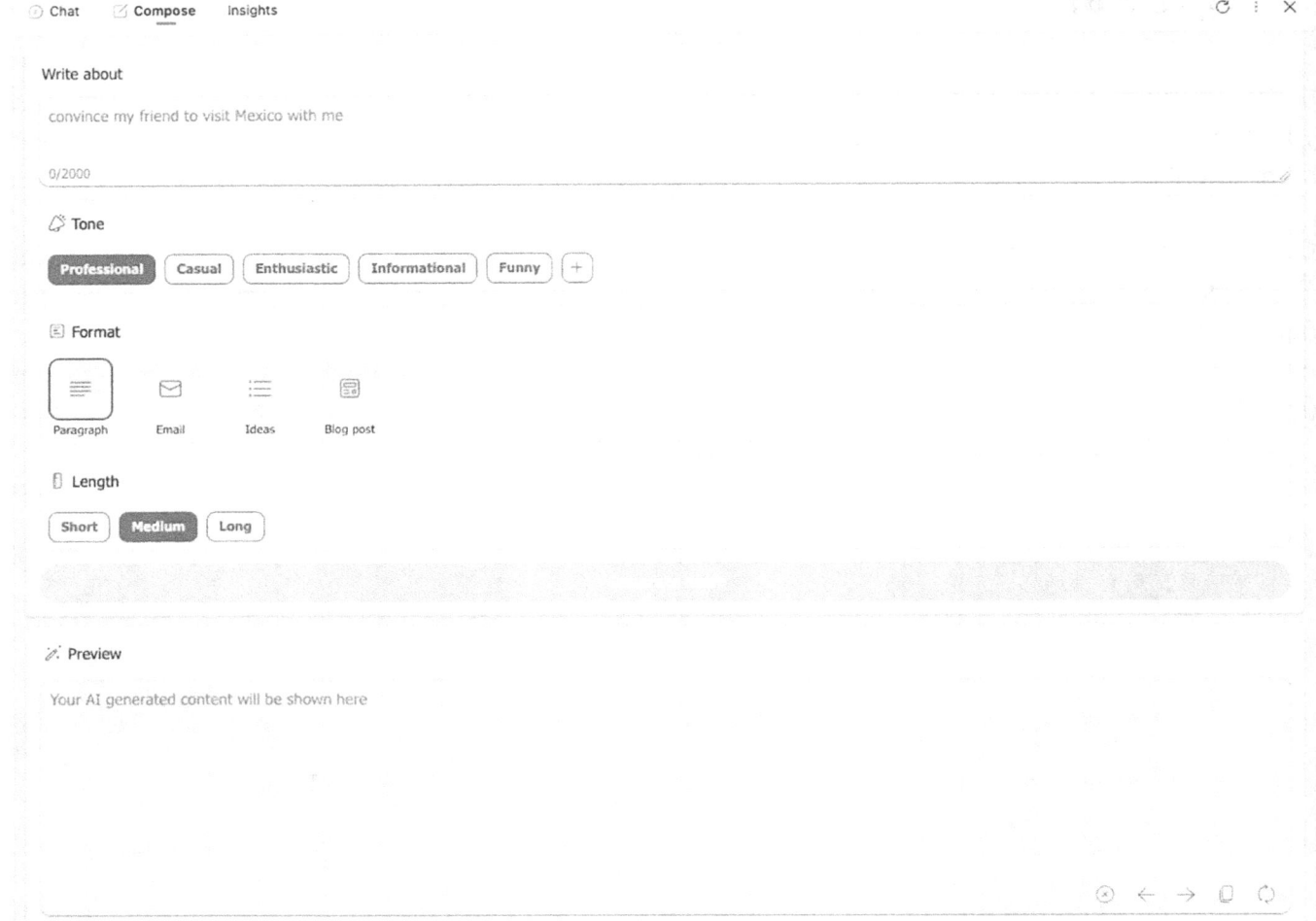

Figure 9.3: Bing Ai compose mode

Compose mode is dedicated to writing a formal text instead of answering a question (see Figure 9.3). That means you could ask it to write a blog post, a chapter of a book, or any other formal document you can think of. Besides that, you can also select the tone, format and length of the document that's being composed so that Bing Ai can zero in on exactly what your needs require.

Bing Ai Insights is a set of features that enhance your search experience on Bing. You can use Bing Ai Insights to get more information about the images, web pages, and entities that you are interested in, as well as to generate suggestions for completing your queries. Here are some examples of how you can use Bing Ai Insights:

- If you want to find out more about the content of an image, you can use Bing Visual Search to find related images, shopping sources, recipes, entity information, and related searches.
- If you want to get suggestions for completing your queries faster and more accurately, you can use Next Phrase Prediction to get full phrase suggestions in real time for long queries.
- If you want to improve your advertising performance and productivity, you can use Performance Insights to get Ai-powered insights into your campaigns and keywords.

- If you want to get insights into the location and proximity of businesses and entities, you can use Local Insights API to get scores based on the distance and accessibility of points of interest.

One of the functions that sets Bing Ai apart from other current chatbots is that it's also able to access DALL-E 3 in order to create images directly in the chatbot. There are two ways to use the Bing Image Creator feature:

- You can use the dedicated Bing Image Creator website (bing.com/create), where you can sign in with your Microsoft account and start creating images.

- You can use the integrated Bing Image Creator tool in the Microsoft Edge browser. You can use it directly within Bing Chat by going to bing.com and clicking the Chat icon. In Bing Chat, start your prompt with "create an image of…" and provide a description of the image you want to create. For example, "create an image of a cat wearing a hat". You can also add more details and context to your prompt, such as location, activity, or art style (see Figure 9.4).

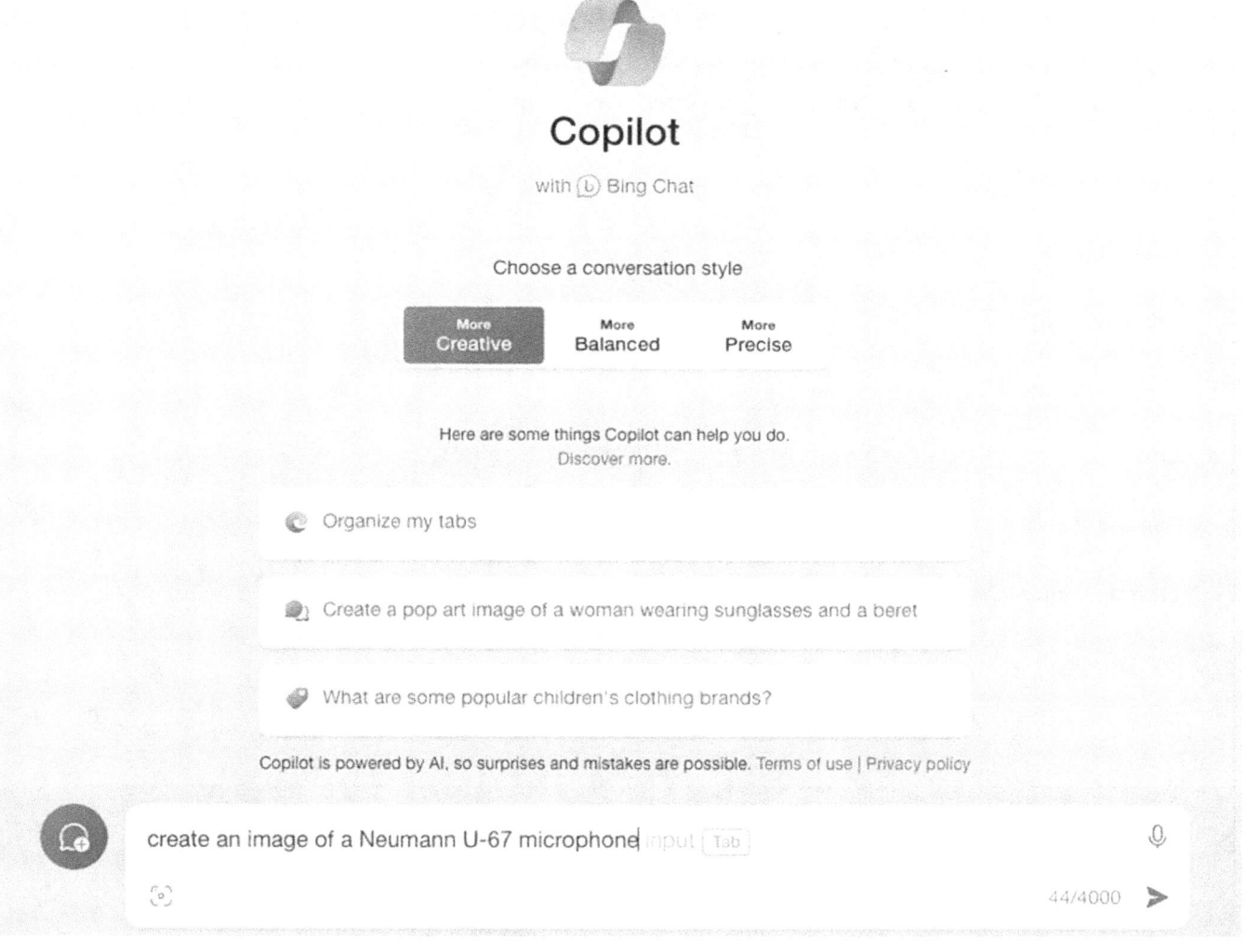

Figure 9.4: Accessing Bing Image Creator from within Bing Ai Chat

As you can see, the three major chatbots are different from each other and they do produce different results. For the longest time, the best results seemed to come from ChatGPT but both Bing Ai and Bard have caught up. While you'll probably settle on one that fits your needs, it's a good idea to try them all and choose the one that you feel most comfortable with.

Other Chatbots

If you just read the headlines about Ai in the press, you're led to believe that the Big 3 are the only chatbots in the technology universe. However, if you've watched this space for any length of time, you know that there are many others available that are excellent and may actually fit you better than one of the Big 3.

For instance, Anthropic's Claude 2 is both formidable and expressive. The latest model is said to have scored 76.5% on the multiple choice section of the Bar exam, up from 73.0% with Claude 1.3. When compared to college students applying to graduate school, Claude 2 scores above the 90th percentile on the GRE reading and writing exams as well. While this isn't something that we'd advocate, it does indicate how successful the platform can be.

Other popular chatbots include Perplexity, Poe, Jasper and Quillbot. Quillbot is especially interesting in that it takes a different approach than other chatbots. For instance, it offers a paraphraser, summarizer, plagiarism detector, citation generator, grammar checker and a translator (see Figure 9.5).

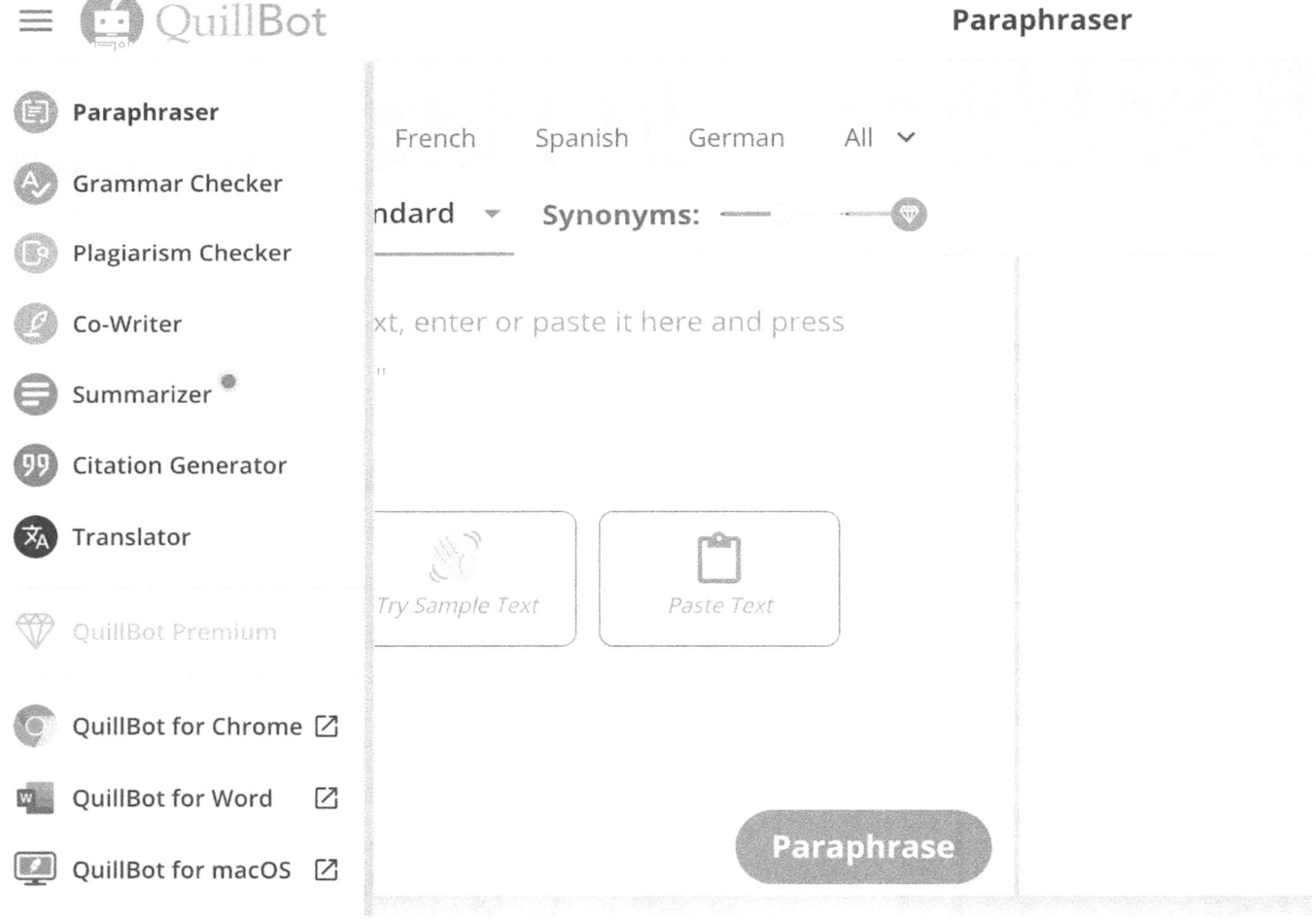

Figure 9.5: Quillbot Paraphraser

Yet another twist on the chatbot is Character Ai, a chatbot that allows you to virtually talk to a large number of virtual entities. These include virtual Elon Musk, Socrates, Napoleon Bonaparte, Albert Einstein, and Nicolai Tesla. On the more practical side, there is also a virtual interviewer, a dating coach, psychologist, English teacher, and a Gamer Boy, all of which can help you think through a particular situation in a more pointed fashion than a general purpose chatbot.

Business Chatbots

All of the major chatbots like ChatGPT, Bing Ai and Claude are available so they can be customized to a particular company's needs. For instance, it can be used for employee or customer training, customer service, and more. This is accomplished via an API (Application Programming Interface - a software interface between two applications so they can talk to one another).

The business has to pay for the use of the API (usually by how much it's used per month), and this is one way that the Ai platform makes money. For instance, companies like Expedia, Slack, Coca-Cola, and even the New York City Public School System use the ChatGPT API.

The Chatbot Copilot

A term you'll be hearing more as time goes on will be "copilot." That means that a chatbot is built-into a platform to help you get the most out of it by automating mundane tasks, analyzing data, and providing support. For instance, a copilot can help users with various scenarios, such as building apps, writing emails, creating presentations, finding insights, and more. Ai copilots can also learn from user feedback and preferences to provide personalized and relevant assistance.

One example of an Ai copilot is Microsoft Copilot, which works alongside popular Microsoft 365 Apps such as Word, Excel, PowerPoint, Outlook, Teams, and more. It also integrates with other CRM systems like Salesforce. Another is Bard for Google Workspace, which offers real-time suggestions, automates repetitive tasks, and even drafts emails or documents. Both of these are add-ons to the services that you have to pay for and so far the reviews of both are mixed. That said, it's still the early days for both and they'll no doubt get better over time.

Another is the GitHub Copilot, which is trained on billions of lines of computer code so that it can provide coding suggestions from simple natural language prompts. And if you've ever used Grammarly to help you with grammar and punctuation, you're using a writing copilot.

Just about every software developer is now looking at a way to integrate Ai into the workflows of its apps. Soon it will just be a normal part of an app without the need to refer to it as a "copilot" or Ai helper.

Chatbot Limitations

While the various chatbots seem like the perfect assistants, they do have their limitations.

They're Not As Smart As You Think

The biggest one is that they're not as smart as many make them out to be. As you've seen with Claude 2, it was only able to achieve a 76% correct score on the U.S. Bar exam. While that's quite laudable, it's not perfect and falls in line with the general intelligence level of today's Ai chatbot.

As said way back in Chapter 1, if you were going to write a term paper on streaming royalties, for instance, you'd no doubt get an F if you turned in a blank page. If you asked any chatbot to write the paper for you, it would probably get a C or maybe even a B- if the prompt was really tweaked well. However, if you tweaked what you received from the chatbot and added your flavor and expertise, then it might rise to the level of an A.

The moral of the story is that the chatbot needs our help both on the input (the prompt) and the output (finishing the product) in order for the result to be its best.

Hallucinations

A hallucination is when an Ai makes something up and presents it as a fact. Chatbots are so good at writing that we believe everything they tell us because it's presented so well, but what it's telling us may not be true at all. This can occur due to a variety of factors, such as programming errors, hardware malfunctions, or because of biased or skewed training data.

High profile examples of when this has happened include an attorney in New York that relied on ChatGPT to write a legal brief for a case in Federal District Court that was filled with judicial opinions and legal citations. When the judge actually researched the cases cited he found that they were pure fiction and didn't exist.

There was also the case of a very high profile NYU professor that had a ChatGPT-generated bio cite a sexual misconduct case against him. There were no such cases ever filed and the professor was not even in the country at the time of the alleged incident.

Hallucinations don't happen very often but they do happen, which is why you must double check everything that a chatbot generates. Yes, that's a pain and calls for more work, but it's the only way to be sure of the veracity of the data.

- Character Ai - Character.ai
- ChatGPT - Chat.openai.com
- Claude 2 - Anthropic.com/index/claude-2

- Google Bard - Bard.google.com
- Jasper - Jasper.ai
- Microsoft Bing Ai - Microsoft.com/en-us/bing
- Perplexity - Perplexity.ai
- Poe - Poe.com
- Quillbot - Quillbot.com

PROMPT ENGINEERING

Prompts are the lifeblood of a chatbot. While a simple prompt may get a helpful result, designing a thorough prompt will provide a more in-depth result that may be more relevant to your initial query.

Creating a successful prompt has an official name and it's called "prompt engineering." Let's take a closer look at what that means.

Types Of Ai Prompts

There are three basic kinds of prompts and a so-called "magic prompt" that sometimes creates an unexpected but useful result.

- **Simple prompt** - This is when you ask the chatbot to do a simple task ("What's a new chord sequence I can try?"). This is beginner mode and you will most likely receive a limited response.
- **Multi-prompt** - This is when you ask it to provide multiple responses ("Where do fans of AC/DC hang out and what are some other bands that they like").
- **Megaprompt** - This is a long and complex prompt but creates the most detailed responses (see below for more).
- **Magic Prompt** - As part of a megaprompt, it's sometimes useful to ask the chatbot what's going on inside your fan's (or music executive or supervisor's) head. NOTE: This only works if you thoroughly describe who your fan is in the first place.

Multi-prompt Example

The following multi-prompt might be better termed a compound simple prompt because it's really just an extended simple prompt like above.

> *"Write some copy that I can use in my social media (or email, video, or any other kind of promotional material) messages to convey the transformation that listening to my music provides.*
>
> *My fan is [insert fan description].*

My music is [insert genre and sub-genre] that [how does it make people feel].

Include 10 headlines, 10 sub-headlines, and 10 bullet points that describe the transformation."

Supercharging A Prompt

There are many techniques that can be used to get better results from a chatbot and it all revolves around supercharging a prompt by adding a few phrases and a different approach. At its most basic, here's what we'd like to do when creating a prompt:

- Create a task
- Outline the steps
- State the goal

Because the chatbot uses a large language model that understands the way you speak, you can construct this prompt in plain language like:

> *"Make a list of venues in Texas that book singer/songwriters. Outline the venues with the highest profiles in each area, then list the manager or promoter for each venue. The goal is to get more gigs in this part of the country."*

While using these three steps gets the job done, you can take your prompt to another level by adding some additional steps.

Visualize A Persona

The first one is to simulate or visualize a persona like:

- "You are an expert music PR person,"
- "Imagine you are a film composer for hit films,"
- "Act like an interviewer."

Believe it or not, by doing this you will get better more informed answers to your queries as the chatbot takes a different approach to the answer.

The other way to approach this step is to have the chatbot assume it's you. In this case you must identify yourself and explain what you do, like:

> *"You are an Americana singer/songwriter touring the club circuit in the Southern portion of the United States."*

Notice that I provided some context here with "touring the club circuit in the Southern portion of the United States." You could have just stopped at "Americana singer/songwriter" but now the chatbot understands more about you and what you're doing so you can proceed to fill in the blanks in providing more information so that it can give you an informed answer to your query.

If you're using a chatbot that's linked to the internet like ChatGPT 4 or Bard, and if you have a great bio on your website or even a Wikipedia entry, you could also approach it this way:

> *"Imagine you are Tom Smith, an Americana singer/songwriter touring the club circuit in the Southern portion of the United States. To better understand Tom's background, study the bio that can be found here https://xxx.xxx"*

Describe The Format You'd Like

If you just stop at the above point in the prompt design, you'll probably get a very helpful answer, but it might ramble on enough that it could take you a while to sort out the useful information later. That's why it's best to give it some parameters about the format you'd like to see the answer in. These could be any of the following:

- "Create 3 paragraphs"
- "Create 10 bullet points"
- "Make a list"
- "In 500 words or more (or less)"
- "Format the output with double spaces between bullets"
- "Provide a summary in the bullet-point format with double spaces between sections"
- "Be sure to include any quotes (along with attributions), facts (with cited sources), statistics (with attribution)"
- or any other format that suits your needs.

The idea here is to have the answer created in a format that you find easy to read and use so you don't have to sort through a few paragraphs of text to dig out the pertinent results yourself.

There are other guidelines that are very helpful that you can add as well, like:

- "Provide clear and tangible steps laid out in bullet points.
- "Explain it to me as if I'm still in high school."
- "Explain it to me as if I'm 5 years old."

Finally, it's sometimes helpful to ask if the chatbot understands what you're asking. A simple question like:

"Do you understand?"

Usually it will come back with something like:

"Yes, I understand the task"

Occasionally it will tell you if it's confused by the prompt. The reason that could happen is because you might have given it conflicting instructions like asking it to find gigs in Texas then asking about venues in Miami in the same prompt.

Regenerate And Tweak

When you ask the chatbot to generate a response it might be brilliant the first time, but even if you like the result, it's a good idea to ask it to regenerate at least a second response and even a third one. You might get new information added to the additional regeneration or it might be laid out in a way that's more understandable. Don't worry, your original response will not be lost and you can easily flip back as necessary.

Some chatbots like Bing Ai automatically generate three responses so a second generation might not be needed. That said, be careful when you get beyond three since the responses at that point will be just different instead of new and all that information can then be difficult to cull.

If you still don't have the response you need you're much better off tweaking your original query to be more precise about what you're looking for. For instance, if your original query was "Make me a list of venues for singer/songwriters in Texas," and you discover that you really only want Austin, Dallas and Houston, then tweak the query to state "Make me a list of venues for singer/songwriters in Austin, Dallas and Houston."

The Megaprompt In 8 Steps

If we take all of the prompt points above and put them into a step-by-step list, this is what we have:

1. **Ask the chatbot to visualize a persona** ("Imagine you are an expert music PR person," or "Imagine you are an expert film music composer,")
2. **Identify who you are and what you do.** ("I am your client and I am a 35 year old male electronic music artist specializing in the Trap style." Continue with more about you.)
3. **Create a specific task**. What are you trying to achieve? ("Write a 6 week marketing plan for the release of my next album which will drop on September 23rd.")

4. **Outline the steps needed.** Point it to places to research as well as tools and resources. ("For more information about me and my music, go to this website.")

5. **State the goal.** ("The goal is to expand my fanbase and expose my music to more people.")

6. **Describe the format you would like.** ("Provide clear and tangible steps laid out in bullet points." "Explain it to me as if I'm still in high school.")

7. **Ask it if it understands.** ("Do you understand?")

8. **Regenerate the result at least once.** You'll most likely find that there are pieces you can use from each generation.

A Megaprompt Example

Here's a great example of a megaprompt. It's geared toward an artist finding out more about his or her fans, but you could replace "fan" with "music exec," "music supervisor," "music publisher," or any other avatar you need to know about.

> *"I'm going to ask a series of questions about my typical fan. Before you start, imagine you are a confident, experienced, and skilled online marketer who understands that the best way to make may fan care about my music is to deeply understand and serve them. Your answers should go beyond the superficial, and really look deeply into the inner conversations that my fans have with themselves.*
>
> *The goal is for me to be able to use these answers to create music and marketing that speaks to what my fan truly cares about on a deep level. For each of these questions please answer with at least five bullet points.*
>
> *My fan is [describe] who [struggles with this problem, cares about this cause or problem, or wants this solution]. I'm creating music that I think that they'll relate to, which will result in them listening to my music and becoming my fan if they're not already. For all further questions, remember those factors. Do you understand the request?*
>
> *First, what are my fan's goals and values? What are their hopes and dreams? Who or what do they aspire to be? Be as specific, tangible, and concrete as possible.*
>
> *Next, what are my fan's greatest opportunities? Are there opportunities they don't even know about yet? Be as specific, tangible, and concrete as possible.*
>
> *What are my fan's problems and challenges? What makes them angry or feel disrespected? In other words, what keeps them up at night? Be as specific, tangible, and concrete as possible.*
>
> *Where does my fan hang out online? What blogs or podcasts or communities do they pay attention to? What social platforms? What gurus, thought leaders, influencers, and artists do they listen to? Be as specific, tangible, and concrete as possible.*

What are my fan's objections? Why might they not listen to my music? Be as specific, tangible, and concrete as possible.

What else is going on in their life that might interfere with them listening to my music? Be as specific, tangible, and concrete as possible.

Who is not my fan? Be as specific, tangible, and concrete as possible."

This megaprompt may take some time to think it through, but the results will be worth the time and effort.

SUMMING IT UP

- The Big 3 Chatbots are ChatGPT, Google Bard, and Microsoft Bing Ai, but there are many other chatbots worth checking out
- Chatbots can be used for any number of music business applications like writing bios and business plans, and planning release schedules and parties
- Ai chatbot copilots are either an add-on to a business suite like Google Workspace or Microsoft 360, or built into many software apps
- Chatbots are subject to limitations like hallucinations and not being as smart as believed
- A chatbot's response is only as good as it's prompt
- Prompt engineering is the process of creating an explicit prompt to get better results from a chatbot
- The more precise the prompt, the better the response
- Use Megaprompts where possible
- Ask the chatbot to imagine that it's you or an expert in a particular field in your prompt
- Ask the chatbot to explain as if you're in high school in your prompt
- Ask the chatbot for clear and tangible steps in your prompt
- Ask the chatbot if it understands in your prompt
- Regenerate the answer at least once
- If you regenerate the response, your initial response will still be saved

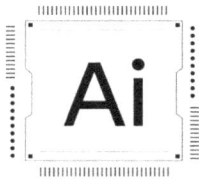

10
THE FUTURE OF Ai MUSIC

Ai music generation and promotion is evolving quickly but as you've seen from this book, it still needs a lot of help from a human to get to a level that a professional can use. It's rough around the edges, but even as those edges get buffed out, Ai is still just a tool like your guitar or DAW.

Synthesizers and MIDI didn't replace keyboard players, drum machines didn't replace drummers, and DAWs didn't replace recording engineers. They made music creation easier, and in the hands of someone skilled, allowed them to make their music even greater than it was before those tools were available.

As you've also seen, much of what's in this book is practical knowledge in Ai that won't be obsolete by the time you read it. Techniques are still techniques, although they may evolve as the technology does. Knowing which DAW inserts to use or which video editing tips will make your video better won't go away any time soon.

That said, we're still not done.

I'm going to give you some recommendations on some Ai toolsets to get you going, and point you in the right direction when confronted with Ai clickbait that is so prevalent in the news.

BUILDING YOUR Ai TOOLSET

There are a lot of Ai tools available and I've given you a list of them in each chapter that are worth checking out. What you'll find here are general recommendations of the type of tools that you'll need for end-to-end Ai music creation and promotion. In some cases I'll provide some specific recommendations, but most of the time there are enough choices that you can find a tool in a particular category that you're comfortable with.

Ai Composition

Many musicians delve into Ai composition because they're curious, others because they want or need new inspiration. You've most likely been making music for a long time without it so this is something that you don't need, but it's always great to have another tool or two to help you when the situation calls for it. If that's you, here are the tools that you'll need in this area:

Ai Composition Tool

It's worth having a subscription to at least one of these Ai composition tools (I particularly like AIVA) if for no other reason than you can get some interesting ideas when you're stuck. Remember that if you generate something that you like, your best bet may be to download the MIDI file and load that into your DAW so you can further develop the idea and tweak the sounds. Also, consider using ChatGPT or a different chatbot as another idea generator.

Ai Lyric Generation Tool

Just like the composition tool, an Ai lyric generation tool can give you some ideas for a word or phrase when you're coming up dry. Sometimes asking it to refine your idea can take you in a new and wonderful direction that you never expected.

Ai Production Tool

Creating new sounds may or may not be your thing, but sometimes it pays to alter a sound just to make it fit in the mix better. Also, the world of virtual vocalists is just beginning where you can tailor the vocal exactly to your musical idea, and a song analyzer can tell you a song's key, scale, BPM and sub-genres.

Ai Audio

The world of ai audio tools is just beginning, and while there aren't many developers in the game as of yet, you'll definitely see more as Ai development tools become more available. In the meantime, an appropriate Ai audio plugin is always worth considering. While a bundle from Sonible, iZotope or Focusrite might be the easiest solution, it might not be the best for your application.

Ai Equalizer Plugin

While we've seen some interesting traditional equalizers powered by Ai, I believe that the future lies more with unmasking plugins like Wavespace Trackspacer or Focusrite Reveal. An automatic EQ that continuously changes with the music like Accentize Spectral Balance is also worth considering.

Ai Compressor Plugin

Personally, if I'm going to use an Ai compressor, then I want something like Sonible's pure:compressor to do all the work for me so I don't have to do much tweaking. That said, others just want to get in the ballpark and then tweak it themselves so Focusrite FAST Compressor or iZotope's Neutron will fit the bill.

Ai Limiter Plugin

A limiter is all about raising the gain of a mix or mix element without it going beyond a pre-set level. There aren't many Ai limiter plugins to choose from just yet, but all of them will do the job. Pick the one that you're most comfortable with.

Ai Gate Plugin

Gates are being used less and less these days thanks to clip gain and automation, so unless your situation very specifically calls for a gate, then you can probably skip this category and never look back.

Ai Reverb Plugin

Setting up a reverb is elusive to many new to mixing, which is why an Ai reverb plugin like iZotope Neoverb can be so useful. That said, the setup process isn't that difficult and as of now you can get better results manually. You can learn this from either the Effects chapter in my Mixing Engineer's Handbook, or from my Music Mixing Primer online course.

Ai Noise Reduction Plugin

Noise reduction is a different case in that one plugin probably won't work well for all the different noisy scenarios that you might run into. The good news is that it's generally not that expensive so having a couple of different choices won't break the bank. Waves Clarity VX is a good low-cost choice, and Accentize dxRevive is amazing on dialog. If string noise is always bugging you, then you might want to invest in iZotope RX just for its Guitar De-Noise module.

Ai Mastering

Mastering is a mysterious process to many but Ai has finally put excellent results within the reach of all musicians. Your only decision is whether you'd like to do it yourself with a plugin like iZotope Ozone or Neutron, or online via a platform like LANDR or eMastered. Be sure to use a reference track and trust what the Ai delivers.

Ai Promotion

When it comes to music promotion, we have more tools available, thanks to their general use in other industries besides music. In this case it might be useful to try a number of different platforms before you decide on the ones you like for each category, but chances are you won't need more than one or two.

Promotion Strategy

Any chatbot that you find comfortable will most likely do this job. However, it's always good to have a second one available just like you would bounce an idea off another person. You'll get a different outlook to the same question. Using a general chatbot like ChatGPT or Bard, then jumping to something distinctly different like Quillbot can be particularly useful.

Ai Video

Although it's nice to have Ai video generation for both music videos and lyric videos in the same platform like Videobolt or Rotor, you may get the best results from having them separate. Be aware that some platforms claim they own the copyright (at least on some tiers), while others like Neural Frames are clear that you own the copyright to any generated work.

Ai Graphics

While you may decide that you can get everything you need from one of the major image platforms like Stable Diffusion or DALL-E, it's nice to have a platform where you can access both from the same interface like NightCafe. These days a photo-oriented platform like Fotor or Photoroom is an essential tool in your toolbox, and an art platform like Illustroke can be invaluable when the need for a vector image arises.

While it's true that you can get by without all these tools in the music world today, having them in your back pocket is certainly useful when the situation calls for it. That's happening more and more every day, as musicians have so much that's demanded of them. These Ai tools are meant to make your music life easier, and if you follow what's outlined in the book, it will be.

YOUR AI MUSIC FUTURE

I'd like to make a few predictions about Ai music and promotion. You might have heard some of them before earlier in this book, but let me be more forthright here.

Ai music generation will become more sophisticated. Yes, this is a given and pretty much a no brainer. Understand what it means though - your music making will get more sophisticated as well, and it will be easier to attain that level of sophistication than ever before. Remember that your competition will also be using these tools.

There will be Ai haves and have-nots. It won't be long before music will be divided into the ones that use Ai and the ones that don't (that time is probably here already). It's inevitable that the technology is here to stay. You've already made the big step to learning as much as you can about Ai and having it work for you. You're way ahead of the ones that are afraid that the robots are taking over their music and their world.

It will be a while (and maybe never) before it can replace a real musician. As you've seen, Ai is a great tool for both creating and promoting your music. It's not good at nuance however, and that's what separates good from great musicians. It turns out nuance separates machines from humans as well. Keep being you, because in this world of Ai, that's your most important quality.

If your music is trying to emulate a machine, the machine will win. Ai is very good at generating electronic-style music. That's not to say that a top producer can't beat it with innovation, but those not as skilled will have a hard time beating the bot in certain genres.

It won't replace a skilled or brilliant human. Ai is going to raise the bar for everyone. If you're mediocre at what you do then you better watch out because it's coming for you. But if you're skilled in your art then it will become your most favorite tool.

Ai audio resolution is still a problem. Obviously this will get worked out as hardware processors and GPU's become more powerful, but it might take longer than you think. As an example of how long some things take, Apple has been collecting high-resolution songs since 2012 and they're still not the norm (or even an option in some cases) in online streaming all these years later. The problem is that professional audio for music, film, games and television uses a higher resolution than the current Ai audio premium standard of 44.1kHz/16bit. That places a serious limitation on what's currently possible from most Ai music platforms.

Anything on a pro level will cost real money. Most tools have a free tier (or are free if they're training on your material), but if you want the pro features and highest resolution results, then it will cost you some money. The good news is almost everything that has an Ai involved is relatively inexpensive compared to the hardware days or even the early years of digital.

Stay On The Path

It's easy to get fooled when reading the news today, especially when it comes to artificial intelligence. Although the following tips are specifically about Ai, they can also apply to just about any other type of news as well.

There are so many who think they know all about a subject because they just read a headline. If they see the same headline over and over they accept it as the truth even though it may just be an altered copy of the same original speculation. To make sure that you don't get caught in that trap, consider the following:

- **Is this just a clickbait headline?** Many times the headline has very little to do with the actual article and is only trying to get you to click. To many online media companies, clicks are the only thing that matters and it's easy to fall victim to that. Learn to recognize this quickly so you don't waste your time reading something that has little substance that's connected to the headline.

- **Is this something that really happened or might happen?** There's a big difference between something that "might" happen and something that really happened or is happening now. Something that might happen is just speculation and the resulting headline may be just a scare tactic to get you to click. Remember, because it "might" happen doesn't mean that it will!

- **Is this a reliable source of Ai information?** There are many sites like Wired and TechCrunch that are skilled in reporting technology. General news sites sometimes miss the most important point(s) of the story or report, which results in incomplete or misleading information.

- **Is the writer relying on another article?** Sometimes writers (myself included) write a post or article based on an article that they've read. That's okay if they put their own unique spin on it and report the facts straight. Many times things get lost in the translation though, and you have an article that misses the point and just confuses readers or sends them in the wrong direction.

I hope you'll consider these points anytime you read the news from now on.

FINALLY...

The whole point of this book is to help you make better music, feel better about what you've done, and get it out to the world more efficiently.

Everything in it may not apply to you. That's okay. Take what's useful and leave the rest. What's important is that you view Ai as a helpful partner and tool and not be afraid or apprehensive that it will usurp your creativity or make you less of a musician.

Because you've read this book you're way ahead of the game. You now have a foundation to go forward and do things that you weren't capable of before.

I congratulate you for taking the leap with me, and I hope to hear your success story soon.

GLOSSARY

Algorithm - A step-by-step set of instructions or rules that a computer program follows to solve a specific problem or perform a task. In Ai, algorithms are essential for tasks like data analysis, learning, and decision-making.

Apple Digital Masters - A protocol set by Apple Music to ensure that the highest quality masters are created for their Apple Music Platform. The preferred resolution is 96kHz/24 bit, and the master file must be submitted by an Apple-certified mastering engineer.

Artificial Intelligence (Ai) - A broad field of computer science focused on creating machines and systems that can perform tasks typically requiring human intelligence, such as problem-solving, learning, reasoning, and perception.

avatar - A representation of your ideal fan or customer—the type of person you want to purchase your products or services.

Big Data - Extremely large and complex datasets that are challenging to process and analyze using traditional methods. Ai and machine learning techniques are often used to derive value from big data.

B-roll - Secondary video footage that's not directly part of the main action

BPM - Beats Per Minute, or the the tempo of the song.

buss - A signal pathway.

ChatBot: A computer program that mimics human conversation, either in written or spoken form, allowing humans to interact with software or digital devices as if they were communicating with an actual person.

ChatGPT - Generative Pre-trained Transformer, which means its an Ai that has been trained before you use it, and is able to transform data from one form to another, like changing languages or converting text into computer code.

cloud - "The cloud" refers to servers that are accessed over the Internet, and the software and databases that run on those servers. Cloud servers are located in data centers all over the world. By using cloud computing, users and companies do not have to manage physical servers themselves or run software applications on their own machines.

codec - Derived from CODer and dECoder, or coder-decoder. A device or software system that can compress the data for an audio or video signal into smaller packets for more efficient transmission, and then convert an incoming digital signal back into audio or video.

copilot - An Ai CoPilot is an artificial intelligence-powered assistant designed to help users with various tasks, often providing guidance, support, and automation in different contexts. Ai CoPilots can be found in applications such as navigation systems, virtual assistants, and software development environments.

copyright - A legal protection given to creators of original works, including music. It allows the creator to control how their work is used and prevents others from using it without permission.

CRM - Customer Relationship Management. Software that supports sales management, delivers insights, integrates with social media and facilitates team communication.

dataset - A dataset is a collection of data related to a particular topic, theme, or industry. Datasets can include different types of information, such as numbers, text, images, videos, and audio.

DAW - Digital Audio Workstation. A software application used to record, edit, and produce audio.

Deep Learning - A subfield of machine learning that uses artificial neural networks with multiple layers (deep neural networks) to model and solve complex problems, often achieving state-of-the-art results in tasks like image and speech recognition.

frequency masking - Frequency masking is a phenomenon that occurs when two or more sounds occupy the same frequency range. The overlapping sound energy causes them to compete for space in the mix. This can result in a muddy or unclear sound that lacks definition and separation.

GAW - Generative Audio Workstation. An Ai-driven software application used to record, edit, and produce audio.

Generative Ai - A type of Ai that creates new content, such as music, images, or text, based on the data it's been trained on. It's responses are often based on patterns it learns from existing data.

ghost notes - Notes or drum hits that are played very softly between the main notes

GPU - Graphics Processing Unit. A specialized processor originally designed to accelerate graphics rendering. GPUs can process many pieces of data simultaneously, making them useful for machine learning, video editing, and gaming applications. They may be integrated into the computer's CPU or offered as a discrete hardware unit.

guardrails - Safeguards to ensure the ethical and responsible use of AI technologies. They include strategies and policies designed to prevent misuse, protect user privacy, and promote transparency and fairness.

hallucination - When an Ai makes something up and presents it as a fact.

hyperparameters - Hyperparameters are external variables that data scientists use to manage machine learning model training. They guide the learning process and impact how the model behaves during training and prediction.

inpainting - An image retouch technology intended to repair or restore certain areas in a photo.

Large Language Model (LLM) - An Ai model trained on a vast amount of text datasets, hence the "language" in the name. They use statistical models to analyze the training data, learning the patterns and connections between words and phrases.

Machine Learning (ML) - A subset of Ai that involves the development of algorithms and models that enable computers to learn from and make predictions or decisions based on data without explicit programming.

masking - See frequency masking

mastering - Mastering a song involves putting the final creative touches on an audio mix by elevating certain sonic characteristics. This can involve aspects like adjusting levels, applying stereo enhancement, and fixing anything that could distract the listener from the music. The end result is a polished, clean sound that is optimized for consistent playback across different formats and systems.

Model - A representation of a system or phenomenon used in machine learning to make predictions or decisions. Models can range from simple linear models to complex deep neural networks.

monetize - To convert something into money. In practice, this means turning things into revenue-generating activities, services, or assets, like turning an artist or band logo into merch.

Natural Language Processing (NLP) - A branch of Ai that focuses on the interaction between computers and human language, enabling machines to understand, interpret, and generate human language.

neural network - A computational model inspired by the human brain, composed of interconnected nodes (neurons) organized in layers. Neural networks are used for tasks like transcribing speech to text, facial recognition, and predicting the weather.

prompt - Any form of text, question, information, or coding that communicates to an Ai what response you're looking for.

public domain - Content that isn't protected by copyright law. Works that are in the public domain may be used freely, without obtaining permission from or compensating a copyright owner.

reference track - A released track that you like the sound of. This will be used by an Ai to mirror the frequency response and compression settings.

regenerate - Asking a chatbot or Ai to generate a new response.

resolution - Resolution refers to how many ones and zeros are used to express a piece of audio or video. The more ones and zeros, the higher the quality the audio or video will be.

rompler - A musical instrument that plays pre-fabricated sounds based on samples. The term rompler is a blend of the terms ROM (Read-Only Memory) and sampler. In contrast to samplers, romplers do not record audio

sidechain - Sidechaining is a production technique used in a wide variety of music genres where an effect on one track is activated from a different audio track.

scraping - The process of using automated bots to extract content or data from a website.

Tonal morphing - The ability to turn an existing sound into a different one, like a voice into a violin, a flute into a trumpet, a male voice into a female voice, or even your voice into someone else's.

Turing Test - A test for intelligence in a computer, where a human is not able to distinguish between an answer from another human and a computer.

upscaler - Using Ai to improve the resolution of an image by increasing the number of pixels in the image or enhancing the existing pixels quality.

vector image - A computer-made image made up of points, lines, and curves that are based upon mathematical equations, not pixels. This allows the image to be scaled up or down without any loss in resolution.

wrapper (audio) - Wrappers allow VST 3 plugin in other plug-in formats with minimum effort to by played on DAWs that might not recognize that plugin format.

Ai MUSIC TOOLS AND SERVICES

The following is a list of all the Ai tools, services and references cited in this book broken down by category.

Ai Text-To-Music Platforms

Aiva - AIVA.ai
Ai Test Kitchen - aitestkitchen.withgoogle.com/
Beathoven - Beatoven.ai
Boomy - Boomy.com
Chordify - Chordify.net
Ecrett Music - Ecrettmusic.com
Loudly - Loudly.com
Magenta - magenta.tensorflow.org
Melodrive - Melodrive.itch.io
Melobytes - Melobytes.com/en
Musenet - openai.com/research/musenet
Musico - Musi-co.com
MusicGen - huggingface.co/spaces/facebook/MusicGen
Splash Music - Splashmusic.com
Soundful - Soundful.com
Soundraw - Soundraw.io

Ai Music Composition Platforms

Aiva - Aiva.ai
Audiocipher - Audiocipher.com
Audiomodern - Audiomodern.com
Bandlab Songstarter - Bandlab.com/songstarter
Captain Chords - Mixedinkey.com/captain-plugins/captain-chords/
Flow Machines - flow-machines.com
Lemonaide - Lemonaide.ai
Melody Sauce - Melody Sauce
Melody Studio - Melodystudio.net
Neutone - Neutone.space
Orb Producer - orbplugins.com/orb-producer-suite/
Pilot Plugins - mixedinkey.com/pilot/
Playbeat - audiomodern.com/shop/plugins/playbeat-3/
Scaler 2 - Scalerplugin.com

Ai Lyric Generator Platforms

Chat GPT - openai.com/blog/chatgpt
Bored Humans - boredhumans.com/?tool=46
Deepbeat - Deepbeat.org
Freshbots - Freshbots.org
Keyword To Lyrics - lyrics.mathigatti.com
LogicBalls - logicballs.com/tools/song-lyrics-generator
Masterpiece Generator - song-lyrics-generator.org.uk/
My Lyrics Maker - apps.apple.com/us/app/my-lyrics-maker/id1609300054
Rytr - rytr.me/use-cases/song-lyrics
Song Lyrics Generator - song-lyrics-generator.org.uk/
These Lyrics Do Not Exist - theselyricsdonotexist.com

Ai Sound Generation Platforms

Algonaut Atlas 2 - Algonaut.audio
Emergent Drums - audialab.com
Jamahook - Jamahook.com
Output Arcade - output.com/landing-pages/arcade/
Quantakor - eplex7.com/quantakor
Samplab - Samplab.com/text-to-sample
Sistema - guk.ai
Steinberg Backbone - steinberg.net/vst-instruments/backbone

Ai Tonal Morphing Platforms

Dreamtonics - dreamtonics.com/synthesizerv/
Eclipsed Sounds- Eclipsedsounds.com
Heard Sounds - Heardsounds.com
Holly+ - Holly.plus
iZotope Nectar 4 Backer - izotope.com/en/products/nectar.html
Kits Ai - Kits.ai
Mawf - Mawf.io
Tone Transfer - sites.research.google/Tonetransfer
UberduckAI - Uberduck.ai

Ai Accompaniment Platforms

EZDrummer 3 - toontrack.com/product/ezdrummer-3/
Melodrive Instant Album - infinitealbum.io/
Musico - Musi-co.com
Playbeat 3 - audiomodern.com/shop/plugins/playbeat-3/

Orb Producer Suite - orbplugins.com/orb-producer-suite/
Unison Bass Dragon - Unison.audio/bass-dragon
Unison Drum Monkey - Unison.audio/drum-monkey

Ai Voice Cloners

Delphi - withdelphi.com
Eleven Labs - beta.elevenlabs.com
Lovo Ai - Lovo.ai
Murf Ai - Murf.ai
Resemble Ai - Resemble.ai/cloned
Respeecher - Respeecher.com

Ai Song Analyzers

Hook Theory - hooktheory.com/trends
Mazmazika Chord Analyzer - mazmazika.com/chordanalyzer
Miked In Key - mixedinkey.com/live/
Moises - moises.ai
Music Genre Finder - chosic.com/music-genre-finder
Song Key And BPM Finder - vocalremover.org/key-bpm-finder

Generative Audio Workstations (GAWs)

Aiva - Aiva.ai
Magix Music Maker - magix.com/us/music-editing/music-maker/
Nodal - Nodalmusic.com
Polymorph - jaytobin.com/polymorph/
Wavtool - Wavtool.com

Ai Track Separation Platforms

Audionamix - Audionamix.com
Acon Digital Remix - acondigital.com/products/remix
Audioshake - Audioshake.ai
Cryo-Mix - Cryo-mix.com/separator
Demixer - Demixer.com
Heard Sounds - Heardsounds.com
Lalal - Lalal.ai
Moises - Moises.ai
RipX Hitnmix - Hitnmix.com
Sounds.studio - Sounds.studio
Spleeter - www.deezer-techservices.com/solutions/spleeter/

Ai Audio Compressor Plugins

Focusrite FAST Compressor - collective.focusrite.com/products/fast-compressor
iZotope Neutron - zotope.com/en/products/neutron.html
iZotope Ozone - izotope.com/en/products/ozone.html
Sonible pure:comp - Sonible.com/purecomp
Sonible smart:comp - Sonible.com/smartcomp

Ai Audio Limiter Plugins

Focusrite FAST Limiter - collective.focusrite.com/products/fast-limiter
iZotope Neutron - izotope.com/en/products/neutron.html
Sonible pure:limit - Sonible.com/purelimit
Sonible smart:limit - Sonible.com/smartlimit

Ai Audio Equalizer Plugins

Accentize Spectral Balance - Accentize.com/spectralbalance
Baby Audio TAIP - babyaud.io/taip-plugin
Focusrite Fast Equaliser - collective.focusrite.com/products/fast-equaliser
iZotope Neutron - izotope.com/en/products/neutron.html
MeldaProduction MDrumStrip - Meldaproduction.com/MDrumStrip
Oeksound Soothe 2 - Oeksound.com/plugins/soothe2
Sonible pure:EQ - Sonible.com/pureeq
Sonible smart:EQ - Sonible.com/smarteq3
Soundtheory Gulfoss - Soundtheory.com
Tone Empire Neural Q - Tone-empire.com

Ai Reverb Plugins

Accentize Chameleon - Accentize.com/chameleon
iZotope Neoverb - izotope.com/en/products/neoverb.html
Focusrite FAST Reverb - collective.focusrite.com/products/fast-verb
Rivium - Riviumsoftware.com
Sonible pure:verb - Sonible.com/pureverb
Sonible smart:reverb - Sonible.com/smartreverb
Zynaptiq Adaptiverb - Zynaptiq.com/adaptiverb

Ai Gate Plugins

Sonible smart:gate - Sonible.com/smartgate
Sonnox Oxford Drum Gate - Sonnox.com/plugin/drumgate

Ai Noise Reduction Tools

Acon Restoration - acondigital.com/products/restoration-suite/
Accentize dxRevive - Accentize.com/dxrevive
Supertone Goyo - Goyo.app
Hush - Hushaudioapp.com
iZotope RX - izotope.com/en/products/rx.html
Waves Clarity VX - Waves.com/plugins/clarity-vx
Waves Clarity VX deReverb - Waves.com/plugins/clarity-vx-dereverb
Zynaptiq Repair - Zynaptiq.com/repair

Ai Mixing Tools

Cryo-mix - Cryo-mix.com
Lawo Automix - Lawo.com/automix
TrackSpacer - wavesfactory.com/audio-plugins/trackspacer/
RoEx Automix - Roexaudio.com
Mix Check - Mixcheck.studio
Focusrite FAST Reveal - collective.focusrite.com/products/fast-reveal
Focusrite FAST Balancer - collective.focusrite.com/products/fast-balancer
iZotope Neutron - izotope.com/en/products/neutron.html

Ai Online Mastering Platforms

Bakauge - Bakauge.com
Cloudbounce - Cloudbounce.com
eMastered - eMastered.com
LANDR - LANDR.com
Maastr - Maastr.com
Masterchannel - Masterchannel.ai
Songmastr - Songmastr.com
Mastering.studio - Mastering.studio
Soundborg - mrmastering.com/soundborg
Virtu - Slatedigital.com/virtu
Waves Mastering - Waves.com/online-mastering

Ai Mastering Plugins

Exonic AI Master - Exonicuk.com/product-page/ai-master
iZotope Audio Lens - izotope.com/en/products/audiolens.html
iZotope Ozone - izotope.com/en/products/ozone.html
iZotope Tonal Balance - izotope.com/en/products/tonal-balance-control-2.html

Ai Text-To-Image Platforms

Adobe Firefly - firefly.adobe.com
Bing Image Creator - Bing.com/create
Craiyon - Craiyon.com
DALL-E 3 - openai.com/dall-e-3
Dreamstudio - Dreamstudio.ai
Fotor Album Cover Generator - fotor.com/features/ai-album-cover-generator/
IMGCreator - IMGCreator.zmo.ai
Leonardo - Leonardo.ai
Midjourney - Midjourney.com
Nightcafe - creator.ightcafe.studio
Stable Diffusion XL - stablediffusionweb.com/StableDiffusionXL

Ai Stock Images

Civit Ai - Civitai.com
Stock Ai - Stockai.com
Stock Image Ai - Stockimage.com

Ai Photo Tools

Cleanup - Cleanup.pictures
Fotor - Fotor.com
Photoroom - Photoroom.com
Pixelcut - Pixelcut.ai

Ai Art Platforms

Artguru - Artguru.ai
Hotpot - Hotpot.ai
Illustroke - Illustroke.com
Lexica Art - Lexica.art
neoSVG - neosvg.com
Vectorizer Ai - Vectorizer.ai

Ai Branding Platforms

Flair Ai - Flair.ai
Looka - Looka.com
Patterned Ai - Patterned.ai

Ai Script Generators

ToolBaz - (toolbaz.com/writer/ai-script-generator)
Vondy - (vondy.com)
DeepStory Ai - (deepstory.ai)

Ai Video Generators

Flexclip - Flexclip
Kaliber - Kaliber
Invideo - Invideo
Make A Video - Make A Video
Neural Frames - Neural Frames
Pika Art - Pika Art
Runway - Runway
Rotor Videos - Rotor Videos
WZRD Ai - WZRD Ai
Videobolt (lyric videos) - Videobolt (lyric videos)

Ai Marketing Platforms

Character Ai - Character.ai
ChatGPT - Chat.openai.com
Claude 2 - Anthropic.com/index/claude-2
Google Bard - Bard.google.com
Jasper - Jasper.ai
Microsoft Bing Ai - Microsoft,com/en-us/bing
Perplexity - Perplexity.ai
Poe - Poe.com
Quillbot - Quillbot.com

Other Ai References

Artist Reference - shellypalmer.com/midjourney-reference-art
Camera Shots - studiobinder.com/blog/ultimate-guide-to-camera-shots.
Lighting Terms - academy.wedio.com/film-lighting-terms
U.S. Copyright Office - copyright.gov/registration

The world of Ai is constantly changing, with new tools and platforms coming online all the time. In order to stay current with the latest Ai releases, here are four sites to check out.

Ai Tools Directory - aitoolsdirectory.com
Futurepedia - futurepedia.io
There's An Ai For That - theresanaiforthat.com
Future Tools - futuretools.io

ABOUT BOBBY OWSINSKI

Producer/engineer Bobby Owsinski is one of the best selling authors in the music industry with 25 books that are now staples in audio recording, music, and music business programs in colleges around the world, These include *The Mixing Engineer's Handbook*, *The Recording Engineer's Handbook*, *Social Media Promotion For Musicians*, and more. He's also a contributor to Forbes writing on the new music business, his popular blogs and Inner Circle podcast have won numerous awards, and he's appeared on CNN and ABC News as a music branding and audio expert.

Visit Bobby's music production blog at bobbyowsinskiblog.com, his Music 3.0 music industry blog at music3point0.com, his podcast at bobbyoinnercircle.com, his online courses at bobbyowsinskicourses.com, and his website at bobbyowsinski.com.

Bobby Owsinski Bibliography

The Mixing Engineer's Handbook 5th Edition (BOMG Publishing)

The Music Mixing Workbook (BOMG Publishing)

The Recording Engineer's Handbook 5th Edition (BOMG Publishing)

The Mastering Engineer's Handbook 4th Edition (BOMG Publishing)

Social Media Promotion For Musicians 3rd Edition - *The Manual For Marketing Yourself, Your Band or your Music Online* (BOMG Publishing)

The Drum Recording Handbook 2nd Edition [with Dennis Moody] (Hal Leonard Publishing)

How To Make Your Band Sound Great (Hal Leonard Publishing)

The Studio Musician's Handbook [with Paul ILL] (Hal Leonard Publishing)

Music 4.1 - A Survival Guide To Making Music In The Internet Age 4th Edition (Hal Leonard Publishing)

The Music Producer's Handbook 2nd Edition (Hal Leonard Publishing)

The Musician's Video Handbook (Hal Leonard Publishing)

Mixing And Mastering With T-Racks: The Official Guide (Course Technology PTR)

The Touring Musician's Handbook (Hal Leonard Publishing)

The Ultimate Guitar Tone Handbook [with Rich Tozzoli] (Alfred Music Publishing)

The Studio Builder's Handbook [with Dennis Moody] (Alfred Music Publishing)

Abbey Road To Ziggy Stardust [with Ken Scott] (Alfred Music Publishing)

The Audio Mixing Bootcamp (Alfred Music Publishing)

Audio Recording Basic Training (Alfred Music Publishing)

Deconstructed Hits: Classic Rock Vol. 1 (Alfred Music Publishing)

Deconstructed Hits: Modern Pop & Hip-Hop (Alfred Music Publishing)

Deconstructed Hits: Modern Rock & Country (Alfred Music Publishing)

The PreSonus StudioLive Mixer Official Manual (Alfred Music Publishing)

You can get more info and read excerpts from each book by visiting the excerpts section of bobbyowsinski.com.

Bobby Owsinski LinkedIn Learning Video Courses

The Audio Mixing Bootcamp Video Course

Audio Recording Techniques

Audio Mastering Techniques

Music Studio Setup and Acoustics

Bobby Owsinski Online Courses

Available at BobbyOwsinskiCourses.com

Vocal Mixing Techniques

The Music Mixing Primer

Top 40 Mixing Secrets

Music Mixing Accelerator

Fully Booked

Bobby Owsinski's Online Connections

Website: bobbyowsinski.com

Courses: bobbyowsinskicourses.com

Podcast: boobbyoinnercircle.com

Music Production Blog: bobbyowsinskiblog.com

Music Industry Blog: music3point0.com

Forbes Blog: forbes.com/sites/bobbyowsinski/

Facebook: facebook.com/bobby.owsinski

YouTube: youtube.com/polymedia

Pinterest: pinterest.com/bobbyowsinski/

Linkedin: linkedin.com/in/bobbyo

Twitter: @bobbyowsinski

For The Best Manual Mix!

Add The Best Selling Book On Mixing Ever Written

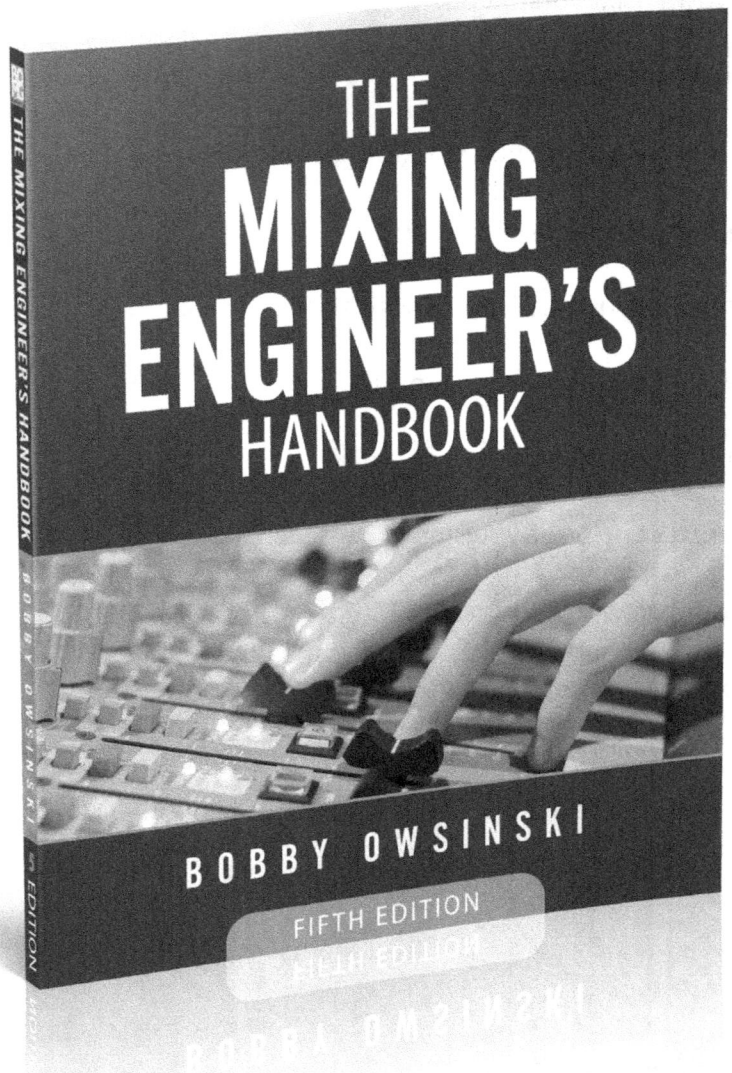

Get 14% off when you order it at bobbyowsinski.com/handbook

(Sorry, due to high shipping costs this offer is only available for customers in the United States, but you can still get it on Amazon)

Ai is quickly evolving, but you can stay on top of it by signing up for free Ai updates, and receive this free bonus too!

Here's An Extra Free Bonus

The Ai Music Cheat Sheet PDF Download

(use the QR Code or go to bobbyowsinskicourses.com/cheatreg)

An Instructor Resource Kit for this book is available to qualified instructors

Everything you need to add *The Musician's Ai Handbook* to your course right now!

Each kit includes:

- Syllabus
- Topics for Demonstrations and Discussions for each chapter
- Test Bank and answer key for 12 week semester
- Powerpoint and Keynote presentations for each chapter

"The Musician's Ai Handbook Instructor Resource Kit is **free to qualified instructors using this book in their in music, recording or production courses.**

Send an email to office@bobbyowsinski.com to receive the download link.

www.ingramcontent.com/pod-product-compliance
Lightning Source LLC
Chambersburg PA
CBHW081744100526
44592CB00015B/2292